REVIEWS AND ARTICLES 2021-2022

REVIEWS & ARTICLES
2021 -2022

JIM BURNS

PENNILESS PRESS PUBLICATIONS
www.pennilesspress.co.uk

Published by
Penniless Press Publications 2022

© Jim Burns

The author asserts his moral right to be identified as the author of the work. All rights reserved. No part of this publication may be reproduced, stored in a retrieval system or transmitted in any form or by any means, electronic, mechanical, photocopying, recording or otherwise, without the prior permission of the publishers.

ISBN 978-1-913144-44-9

Cover: Some books reviewed

CONTENTS

Sex And Sexuality In Georgian Britain	7
100 Posters That Changed The World	13
The Secret War Against The Arts	19
The Joan Anderson Letter	25
The Paper Chase	29
The Brothers Mankiewicz	35
Patterns Of Russia : History, Culture, Spaces	41
The Fighter Fell In Love: A Spanish Civil War Memoir	45
Peel Me A Lotus	50
Nina Hamnett	56
In Love With Hell : Drink In The Lives & Work Of 11 Writers	61
Unbury Our Dead With Song	67
On The Mesa : An Anthology Of Bolinas Writing	70
Arvin Garrison	75
Kerouac's Miles : Jack Kerouac And The Music Of Miles Davis	81
Ross Russell And Bebop	85
Picturing A Nation : The Art And Life Of A.H. Fullwood	91
Cold War Secrets	97
Alston Anderson : Dance Of The Infidels	103
Spanish Republicans And The Second World War	107
American Sherlocks	113
The Last Bohemian : Augustus John	119
The Spanish Civil War At Sea	121
Art Along The South Coast	127
The Belle Époque	131
Humankind : Ruskin Spear	137
The Siege That Changed The World Paris 1870-1871	143
The National Gallery Masterpiece Tour	149
The Poet And The Publisher: The Case Of Alexander Pope	152
Unknown No More: Recovering Sanora Babb	158
Harold Rosenberg : A Critic's Life	164

Suzanne Valadon : Model, Painter, Rebel	171
Sickert : A Life In Art	177
Beyond Bloomsbury : Life, Love And Legacy	181
Light On Fire : The Art And Life Of Sam Francis	183
London Yiddishtown : East End Jewish Life	189
Alias Akbar Del Piombo ; Annotations On The Life And Work Of Norman Rubington	195
The Worst Military Leaders In History	198
British Army Of The Rhine : The BAOR 1945-1993	204
Clem Beckett: Motor Cycle Legend and War Hero	209
Writing in the Dark	215
Nothing to Lose But Our Chains	221
1922; Scenes from a Turbulent Year	226
Eileen Agar: Angel of Anarchy	231
Americans Abroad (Sherry Mangan)	234
Polperro: Cornwall's Forgotten Arts Centre	240
Victor Grayson: In Search of Britain's Revolutionary	244
Writing Red: American Women Writers 1930-1940	250
Magritte: A Life	257
The Haunted Life of Jean Rhys	264
Defining the Age: Daniel Bell	270
Between Two Hells; The Irish Civil War	275
Paul Potts	280
Bohemia – John Taylor Williams & Hayden Herrera	287
Just Go Down the Road - James Campbell	297
Mina Loy: Apology of Genius	301
The Little Art Colony and US Modernism	308
Queer St Ives and Other Stories	315
Cold War Counterfeit Spies	321
Trotsky The Passionate Revolutionary	326
Kiki Man Ray	332

SEX AND SEXUALITY IN GEORGIAN BRITAIN

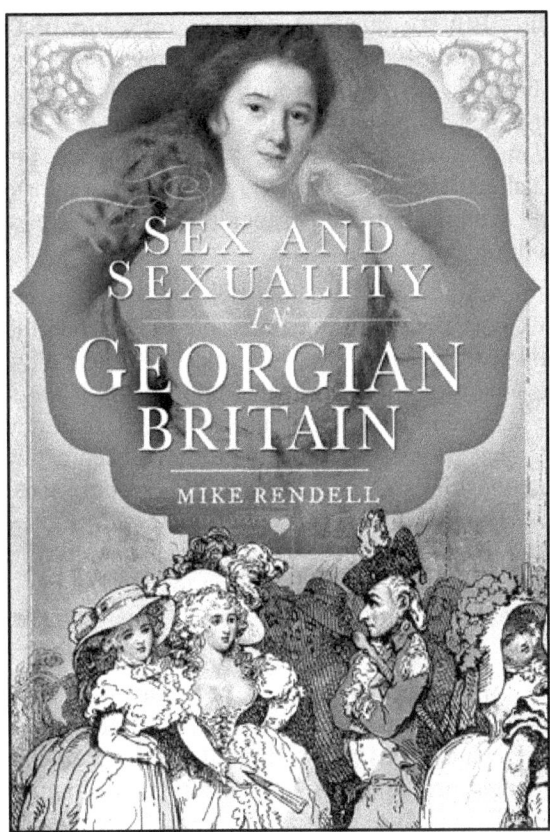

We live in an age of supposed sexual liberation and yet it's true to say that certain attitudes remain much the same as they were three hundred or so years ago. A man who brags about how many women he's slept with will be considered a bit of a lad and is sure to be admired by numerous people. Let a woman admit to all the men she's had in her bed and she will be looked on with scorn, and often by those of the same sex as well as by men. We really do revel in hypocrisy.

Mike Rendell's lively survey of sex and sexuality in Georgian Britain (mostly Georgian London, if the truth be told) makes no bones about the fact that it was largely a time when men were firmly in control and determined to keep it that way. When women did succeed it was usually because they knew how to exploit their availability as objects of sexual desire. But the numbers achieving any sort of status or wealth were few. For most women life was a limited affair, and those attempting to break away from it through the use of their bodies more often than not ended up poverty-stricken and diseased. The heroine of *Fanny Hill* may have been shown to have romped through a variety of sexual adventures without too much suffering, or bouts of gonorrhoea and syphilis, but like pornography in any period it didn't represent how things truly were.

Why has the Georgian age – Rendell defines it as between 1714, when the first George became monarch, and 1837, when the young Victoria ascended to the throne - exerted such a fascination on our imaginations? What do we see in it that appeals? Is it the seeming openness, the apparent bawdiness, the supposed opportunity for unlicensed personal behaviour? It seems to have been a time when rogues and rascals flourished and don't we all secretly like to read about them? Books like *Fanny Hill* and *Moll Flanders,* and especially films like *Tom Jones* and *Barry Lyndon,* have perhaps painted a picture for us that doesn't offer a totally accurate view of what it was like to be around in the stench and squalor of the eighteenth century. But we prefer the romance to the reality.

If the comments of foreign observers are to be believed, London did offer open displays of sexual availability that surprised them. As one of them said: "Debauch runs riot with an unblushing countenance". Another commented on the number of prostitutes accosting passers-by "in broad daylight". And a third remarked on the availability of young girls of the age of twelve or thereabouts. Twelve had been the age of consent for "some 500 years", according to Rendell, and when those who could afford it believed that deflowering a young virgin was a cure for syphilis, it's easy to understand why child prostitution was not seen by many men as something to be abhorred.

Prostitution generally was a way out of poverty, or so it seemed, though the financial rewards could often be meagre. And it's more than likely that some of the females only took to it on an occasional basis. It helped to boost the low wages they earned as milliners, shop assistants, and such. But there were rich pickings to be had, provided a pretty woman had the ability to dress well, conduct herself with decorum in fashionable company, and the intelligence to discuss matters beyond the purely mercenary. The kind and quality of the sexual services on offer would also have been a key factor in any arrangement.

The well-known women – courtesans – who took up with a variety of wealthy patrons were written about in the newspapers and magazines of the day, recognised on the streets, and frequently satirised by illustrators such as Gillray, Cruikshank and Rowlandson. Hogarth I see as something of an exception in that he was more of a moralist than the others. His wonderful works, *The Harlot's Progress, The Rake's Progress* and *Marriage a la Mode,* point to how easily someone could slip into debt, disease, and death by being involved with loose living. It's interesting to note that the first illustration in *The Harlot's Progress*, where the innocent country girl comes to town and is greeted by a procuress, alluded to two well-known characters of the time. The procuress was Elizabeth Needham, a noted brothel keeper, and lurking in the background was the notorious Colonel Francis Charteris, a man who could rape with impunity knowing that his "friends in high places" would soon secure his release if he was arrested and imprisoned.

It's a fact that a few of the courtesans did manage to survive and milk enough money out of their admirers, sometimes by marriage, sometimes by other means. Harriette Wilson wrote her memoirs and mentioned many of her lovers, but withheld some names if paid enough to do so. One of her liaisons had been with the Duke of Wellington, and when she attempted to blackmail him he responded with the now-famous phrase, "Publish and be damned". Rendell runs through a short-list of a few of the better-remembered ladies, including Kitty Fisher, Frances Abington ("she finally retired at the age of sixty and spent her last seventeen years in comparative wealth, courtesy of an inheritance from a wealthy admirer"), and Elizabeth Armistead, who took up with Charles James Fox, a politician, gambler, womaniser, and drinker. They seemed an odd couple but were genuinely fond of each other, and her charm, good nature, and tolerance won people over. She lived until she was ninety-one, and was "untouched by scandal, never once attempted to 'kiss and tell', and died beloved by the local community".

Providers of sexual services at the brothels they ran could also sometimes come out on top in financial terms. Rendell relates how

Theresa Berkley, who had an establishment that concentrated on flagellation and other deviances, was highly successful. Her services had a price, of course, and when she died she left an estate valued at £100,000, a tremendous sum at the time. Her brother, a missionary among the aborigines, returned to claim his inheritance, but on learning where the money came from fled back to Australia. The Government wasn't as fussy and stepped in to seize it.

It's interesting to note that several of the courtesans were painted by one or other of the leading artists of the day. And some had worked as actresses on the London stage. Models and actresses were often considered as no better than common prostitutes. Sir Joshua Reynolds produced a portrait of Kitty Fisher, and another of Francis Abington. George Romney painted Emma Hamilton long before she became associated with Horatio Nelson. Rendell says that she had worked in a brothel as a "posture moll", the slang name for a girl who didn't engage in direct sexual contact but posed naked so that men could inspect her closely. Rowlandson, of course, came up with an illustration entitled "The Cunnyseurs" which showed a trio of elderly males peering at a young woman's private parts. Reynolds and Romney were far more respectful of their models. But it is amusing to think that, when their pictures were exhibited at the Royal Academy, they were shown alongside portraits of members of the supposed great and good.

Rendell points to the "terrifying increase in incidents of venereal disease", and there was a popular phrase which said, "One night with Venus, a lifetime with mercury". Cures for syphilis were often based around the use of mercury, and that in itself could be a cause of death. Quack doctors added to the confusion with claims of special remedies. And there was a widespread belief, even among so-called qualified doctors, that it was women who were responsible for the spread of venereal afflictions and not men. Rendell writes about a Doctor Rock who advertised that if people called on him at the Golden Head and Key they could purchase for six shillings a pot of his "miraculous cure-all". Hogarth pictured Rock arguing with another quack in the fifth scene of *The Harlot's Progress"* "while their patient lies dying from venereal disease".

It's easy to mock the quack doctors, but some of the beliefs of the medical profession generally do tend to make one wonder just how much they knew. There was a famous case in 1726 when a woman named Mary Toft claimed to have given birth to rabbits. Various people, including some from the ranks of professional doctors, visited her and backed up her claim. In time it all turned out to be faked. But one of the doctors who believed her, John Maubray, a "qualified physician and a teacher of midwifery", had written that in pregnant women "an overfamiliarity with household pets could cause their children to resemble those pets". Mary Toft had worked in fields where rabbits were seen, so he perhaps thought it added weight to his theories?

There were some quacks who, even if they weren't medically qualified, did possibly propagate a few useful ideas. Doctor Graham's Temple of Hymen and Health had lectures which "propounded on women's rights, promoted vegetarianism, and drove home the qualities of exercise in the fresh air. Above all he promoted personal hygiene in an age when cleanliness was definitely not next to godliness". Doctor Graham seems to have been well ahead of his time in some respects.

As I noted earlier, Rendell's book is essentially about London, and the rest of the country is allocated only brief asides. There were obviously prostitutes in most towns and cities, and particularly in ports where sailors came ashore to spend their earnings and let off steam. But London had a large and growing population, the court was there, and the nobility, even if they had estates in the counties, gathered in the city to socialise and, as we've seen with regard to the males, sow a few wild oats. The pleasure gardens like Vauxhall and Ranelagh laid on pageants and other performances, and the bushes and trees and shady nooks were ideal for assignations. As we know from our own recent experiences, people gathering together and losing some of their inhibitions can make for an ideal situation in which viruses (and in Georgian times venereal infections) can easily spread.

If it sometimes seems that the whole population of London was engaged in one long, unregulated orgy, it wasn't quite the case. The authorities, at least the more-responsible of them, did attempt to keep some sort of order, though their efforts were often hindered by long-established habits of thought regarding the role of women in society and what were seen as the "rights" of Englishmen to mostly do what they wanted without restriction. This was especially true of the upper classes. They were more concerned about robbery rather than rape, so the theft of a handkerchief might be seen as deserving a heavier punishment than the ravishing of a child.

There was a Society for the Reformation of Manners (for "manners" read "moral behaviour", says Rendell) and it co-operated with the police in trying to limit the number of brothels, molly houses, and other establishments catering for various sexual activities. The churches often campaigned against licentious behaviour, and Rendell has them active with regard to the practice of masquerades. It was considered that allowing people to mix freely while wearing masks could lead to a breakdown in "social distancing" in the sense of different classes coming together without restriction. And prostitutes were able to practice their trade more easily. A mask could hide a syphilitic face with its recognisable sores.

It is, I suppose, an undeniable fact that the Georgian years seem colourful in many ways. Rendell takes the reader on a tour of the brothels, and discusses dildos, homosexuals, lesbians, cross-dressers, bigamy, aphrodisiacs, and a few more subjects of a similar nature. It's not the whole story, of course, but he tells it in a spirited manner, and he is alert to the fact that it was not a good time for women generally, that paedophilia thrived, and the prevalence of venereal diseases brought misery to many people, including those who were innocent but were infected by those who weren't. They suffered terribly through no fault of their own.

SEX AND SEXUALITY IN GEORGIAN BRITAIN
By Mike Rendell
Pen & Sword Books. 191 pages. £14.99. ISBN 978-1-52675-562-9

100 POSTERS THAT CHANGED THE WORLD

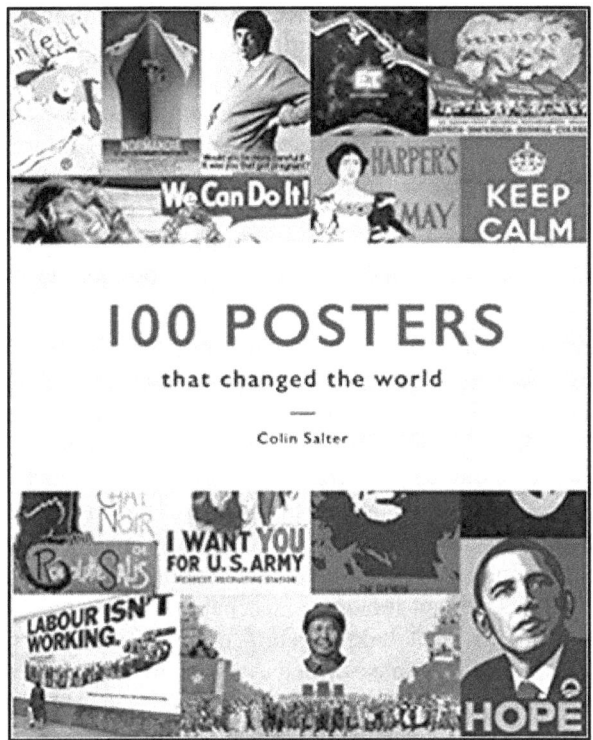

Posters are always all around us. When I'm out and about these days they're telling me to wear a face mask, wash my hands regularly, and stay a safe distance from other people. If I look back seventy-five years I can recall posters that told people to "Dig for Victory" (the image of a booted foot pressing down on a spade has stayed in my mind) and warning them that "careless talk costs lives". Posters such as these signify just one use of them- to keep us alert to possible dangers – but there have been plenty of other posters, providing information, entertainment, propaganda, that have adorned walls, windows, and a variety of places where passers-by might see them. That's the idea of a poster – to catch your eye and tell you something. Colin Salter refers to the Russian poet Mayakovsky, who said, "that if a poster could not bring a running man to a halt it had not done its job".

In its simplest form a poster may just contain text. Salter reproduces a proclamation that was issued by Parliament for the apprehension of "Charls Stuart" (the future Charles the Second) following the Royalist defeat at Worcester in 1651. It's plain and straightforward in its presentation, and if displayed in a public place would presumably have been read aloud for the benefit of those who were unable to read. By contrast, a 1930s poster advertising rewards for information leading to the capture of the notorious gangster John Dillinger, had not only photos of him but also the sums of money involved highlighted in larger lettering. The aim of both posters was the same, to lead to an arrest, but technology had made it possible to change ways of attracting the attention of likely informants.

It was technology, primarily the development of lithography and the use of colour, that led to the explosion of poster displays in the late-nineteenth century. The posters that Toulouse-Lautrec created to publicise The Moulin Rouge and its performers have shaped our ideas of 1890s Paris to the point where it's almost impossible to think of that era without one of his posters in mind. But he wasn't the only artist producing posters to celebrate the clubs and cabarets of Montmartre. Théophile Alexandre Steinlen's poster advertising Le Chat Noir, with its defiant-looking black cat staring at the viewer, and what appears to be a halo of sorts around its head perhaps mocking the work of Alphonse Mucha, seems to me important in terms of typifying a specific period in Paris. It might also be appropriate to mention Jules Chéret. He was one of the most prolific poster artists of his time and the pretty girls he portrayed became known as Cherettes and achieved great popularity among Parisians.

Posters were not only known for their links to Montmartre and its night-time entertainments. The late-nineteenth century saw the rise of a middle-class with money to spend on more than the basic requirements of life. Advertising, as it always is, was directed towards those with the funds and the time to frequent cafés and other leisure centres. Posters advocating the pleasures of alcohol of one kind or another could be seen in the streets. Salter has one for absinthe which is quite provocative in its way. It shows a couple seated at a table with the well-dressed man watching a young woman tentatively sipping at a glass of the green liquid. Is there something in his look that suggests seduction? Salter at one point talks about "persuasion by association" and it could be that was what was in the mind of the artist. Persuade a woman to drink absinthe and she's yours? Suggestion can be a key factor in advertising. Were the 1940s/1950s advertisements for Chesterfield cigarettes only drawing attention to the product when they used phrases such as, "Like your pleasures BIG?" and "Man-Size Satisfaction"?

Good-looking females were and still are a standard item in advertising. Males, too, though the emphasis has mostly been on women. I've mentioned Chéret's pretty girls and their roles in pushing various products and much later PETA (People for the Ethical Treatment of Animals) put a nude model on a poster protesting against the use of fur. Not everyone was happy about it. They felt, not without reason, that there was a doubtful aspect to illustrating a message with a picture of a naked woman. And wasn't it likely to pull attention away from the message and focus it on her body? I was intrigued by what Salter describes as "the biggest-selling poster of all time, shifting 20 million copies". It's of Farrah Fawcett in a red swimsuit, and according to Salter "adorned the bedroom walls of many adolescent boys". It's quite innocuous, especially by today's standards, though might have been thought daring when I was a teenager.

The fact that it "shifted 20 million copies" points to how posters became items manufactured for sale and decoration rather than for use in advertising. Almost from the start they had been sought after by collectors, and it didn't take long for galleries to mount exhibitions of posters, and for shops that sold them to open. In the early days it's said that posters would often be removed almost as soon as they'd been pasted up on walls and hoardings. The thieves, if that's what they were, had an eye to the artistic qualities of posters by Toulouse-Lautrec, Chéret, Steinlen, and others. Or perhaps realised that they would increase in monetary value as the years passed.

There was often a serious purpose behind the production of posters. They weren't all designed to sell silk stockings, bicycles, beer, and biscuits. Political posters came in a variety of forms, ranging from encouragement to vote in a certain way to emphasising the solid virtues of a leader. The cult of personality that surrounded Stalin was accented in numerous examples of the stern but just leader, the friendly leader, and the wise leader. Salter uses one or two good ones to illustrate his comments. One shows Stalin holding a small child waving a flag. His look is benevolent. I recall a few years ago seeing an exhibition of Soviet social-realist art at the Russian Museum in

Málaga, and it struck me that Stalin seemed to be in just about every other painting. He was seen addressing workers on collective farms, chairing meetIngs of the Politburo, and poring over documents. None of the representations of the Great Leader naturally gave an indication of his lust for power and his cruelty. As with an advertising executive constructing an image for a politician only the positive could be emphasised.

With political posters it is always possible to draw attention to negative matters. Salter uses the famous (perhaps infamous, depending on your political leanings) Conservative Party poster, "Labour isn't Working", which showed what appeared to be a queue trailing back into the distance while the head of the queue enters the Unemployment Office, or the Dole as I would have known it. It was, like it or not, a striking and effective image and may have been at least partly responsible for the Tories winning the 1979 General Election. Salter has some interesting things to say about how Saatchi & Saatchi created this poster. If questions can be asked about some of his choices of posters and their supposed impacts, there's no doubt that this one did contribute towards change.

War being politics by other means, posters plainly come into their own when it's necessary to persuade people to join up, work harder, make sacrifices, and generally fall in behind whichever government wants their support. There are famous posters which seem to represent the mood of the moment, such as that of Kitchener pointing his finger towards whoever is looking at the poster and demanding that he should "Join Your Country's Army". It appeared in 1915 as the need for men became increasingly obvious. From the Second World War, and more to do with the home front in the United States, there was the well-known "Rosie the Riveter" poster which celebrated the role that women had to play by replacing men in the factories turning out tanks, planes, and other armaments.

Motivating the civilian population was a concern in wartime, and in 1915 worries extended to the effect that alcohol consumption was having on factory workers, miners, and many others. Lloyd George proclaimed on a poster that "We are fighting Germany, Austria and Drink…..and the Greatest of these three Deadly Foes is Drink". It was during the First World War that the licensing laws we lived with for so long were brought into effect. At the time of the Second World

War there were poster campaigns to warn servicemen of the dangers of sexual diseases: "You can't beat the Axis if you get VD".

The wars, First and Second, did allow may women to lead independent lives, though the post-war situations often found that independence under attack. It wasn't just a case of men not liking the idea of women doing jobs that had traditionally belonged to them. Their new-found confidence made men feel uneasy. But any attempts by women to move out of their "proper" roles had long been frowned on, as the Suffragettes discovered when they agitated for the vote. Salter presents posters from both sides of the story, with one demonstrating what happens when working-class women get mixed up with suffragette concerns and as a result neglect their homes and children. Of the pro-suffragette statements I like an American example where Rose O'Neill employed her Kewpie characters from the strip cartoons she did for *The Ladies Home Companion* and other publications for a poster on which they ask that their mothers be given the vote: "Isn't it a funny thing/That father cannot see/Why mother ought to have a vote/On how these things should be?" The "things" were food, health, schools and other matters affecting children. The Kewpies were cute and popular and would have caught the attention of the general public.

Salter's survey doesn't only look at posters from the past, and in fact his book has one from a 2019 Extinction Rebellion campaign. It could, perhaps, be argued that the period from 1960 on has been a golden one for poster designers and printers. The 1960s had a resurgence of Art Nouveau which tied in easily with the psychedelic layouts favoured by the so-called "underground" with its hippy devotees. Posters advertised Woodstock and rock music. Out of the same era came posters opposing the Vietnam War and stirring up events in Paris. Film posters explored new angles, exploiting sex and shock tactics to make people stop and, hopefully, think they might like to see the film concerned. Salter uses a poster advertising *Jaws*, with the shark's teeth prominently displayed.

It's always been debatable if poster art, which is essentially commercial art, can, at its best, be moved into a fine art category. There are all kinds of interesting questions raised in this connection. If I see a poster advertising an exhibition of a famous artist's work, and on which there is one of his paintings, has that work been reduced in status by its use for a commercial purpose? I doubt that any of us would think so. And we now happily accept Toulouse-Lautrec's work as art, even if it was done for the purpose of advertising. I have to say that I've seen posters, many of them skilled in their drawing and painting techniques, which seem to me to be more interesting than a lot of the routine portrait and landscapes found in galleries. Remove the brand name or slogan from a poster and it could be viewed as a work of art and not just an advertisement.

Colin Salter has put together an entertaining and informative book. It covers much more ground than I've been able to indicate in this review. Liberally illustrated, and with useful accompanying text, it provides a good guide to the qualities and uses of posters.

100 POSTERS THAT CHANGED THE WORLD

By Colin Salter

Pavilion Books. 224 pages. £14.99. ISBN 978-1-911641-45-2

THE SECRET WAR AGAINST THE ARTS : HOW MI5 TARGETED LEFT-WING WRITERS & ARTISTS 1936-1956

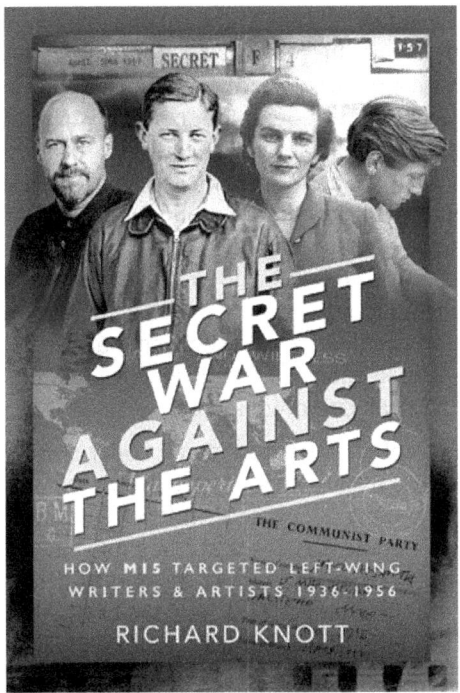

We live in a democracy. There may be various interpretations of what that word means, but we generally agree that the rule of law should apply fairly and freely to all, and that we are on the whole at liberty to read what we want, and express our opinions about most things without falling foul of the institutions of the state. We assume that our homes will be respected and not raided, that the police will leave us alone if we don't commit crimes, that we can move around without hindrance, and that we can communicate openly with other people and not be pilloried for doing so.

Well, that's what should happen, and often does for most people. There are always exceptions to any law or matter of understanding, and we'd no doubt accept many of them on the grounds that the general good requires us to make concessions. Only an extreme libertarian would argue that terrorist material should be easily available, that certain kinds of pornography ought not to be censored, or that everyone has the right to own guns and ammunition. It's also necessary to point out that recent events have shown how quickly some of our "rights" can be tinkered with when governments think it necessary.

A difficulty often arises in relation to political aims and ideas. Provided you don't conspire to overthrow the state by force of arms it might be thought that we ought to be able to read and write anything we please. But the state will most likely claim that it needs to keep an eye on what we are doing in case words turn into actions. And this argument was particularly pronounced during the period covered by Richard Knott's book when communism was the bogey word. Writers and artists, few of who were active in a direct sense, were closely watched and reported on. It was a situation which led to moments of some amusement when people found themselves subject to surveillance, but also times of stress when authors and painters were blacklisted and unable to obtain work.

Clive Branson and Paul Hogarth both came under suspicion because of their links to the Communist Party. Branson was born into comfortable surroundings – Knott refers to his parents as "conventional upper middle class" – and had a good education. When he left Bedford School he worked in an insurance office, but nursed ambitions to become an artist. His parents eventually agreed to provide him with a small allowance while he became a student at the Slade. He didn't settle at the Slade, finding the teaching uninspiring, and left to follow what I suppose would be called a bohemian lifestyle while pursuing a lone path with his artistic aspirations. An inheritance gave him freedom from financial worries, but his eyes had been opened to the poverty and distress evident around him, and he became radicalised. He had met Noreen Browne, who came from a family with aristocratic connections, but was. like Branson, growing more aware of the social and political problems of the period. A short stay in the Independent Labour Party (ILP) led them to the Communist Party.

Paul Hogarth was also destined to become a Party member, but his background was a world away from that of Branson. Born in Kendal, and brought up in Manchester, his father was a small shopkeeper who frowned on his son's interest in books and art. Hogarth attended the Manchester School of Art but left home when he was seventeen, and took an interest in politics. When the Civil War broke out in Spain in 1936 Hogarth was an early volunteer, along with Clive

Branson. It was a decision that heightened the interest taken in them by both local police and MI5.

That interest, with files kept on their involvements and movements, lasted for years in Hogarth's case. With regard to Branson, his death in action in Burma in 1944, while serving in the British Army, brought matters to an end, though Noreen Branson's continued membership in the Party meant that she was always likely to be watched. Likewise with Hogarth, and he was discharged from the army after a few months even though he was keen to carry on serving in its ranks. His "premature anti-fascism" was held against him. He resigned from the Party in 1957, but was still denied entry to the USA in 1991 because of his one-time Communist Party membership, which the Americans probably knew about thanks to MI5. It might be seen that it was "quixotically British" when he was awarded an OBE in 1989, and was elected to full membership of the Royal Academy.

Branson and Hogarth are just two of the artists Knott deals with. Others include the now, I would guess, largely forgotten Ralph Bates, a novelist and short-story writer with involvements in Spain, who "was deemed to be a potential Red following the discovery of a copy of Stendhal's *The Red and the Black* in his luggage". When Bates made an appeal for aid for the Spanish Republic at a meeting in Conway Hall it was reported that "the audience appeared to be made up of Jewish and intellectual types of communists".

Throughout his book Knott points out how "personal idiosyncrasies" were often noted in reports about supposed communists. It was said of the painter Julian Trevelyan that "he sometimes wears sandals" George Orwell's inclination to "dress like a bohemian" was registered.. A red bow-tie, or owning a pair of red silk-stockings was enough to arouse suspicion, as was merely being seen in the presence of a known radical. It does occur to me to wonder if simply being interested in the arts was considered a questionable activity in the eyes of many policemen, and therefore worthy of attention? Contact tracing was in operation long before Covid19 arrived on the scene.

George Orwell, despite his background at public school and in the Colonial police, was looked on as potentially dangerous by the security services. The fact that he was firmly anti-communist may have been recognised, but it didn't stop Special Branch and MI5 keeping files on him. He'd fought in Spain, but with a non-communist Marxist organisation, though that difference probably didn't count for much with the authorities. The nuances of left-wing thought confused many people. And his attitude towards the police was suspicious, especially when he said of a campaign to have the Scotland Yard surveillance files destroyed if it looked like the Germans might invade: "Some hope. The police are the very people who would go over to Hitler once they were certain he had won".

Knott does refer to what some commentators see as a blot on Orwell's record of opposition to authority, his list of communists and fellow-travellers that he handed to MI5 in 1949. Excuses can be made for his action. He was in poor health, he was possibly influenced by the attentions of a female MI5 agent, and he was genuinely concerned about what communists were planning in terms of infiltrating various organisations. It's difficult to now understand what the atmosphere was like in the late-1940s and early-1950s. There was a general hostility to communism, especially because of the Cold War and the Russian activities in Eastern Europe. Naming names is not necessarily a practice to be approved of, particularly when some of the names might belong to people who are not in any way dangerous, but we may want to allow for special circumstances at times.

It would be difficult to ascertain just how many lives were affected by the presence in them of the operatives from MI5 and the police. Knott inevitably focuses on some of the better-known names in the arts. But I suspect that others were also caught up in the dragnet, with Special Branch officers from local police forces, and informants, feeding details to MI5. It's highly likely that some of the details had more to do with the social prejudices of the observers rather than any actual activities on the part of the observed. Dressing a little differently, being interested in things most people ignored, and not openly participating in what might be called normal day-to-day involvements, were all possible grounds for comment.

Shopkeepers, postmen, and neighbours, would know which newspapers and magazines were read, where mail came from, and how many curious-looking visitors arrived. The authorities tapped telephone and opened letters to obtain information. It's no secret that Communist Party headquarters in London were bugged and burgled. But what about the provinces where the unusual might be more noticeable than in London? Which painter or poet in Birmingham or

Manchester had his ideas and opinions scrutinised? The answers might be in the archives, if they still exist, of local Special Branch units, but accessing them might not be easy. And though Knott can come up with evidence of blacklists which prevented some people from working for the BBC and other organisations, I began to wonder how many others were denied employment with local authorities and private companies because the police or MI5 had advised against them being hired?

Such questions are outside the scope of Knott's book, and his focus is on someone like the poet Randall Swingler. There has been a revival of interest in his life and work in recent years, thanks to the efforts of Andy Croft who has written extensively about him. Swingler had served with some distinction in the British Army in the Second World War, but his continued commitment to communism meant that he found it difficult to obtain suitable employment in the post-war years, and so scuffled to earn a living. He had personal problems, which could have been partly caused by the predicament in which he found himself, and collapsed and died in a Soho street when leaving a pub.

Swingler is a valuable case to study when it comes to how easily a writer can disappear from sight. His writing, and his literary involvements in the 1930s and 1940s, seem impressive, but the onset of the Cold War caused him to be almost "airbrushed" out of history. His radicalism counted against him. It's also true that his poems would probably not have found favour with the Movement poets of the 1950s, nor with the so-called "underground" poets of the 1960s. The majority of poets are fated to be forgotten, but Swingler probably suffered from neglect more than most.

There is a dark humour to be gained from the fact that, while MI5 were harassing writers and artists, most of who were never likely to engage in espionage or other illegal activities, more than a few real spies were escaping its attention. The stories of Blunt, Philby, Burgess, Maclean, and more, are too well-known to need noticing here. While Auden, Spender, the artist James Boswell, the composer Alan Bush, the novelist Doris Lessing, and the theatre activist Joan Littlewood, were all regularly investigated, information of value to the Russians was flowing freely from highly-placed sources.

The Secret War Against the Arts can't possibly tell the whole story of how MI5 and Special Branch harassed writers and artists and what the effects were on their work. Did publishers fight shy of poetry by left-wingers and galleries turn down paintings by artists known to be political radicals? Knott says that the Leicester Galleries, his regular outlet, refused to display Paul Hogarth's drawings from a 1956 trip to Africa, "because of their challenging content". It isn't specified what was "challenging" about the drawings, but it's not unreasonable to assume that what they showed was not In accord with official policy about the colonies. MI5 had informed the police in South Africa and Southern Rhodesia that Hogarth and Lessing were on their way. Knott says that both had their luggage searched before they left England. The authorities presumably knew that funds for the trip, which was in connection with a book Lessing was writing and Hogarth illustrating, had been provided by the Soviet News Agency, TASS.

Richard Knott has written a lively and thought-provoking book. It won't be the last word on the subject. He notes that researchers continue to be denied access to some files, and that those that are made available are often heavily-redacted. "National security" is the usual excuse for limits imposed on allowing access to files or redacting them.. The names of informants are blacked out. The state doesn't want us to know too much about how and why we've been watched. Which makes one think about who is being observed now besides suspected terrorists? Police in recent years have infiltrated a variety of protest groups, And the growth of surveillance equipment means that we're all watched a lot of the time. Technology enables investigators to follow our movements, find out what we buy and who we meet. It's no longer a case of a local policeman sending in a report to say that someone has the appearance of a "bohemian" or sports a red tie. MI5 will now already know much more than that.

THE SECRET WAR AGAINST THE ARTS : HOW MI5 TARGETED LEFT-WING WRITERS & ARTISTS 1936-1956

By Richard Knott

Pen & Sword Books. 226 pages. £25. ISBN 978-1-52677—031-8

THE JOAN ANDERSON LETTER:
THE HOLY GRAIL OF THE BEAT GENERATION

According to Jack Kerouac the "Joan Anderson Letter" was "The greatest piece of writing I ever saw", an enthusiastic approbation by a man given to spontaneous responses to a variety of experiences. Did Kerouac really feel that way? And did the letter truly influence the writing of *On the Road*, the book that launched him into the limelight and created the myth of Dean Moriarty, the fictional character based on the real-life Neal Cassady? There are those who believe that there is little to choose between the two, but *On the Road* is a novel and best read as such.

So what was the "Joan Anderson Letter", and why is it said to have made such an impression on Kerouac? It was sent by Cassady to Kerouac in December, 1950, and laid, out in some detail, Cassady's activities in Denver during a period around 1945/46. Perhaps I should qualify this and say that the letter mostly involves his encounters with various young females, including Joan Anderson. A. Robert Lee, in an informative introduction, rightly points out that Cassady was writing as much for Kerouac as to him. He knew what Kerouac wanted to hear in a way that would help create an image of Cassady as a dynamic and hyper-active new hero. Writers and intellectuals, engaged as they are in largely sedentary occupations, often admire others who are more physically active. And for Kerouac and Ginsberg, Cassady seemed to "embody the figure of life-force and resuscitation, little short of a Rocky Mountain messiah". Others, like John Clellon Holmes and Alan Harrington, had a more down-to-earth notion of him. Holmes' portrayal of Cassady as Hart Kennedy in *Go* certainly doesn't invest him with legendary qualities. And Harrington once said that, by any definition he knew, Cassady was a "complete psychopath".

Cassady claimed to have stolen hundreds of cars, seduced any number of women, and had seen the inside of prison cells. His childhood had involved being dragged around hobo hangouts, bar-rooms, and doss-houses by an alcoholic father, That he had managed to pick up some sort of education on the way is to his credit. Those who knew him said he read voraciously, and he did have ambitions to become a writer. He drops the names of Celine, Dostoyevsky, and Herman Melville into the rush of words in the letter. And some time later he did manage to put together a narrative of his early life that Lawrence Ferlinghetti's City Lights Books published with the title, *The First Third & Other Writings*, the latter being a handful of fragments. But *The First Third* is a more-sustained piece of work. If someone who now only knows Cassady's writing through the Anderson letter reads it they might be surprised by the relative formality of the prose. But letters frequently are looser in their use of language, unless the writer is aware that he's writing for posterity to read. I doubt that Cassady had any such aim in mind when he sent his letter to Kerouac.

The letter, however, achieved legendary status over the years. People talked about it, but no-one seemed to know where it was or if it still existed. It was said by Kerouac to have been 40,000 words long, but was actually nearer 16,000. At some point it was passed to the poet Gerd Stern in the hope that he might persuade Carl Solomon's uncle, who ran Ace Books, to publish it. Ace published William

Burroughs' *Junkie*, but that had commercial potential as a pulp paperback. When nothing happened Stern then sent the letter to the publishers of *The Golden Goose*, a West Coast little magazine. Its editor later gave it to the owner of Gold Coast Records, and it stayed with him, hidden in a box, until his daughter discovered it when sorting out his possessions in 2011. What happened after that, in terms of the letter accumulating in value and being auctioned, is explained by A. Robert Lee. It might be worth mentioning that, during the years it was assumed "lost", Allen Ginsberg added fuel to the fire by suggesting that Gerd Stern had destroyed it. This no doubt heightened the legendary status of the letter as people thought about what might have been in it, and why it had been so highly rated by Kerouac and Ginsberg.

Now, seventy or so years after it was written, it can be looked at with a degree of detachment. It certainly does seem to have had an effect on Kerouac. He had produced one novel, *The Town and the City* which was straightforward in terms of its overall structure and writing style. It did hint at some of his later concerns when it talked about night-life in New York and what might be seen as the first stirrings of the Beat Generation. But Kerouac was looking for something different, and it's debatable if he would have led a writing life of literary conventionality had Cassady and his letter not arrived on the scene. Cassady's loose oral style, with asides and interventions, and the words tumbling over reach other, supposedly led Kerouac to writing *On the Road* in the way that he did. But It does occur to me to consider whether or not Kerouac would have produced a fresh style, anyway, if Cassady had not written to him? Other people had urged him to look at prose in a different way, suggesting he write quickly and in a sketch-like manner.

Lee says that "Kerouac's styling of the novel lies as much at the centre of its appeal as the events it records". And that's true enough. I've met people with no particular interest in the Beats, and no idea of who Dean Moriarty was created from, but who have enjoyed *On the Road*. They may not have thought too much about what the characters get up to – "So, what's new?" one person said with a shrug. But they liked the pace, the energy, the enthusiasm in the narrative. The same could be said about Cassady's letter. There isn't all that much under the surface of what he's saying, but the account is racy and bright and keeps going on its speed and enthusiasm. The difference between the letter and the book is that Kerouac had a better idea of how to "style" his novel. I've also long been of the opinion that some editing was involved. The book gave the impression of spontaneity, but had been shaped to do that.

I mentioned earlier that Alan Harrington thought of Cassady as a "complete psychopath". It's a comment he made in his book, *Psychopaths* (Simon & Schuster, New York, 1973), and his general view of Cassady is a fairly critical one, and based on personal observation. Harrington appears in *On the Road* as Hal Hingham. Was his description of Cassady accurate? Certainly the personality that comes across from the letter would suggest that it is. In his behaviour with women generally he appears to have little or no sense of responsibility. His relationship with Joan Anderson is such that she attempts suicide at one point. Other females, including a sixteen year old, are treated in an offhand manner and, like the cars he stole, are abandoned once he has used them for his own gratification. Perhaps we shouldn't comment on Cassady's character, and his moral flaws, and should simply look at the letter now in terms of its literary value in relation to *On the Road*, and its place in Beat history. But it's frankly hard not to wonder why people ever saw Neal Cassady in any sort of positive light.

It's useful that the Joan Anderson letter finally came to light, and that it's now available in an edition making it available to a wide audience. The introduction by A. Robert Lee places Cassady and the letter in a wider Beat context. There are useful notes, and an ample bibliography.

THE JOAN ANDERSON LETTER: THE HOLY GRAIL OF THE BEAT GENERATION

By Neal Cassady (Introduction by A. Robert Lee)

Black Spring Press. 188 pages. £20. ISBN 978-1-913606-33-6

THE PAPER CHASE: THE PRINTER, THE SPYMASTER & THE HUNT FOR THE REBEL PAMPHLETEERS

London in 1705 was awash with conspiracies, plots, schemes, and rivalries. It hadn't been long since James the Second, a Catholic sympathiser, had lost his throne when an invasion force from Holland, led by William of Orange and his English wife, Mary, landed and in due course took over the country. But there were still many people sympathetic to James. Jacobite supporters could be found everywhere, including Parliament, though it wasn't always wise to be outspoken about it. In 1702 Anne, the daughter of James, had been proclaimed Queen following the death of William. She had been brought up in the Anglican faith and ruled over a kingdom that was still bitterly divided in many ways. And Britain was at war with France.

Before 1695 it had been necessary to submit printed matter for inspection, and possible censorship, prior to publication. The law was changed so that "government licensing of books, newspapers, and pamphlets officially came to an end". It might seem that this, in effect, allowed anyone to write and publish anything they wanted. It wasn't the case, of course, and there were strict laws which referred to treason, libel, and other matters that could lead to prosecution, possible imprisonment, and even the death penalty. Free expression was still a risky business. Even if the law didn't take action against offenders, powerful people had their own ways of dealing with a writer or printer they thought had offended them. Threats, mysterious disappearances, and murders were not uncommon. It was little wonder that authors often chose to remain anonymous.

It was in this kind of atmosphere, in a London that could be violent, and where gossip and innuendo flourished in the coffee-houses and taverns, that hack writers, and even more-polished ones, churned out poems and prose works commenting on the politics of the day and the personalities involved. There were always plenty of printers waiting to produce a pamphlet or a leaflet and numerous bookshops or street stalls where they might be bought. As noted, it could be dangerous to print something controversial, but printers often had political leanings that persuaded them to handle what was risky. They attempted to evade being identified by omitting their addresses. This wasn't always a sure way of avoiding attention. Spies and informers abounded, and other printers sometimes recognised a publication's origins from the kind of paper and type used.

David Edwards, a printer with premises in Nevil's Alley, just off Fetter Lane in Holborn, was wary when in 1705 a masked woman turned up and handed him a manuscript she wanted him to print as a pamphlet. Edwards looked at the document, which bore the title, *The Memorial of the Church of England.* It was anonymous and appeared to be an attack on the church for allegedly watering-down its principles by allowing dissenters to be included in its ranks. It was clearly stating a case that had Tory backing. Joseph Hone says that "Dissenters and broadminded conformists gathered under the Whig banner to fight what they viewed as renewed tyranny and absolutism" whereas for the Tories, "Conformists and churchmen all….Monarchy remained sacred in Tory doctrine and the king was owed blind, passive obedience by his subjects". Add to this a very strong current of Jacobitism and a divided view of Catholicism. Both parties were anti-Catholic, but some Whigs were perhaps inclined to be more tolerant of their presence in the interests of maintaining a broad-based form of government. There were English Catholics who still supported the Stuart claims to the English throne, and responded when the "Old Pretender" marched down into England from Scotland in 1715. The overall situation in England in the early-1700s can best be described as unstable.

Edwards' doubts about accepting the commission to print *The Memorial of the Church of England* were overcome by the fee offered, and perhaps his political commitments. His wife, Mary, was a Catholic, whereas he was Church of England. But both were of the opinion that, "the exiled King James had been treated abominably and that King William was nothing more than a usurper". The sentiments expressed in the pamphlet would have appealed to them. They would have known the dangers inherent in what they were doing. Edwards had been in trouble before when he printed works by Catholic theologians. And he was fined and spent time in the pillory for printing *The Anti-Curse,* a pro-King James tract. As Hone puts it, "Ever since the outbreak of civil war, printed pamphlets had been the principal vessel for public debate". Sold by hawkers in the streets, circulated in the coffee-houses where people, if inclined, talked about what was in the news, and passed from hand to hand, they were seen as dangerous when they attacked, often by way of satire, those in positions of power.

Once Edwards and his wife had produced the pamphlet the plot began to thicken. The mysterious veiled lady had re-appeared, and various others, such as porters who carried messages across London, became involved. No-one knew the identity of the lady, nor that of another woman who arrived with her but stayed outside the printer's premises. When the document came to the attention of the authorities the hunt began to ascertain who wrote the pamphlet and who printed it. Robert Harley, the Secretary of State, led the investigation, employing informants and "messengers", men who were authorised to act in tracking down anyone suspected of subversion. In this case its contents added up to allegations of "corruption, greed, and perversion within the corridors of power, a 'heretick fever' lurking in the bowels of church and state". It is, perhaps, not always easy to understand that, at the time concerned, the interests of church and state were frequently closely combined.

As Hone says, "religion served government by regulating social behaviour".

One of the joys of reading *The Paper Chase* is encountering the wide range of characters that Hone introduces into the narrative. William Pittis, for example, "abandoned a prestigious junior fellowship at Oxford in 1695 to pursue a literary career in London". He soon became associated with "an unruly crowd" which included Grub Street writers like Ned Ward, Thomas D'Urfey, and Tom Brown, who met at the Rose Tavern "on the corner of Cross Keys Alley and the Strand". Pittis was "a drinker among drinkers", and was said to be "brash in conversation and careless in the company he kept". John Dunton, described in Pope's *The Dunciad,* as a "broken bookseller and abusive scribbler", said of Pittis that: "He can guzzle more at a sitting than wou'd keep a family a month". It's significant that Pittis and his cronies launched a monthly "poetic journal" with the title, *Miscellanies Over Claret,* from The Rose, though Hone doesn't say how long it lasted.

The net was closing in on Edwards, but he had disappeared (he had fled to his native Wales), so his wife was arrested and questioned. She was eventually released, mainly so that she could be followed in the hope that she would lead the watchers to her husband. In the meantime suspicion had fallen on Thomas Mackworth, "a leading Tory backbencher" and Henry Poley, "a Lincoln's Inn lawyer" as possible authors of the pamphlet. Poley was also a Tory backbencher. Mary had been roaming London, looking for the masked lady and her associates, and in many ways functioning as a detective in a more-convincing manner than most of Harley's spies and enforcers.

Edwards eventually agreed to return to London and co-operate with any enquiries into who wrote *The Memorial,* provided he was indemnified against prosecution. He felt, not without reason, that he had been abandoned by those who had written and financed the pamphlet, despite the masked lady assuring him that powerful men were behind it and would protect him in the event of trouble. They obviously had little or no intention of honouring any promises the lady had made – were they her own invention? – and Edwards therefore felt justified in defending his and Mary's interests by telling what he knew.

His actions may have seemed necessary, given that he was living in impoverished circumstances. The news that he had agreed to act as an investigator and informer for Harley soon circulated among writers and printers in London. The result was that he "alienated many of his old friends. Men like William Pittis and Ned Ward, who had defended the *Memorial* in the press at great personal cost, would no longer even look at him". Hone suggests that, in fact, much of the information that Edwards may have passed to Harley probably originated from Mary whose talents for tracking down suspects and unearthing details of their activities had come to the fore when Edwards was in hiding: "Having spent her childhood running errands for her stepfather and his shady associates in the Catholic book trade, it was a part Mary was born to play".

That Edwards was not the only one who could switch sides was shown when Harley resigned from his position as Secretary of State due to a scandal involving a member of his staff. William Greg, a junior clerk, had been selling secret documents to the French. He had been given a job by Harley after playing a useful part in reporting on Jacobite activities in Scotland. There was nothing to suggest that Harley knew about Greg's treachery, though he had little option but to resign. To retain a position in politics, he began to ingratiate himself with the Tories.

Interest in the *Memorial* faded with Harley's fall from grace. There was, a few years later, a second edition, by which time it was said to be partly the work of Dr James Drake, along with Thomas Mackworth and Henry Poley. But neither Harley nor Edwards responded in print to its appearance. Hone says that Edwards could have commented on how and why the first edition was printed, and who was possibly behind it, but chose to stay silent: "Experience had taught him to avoid the fray". He had, thanks to Harley's influence, been given a job in the Thames customs office, "inspecting and collecting duties on high-value goods from the East Indies, mostly silks and spices". While his wife "continued occasionally to print and sell books from her stall on Fetter Lane, the press on Nevil's Alley was mostly dormant". She presumably played it safe by not printing anything likely to attract hostile attention, and the new edition of *Memorial* didn't come from her print shop. The couple appear to have disappeared from history at that point.

The Paper Chase is an engaging book. It successfully mixes the personal stories of David and Mary Edwards with the wider account of the complex politics of the reign of Queen Anne. With memories of the Civil War and the Restoration still in mind, the Jacobite threat, the Glorious Revolution, and the general shifting nature of British society at the time, it was a turbulent period. It was also a colourful one, if sometimes brutal. Hone touches on the Grub Street writers and the taverns where they gathered and laid down plans for new publications, many of them admittedly not destined to have long lives. Not all of what was written and published had a political edge, nor was it meant to be taken seriously. But there were writers willing to engage in political matters, and printers who would risk publishing controversial material. Joseph Hone brings this world alive in *The Paper Chase*. His book is well-researched, with ample notes, and a useful bibliographical essay.

THE PAPER CHASE: THE PRINTER, THE SPYMASTER & THE HUNT FOR THE REBEL PAMPHLETEERS
By Joseph Hone
Chatto & Windus. 251 pages. £18.99. ISBN 978-1-784-74306-2

THE BROTHERS MANKIEWICZ: HOPE, HEARTBREAK, AND HOLLYWOOD CLASSICS

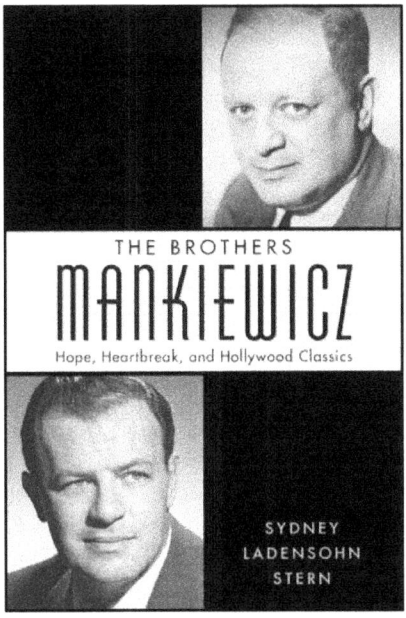

The life of a screenwriter in Hollywood was never all that easy. Writers hardly rated highly in the studio pecking order, and their work, if it wasn't already the result of a collaborative effort with several additional writers, could be re-written by directors, producers, and actors. It was true that writers could be well-paid by the standards that applied outside the film industry, but they were poorly paid in comparison to the people who could interfere with their scripts. And their terms of employment were often temporary. Short-term contracts were not renewed if a writer couldn't produce what was wanted quickly. It was often a case of "We don't want it good, we want it Tuesday". More writers could always be brought in to improve it. Studios were like factories and designed to produce a product called movies.

The brothers Mankiewicz – Herman and Joseph – stayed the course in Hollywood, and were usually in receipt of earnings that others might envy. They were both linked to films that have a place in screen history, and their names are remembered because of that fact. But not everything ran smoothly for them, and, for varying reasons, they had their share of the many difficulties that a career in films almost inevitably involved.

Herman, the older of the two, was born in 1897, and Joseph in 1909. In childhood Joseph always looked up to Herman, and later in life he took on the responsibilities of picking up the pieces as his older brother's life began to fall apart. They were both heavily influenced by their father, a teacher and later professor who expected high standards and was not in favour of popular culture, including the cinema. Sydney Ladensohn Stern describes him as a "harsh parent". She also tells the story of Herman's feelings when a bicycle he had been given as a Christmas present was stolen. It was an incident that imprinted itself on him and was a shaping factor when, much later, he worked on the screenplay for *Citizen Kane.*

A bright student, Herman applied to go to Columbia University in New York, but because of his age had to wait a year before acceptance. His father sent him to work in the coal mines near Wilkes-Barre in Pennsylvania, where the family was then living. Stern says that Herman always valued the experience of working with the miners, who taught him to smoke and drink, and he admired their camaraderie. But he was never a radical, and in the 1930s, when the Screen Writers Guild was established, he refused to join it, and instead aligned himself with a rival, more-conservative organisation designed to represent the interests of writers in the studio system.

Herman had an active life as a student and enlisted in the armed forces in 1918. He arrived in France in early November, but was too late to find himself in a combat situation. Before leaving New York he had started writing book reviews and articles for the *New York Tribune*, and when he returned from Europe he continued to pursue a career in journalism. He was also deeply interested in the theatre and anxious to write plays. I'm not giving a complete account of Herman's travels and experiences in the early 1920s. He visited Paris and Berlin, and in New York wrote for the *New York Times* and the newly-started *New Yorker.* His work as a theatre critic introduced him to the legendary Algonquin Round Table, and its often hard-drinking characters like Dorothy Parker, Alexander Woollcott and

George S. Kaufman. He also knew Ben Hecht, Louise Brooks and Harpo Marx.

In 1926 the lively and likeable Herman moved to Hollywood, attracted by stories of the high salaries paid for turning out what appeared to be routine scenarios. His intention was to earn enough to settle some debts – he gambled as well as drank – and then return to New York. Like others at the time, he had little fondness for the cinema and saw it as inferior in both content and intention to the theatre. Working in Hollywood, Herman had to adhere to its conventions. As Stern puts it, "Movies grew out of peep shows and vaudeville. They started as commerce and developed into art", and art was ok provided it made money. She quotes Herman as saying: "When the producer says to you, 'Now in Reel Three the fellow shouldn't kiss the girl, he should kiss the cow', that fellow was going to kiss the cow and there wasn't a thing the writer could do about it".

Faced with situations like that, Herman rarely took his work in Hollywood too seriously. Perhaps his general view was summed up in a telegram to Ben Hecht encouraging him to come to Hollywood, part of which read, "Millions are to be grabbed out here, and your only competition is idiots". And Herman, although he had a wife and children to support, took advantage of his capacity to earn high fees for what he wrote by spending much of his income on drinking and gambling. And he continued to yearn for a move back to New York and the world of the theatre.

Did Herman connect with any major films during his time in Hollywood? *Citizen Kane* (1938) is probably the only one, and his contribution to that was for a long time disputed. Orson Welles often claimed to have written most of the screenplay, and downplayed what Herman had added. But Stern makes a convincing case for Herman being the main source of it, and she points out that his memories of the bicycle he lost when young were likely behind the word "Rosebud" that Kane utters as he dies. The bicycle and the sledge represented lost innocence.

It would be unfair to overlook some other films that Herman had links to. He worked on *Monkey Business* (1931) with the Marx Brothers, and on *Dinner at Eight* (1933) which, as a stage play, had been a hit on Broadway, and became a popular film. There was *Million Dollar Legs* (1932), hailed as a "surrealist masterpiece" by the artist and photographer, Man Ray. Later, he wrote *Christmas*

Holiday (1944), often included in lists of film noir material and notable for Deanna Durbin and Gene Kelly playing uncharacteristic roles. Some attention should also be paid to *Mad Dog of Europe*, an attack on Hitler and the rise of the Nazis that Herman struggled in vain to get into production. Despite his reputation for drinking and flippancy he was politically astute enough to understand what was happening in Germany and elsewhere as state-sponsored anti-Semitism gained a foothold in various countries.

Joseph Mankiewicz, who still looked up to his brother, had followed him to Hollywood. Like Herman, he thought of the cinema as having less importance than the theatre. Both brothers can be seen as wanting to please their father by creating something good in his terms, which may not have been the best sort of influence for them. If someone has their mind set against something they are convinced is inferior then it's difficult to convince them that it can have qualities worthy of attention. "Pop" Mankiewicz never did think much of films as art.

Joseph's first film for MGM was *Manhattan Melodrama* (1934) which featured Myrna Loy and William Powell, and turned out to be a box-office success. He shared credit for the screenplay with Oliver H.P. Garrett, He also contributed dialogue to King Vidor's *Our Daily Bread* (1934), a socially-conscious film about a collective farm during the Depression. Vidor later disparaged Joseph's contributions to the script, saying they were no more than a few adjustments here and there.

Persuaded to take on the role of a producer, Joseph spent some time overseeing the work of other writers and directors.. It was not a task he was completely happy with, though it raised his earnings beyond what he would have received writing screenplays. And he needed the money. Herman was frequently in debt or trouble of one sort or another, and relied on Joseph to come to his rescue. But one advantage that being a producer brought was the power to order re-writes when necessary. Joseph, as a producer, could not claim any screenwriting credits unless he had written the full script, but he was in a position to make revisions and replace writers when required.

An example was when he brought in F. Scott Fitzgerald to work on *Three Comrades* 1938) which, in Stern's words, "could have been the industry's first major openly anti-Nazi film". But it was based on a novel by Erich Maria Remarque, whose books had been burned by the Nazis, and interference by the German Consul in Los Angeles, the Catholic Legion of Decency, film censor Joseph Breen, and studio heads worried about possible effects on the sales of their films in Germany, led to references to Jews and Catholics being removed from the script: "Remarque's powerful political drama was reduced to romantic melodrama". Breen even wanted the Nazi thugs changed into communists.

Joseph left MGM and went to work at Twentieth Century Fox. He wrote and directed *A Letter to Three Wives* (1949), which was both a critical and commercial success. And gave him some standing as an astute social critic. This was further enhanced when he used his skills as writer/director for *All About Eve* (1949), a sharp observation of the world of the theatre in which an ambitious young woman ruthlessly claws her way to stardom by exploiting her relationship with an older, established actress. It's a film that has become something of a cult classic over the years and bears repeated watching for Mankiewicz's work and his capacity to get the best out of his actors, including Bette Davies and Ann Baxter.

Herman's career had been in decline as he drank his way through the late-1940s and early-1950s, and he died in 1953. Joseph continued to work steadily. He directed *Julius Caesar* (1953), which starred Rex Harrison, John Gielgud and Marlon Brando. He then turned his attention to Hollywood and, almost biting the hand that fed him, wrote and directed *The Barefoot Contessa* (1954), in which Ava Gardner played a Spanish dancer discovered by a wealthy man anxious to put money into a film. He's accompanied by a washed-out, cynical director (played by Humphrey Bogart) and an obsequious publicity man (Edmond O'Brien in excellent form), both of them anxious to please the man with the money. The film wasn't a complete success, perhaps partly because of a somewhat contrived ending. And there had been intrusions from Howard Hughes, who suspected, not without reason, that the money man was based on him. Nor had everything been comfortable among the cast. Bogart had little regard for Gardner's talents as an actress.

If there had been difficulties with *The Barefoot Contessa* they were nothing compared to what Joseph experienced when he directed *Cleopatra* (1963), an extravaganza that featured Elizabeth Taylor, Richard Burton, and Rex Harrison. It was an experience from which, according to Stern, Joseph "never really recovered". There have been books and documentaries about the making of the film. It ran wildly over-budget, suffered from studio interference, was affected by the behaviour of its stars, and in the end didn't impress the critics. There was even a dispute about screenwriting credits, and finally Joseph, Ranald MacDougall, and Sidney Buchman shared them. Buchman was a blacklisted writer living in Europe.

It might have seemed that Joseph's career would end with a failure, but he did close it with *Sleuth* (1972) and its fine performances from Laurence Olivier and Michael Caine. He died in 1993.

I've only managed to refer to a few of the films that Herman and Joseph Mankiewicz were involved with. Some of their work was admittedly routine, and in Herman's case was obviously badly affected by his alcoholism. But they both were also responsible for films that have stood the test of time. And even in their minor moments there are flashes of dialogue or direction that come alive. It wasn't easy creating art in Hollywood, where the dollar reigned supreme and everyone had a better idea about how a film should be made than the writers and directors, but Herman and Joseph Mankiewicz did at times achieve it.

The Brothers Mankiewicz is informative and entertaining. It has numerous notes and a useful bibliography, and testifies to some dedicated research. I should add that the emphasis in the book is rightly on their activities with regard to working in Hollywood. But there are sufficient details about their personal lives, in terms of wives, children, and other relationships, to round out their stories.

THE BROTHERS MANKIEWICZ: HOPE, HEARTBREAK, AND HOLLYWOOD CLASSICS

By Sydney Ladensohn Stern

University Press of Mississippi. 468 pages. £34.95. ISBN 978-1-61703-267-7

PATTERNS OF RUSSIA : HISTORY, CULTURE, SPACES

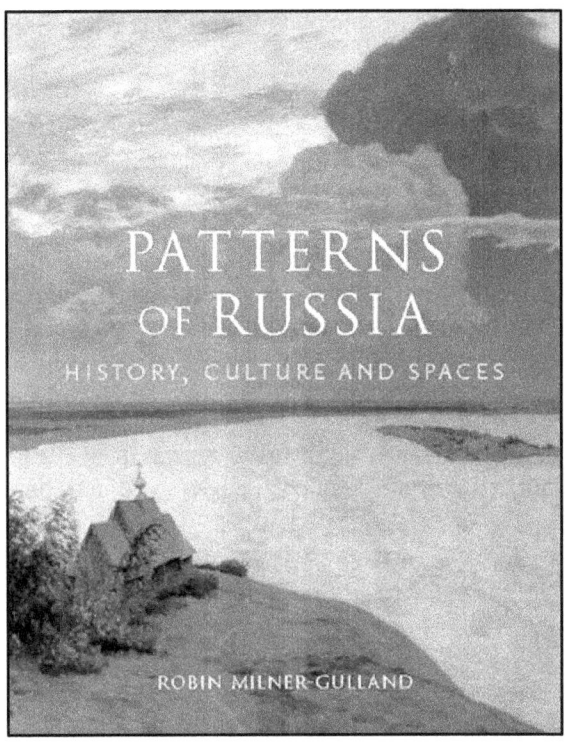

What do we know about Russia? I don't mean the Russia presented to us by politicians and political commentators, with their emphasis on its current difficulties and its supposed, and perhaps real, threat to our lives and liberties. I'm thinking more in terms of Russian history, its traditions, and the vastness of a country that encompasses millions of people from a variety of backgrounds and with a variety of beliefs and interests.

The complicated beginnings of what became known as Russia are outlined by Robin Milner-Gulland in a brisk, informative manner. There were shifts of power with leaders rising and falling and, at one time or another, "the Russian metropolitan seat" was located in Kiev, Vladimir, and then Moscow in 1321. St. Petersburg as a centre of culture and political power came later. It's worth noting this because it indicates how, under Peter the Great's direction, influences from the West began to play a relevant part in shaping Russia. But, as is made clear by Milner-Gulland, at the same time "the Russian Church became all the more significant as an all-Russian unifying force, enhanced by reinvigorated monasticism".

Discussing "Art and Artists of Old Russia" he points out that artists, as we think of them, "did not, strictly speaking, exist". There was plenty of art around, but it was primarily related to religion. And it didn't occur to people to think of it as art until the seventeenth century. Before that, `art' "as a generality meant nothing and could not have done……An `artist', too, could only have been perceived as a craftsman in one or another trade who carried out a specific task to the satisfaction of those by whom it was required". Icons were of key importance in this respect and Milner-Gulland devotes a fair amount of space to discussing them and what their uses were. We may now look at them as art, but in their day they often had more practical applications: "Simple people might treat them as if alive: blaming, even punishing them if the result of prayers did not live up to expectations".

What had become established in the West – portraiture and landscapes – arrived in Russia relatively late, and Milner-Gulland states that: "Post-Renaissance linear perspective did not affect Russian art (even on a sophisticated, let alone folk level) until the mid-seventeenth century, and even then only tentatively". But artists from outside began to work in Russia, and Peter the Great encouraged young would-be artists to go to Italy, for example, to study painting and sculpture: "It all worked well, with early eighteenth-century Russian artists (for example, the Nikitin brothers) speedy at adopting European techniques". There is a painting reproduced in the book – "In the Ploughing Field, Spring" by Aleksey Venetsianov – which shows how, by the early nineteenth-century, European influences had been absorbed, in more ways than one. The tranquil and idealised scene of peasant life was clearly designed to appeal to stratas of society that were financially and socially comfortable and did not want to be reminded of the true realities of agricultural labour.

When Milner-Gulland moves into the nineteenth-century, and what he refers to as "art for galleries, and not living rooms," I was reminded of an exhibition at the Russian Museum in Málaga some years ago. If memory serves me right, it was called *The Four Seasons* and tracked them through mostly nineteenth-century paintings. Many of them were large, and impressive in their realisation. Milner-Gulland mentions Ivan Shishkin who was accorded the perhaps back-handed compliment of being described as "the accountant of leaves" because of the precision of his paintings. Another artist, Isaac Levitan, is said to have produced canvases in which "nothing is fugitive", with his "poeticization of apparently unremarkable themes often compared with the literary methods of his lifelong friend (if occasional enemy) Anton Chekhov". Levitan's "The Vladimir Road" is reproduced in *Patterns of Russia"*, and shows "the first stage of convicts' journeys to Siberian exile". I recall seeing this painting in an exhibition at the National Gallery some years ago, and being struck by the way in which the seemingly sparse landscape captures the endless and empty futures awaiting the prisoners.

The reference to Levitan sent me hunting for a book, *The Itinerants*, published in Leningrad in 1974, which focused on the painters who came together in the Association of Itinerant Artists and exhibited their work in St. Petersburg, Moscow, and various provincial towns and cities. Milner-Gulland describes them as a "motive force for the so-called Socialist-Realist method of artistic production and propagation from the Soviet 1930s onwards; incidentally it is noteworthy to this day how many Russian provincial capitals have remarkable art museums".

It's said, by Milner-Gulland, that the tradition of "the Russian artists' conquest (or portrait) of land and landscape…..continued with a mild and belated, if competent, version of Impressionism much appreciated in the Soviet Union". I wondered about the comment regarding Impressionism being "much appreciated in the Soviet Union", an idea having been implanted In my mind somewhere along the way that it was largely a decadent, bourgeois form which was frowned on by the authorities. As a result, Impressionist art tended to be hidden in the storage spaces of museums or was secretly in private hands. But then I looked at the aforementioned book about the Itinerants alongside the catalogue for the exhibition of Russian Impressionism due to be held in Potsdam and Baden-Baden in 2020/2021. I'm not sure if it was affected by the Covid crisis.

What is obvious is that some of the artists in *The Itinerants* can also be seen as Impressionists. From this point of view I've long had a notion that "impressionism" is now something of a catch-all term widely applied to many late-nineteenth century paintings. There were a few original Impressionists, but lots of artists who looked at Monet and others and took away some aspects of their work. So, there can be a fairly clear relationship between the paintings by Isaac Levitan, Ilya Repin, and Vasily Polenov, to name three, that are featured in both books. They had all spent time in Paris. And Valentine Serov's "By the Window", in the Russian Impressionists catalogue, would not have seemed out-of-place in the book about the Itinerants.

When Milner-Gulland turns his attention to St. Petersburg (also called Petrograd and Leningrad, at various times), he provides an account of the establishment of the city, and its place in Russian history with regard to politics and culture. As a construct of the eighteenth-century it wasn't as established as Moscow, and there was always a certain amount of tension between the two cities. And St. Petersburg always had an eye on Europe. Milner-Gulland stresses the cultural importance of the city, where Pushkin's "The Bronze Horseman" exerted its influence, Andrey Beliy's vast novel, *Petersburg*, was set, and poets like Alexander Blok, Vladimir Mayakovsky, and Anna Akhmatova performed at the Stray Dog Cabaret before the First World War.

Patterns of Russia is a stimulating book with much to recommend it in terms of information and ideas. I'm conscious of having only given a broad indication of its values, and I admit to having indulged myself by looking closer at Russian art than other aspects of the country's history, culture, and spaces. But Robin Milner-Gulland makes them all worthy of attention.

PATTERNS OF RUSSIA : HISTORY, CULTURE, SPACES
By Robin Milner-Gulland
Reaktion Books. 237 pages. £25. ISBN 978-1-78914-225-9

**THE FIGHTER FELL IN LOVE:
A SPANISH CIVIL WAR MEMOIR**

A couple of recent books about the Spanish Civil War have focused on the broad involvement of the International Brigades in the conflict. Alexander Clifford's *Fighting for Spain: The International Brigades in the Civil War 1936-1939* (Pen & Sword Books, 2020) and Giles Tremlett's *The International Brigades: Fascism, Freedom and the Spanish Civil War* (Bloomsbury, 2020) are both worth reading, with Tremlett's 700 page history perhaps being the definitive English-language book on the subject. It's worth noting that Richard Baxell's *Unlikely Warriors:The British in the Spanish Civil War and the Struggle Against Fascism* (Aarum Press, 2012) provides a closer examination of a specific group of volunteers.

Such books can, of course, include references to the experiences of individuals who fought in Spain, as well as outlining the broad strategy of the war, but they rarely go into great detail about the day-to-day activities of the average soldier. As anyone who has spent time in an army, whether in peacetime or a war setting, will tell you, much of military life is a question of routine. No matter the circumstances there are numerous jobs that need to be done to keep a unit functioning in an efficient manner. Soldiers have to be clothed, accommodated, fed, and paid. Mundane tasks but nonetheless essential. They are often not given too much attention by historians, and we may need to turn to memoirs such as the one under review to get an idea of what life was like a lot of the time when someone wasn't directly under fire.

James R. Jump – known as Jimmy to his fellow-Brigaders – was 21 when he decided to go to Spain. He wasn't an early-volunteer – it was late-1937 before he made his decision – but he had been active in local Labour politics in the South-East, where he worked as a journalist for the *Worthing Herald*. He had been taught Spanish while at school, and he was engaged to a Spanish woman, Cayetana, who had come to England with a party of Basque refugee children. The fact that he spoke Spanish was to play a part in what happened once he arrived in Spain. It's useful to know, in this context, that casualty rates were high among Brigaders. As an example, of the just over 2,000 men in the British Battalion, around 500 were killed and many others wounded, sometimes more than once. By the end of 1937 half of the International Brigades "consisted of Spanish conscripts".

There have been other accounts of what it was like to make the journey, via Paris, to Spain, with its subterfuge, assistance from French communists, and the long hike across the mountains between the two countries. Jump's story is still relevant. He kept a diary of his activities and noted details of where he was and who he met. He didn't travel alone and at one point in Paris, while waiting to be interviewed and medically examined, "My ears caught the sounds of German, Italian, French and American English, but there were other languages that I did not recognise".

When he finally got to Spain and the International Brigade headquarters at Albacete, he was issued with items of equipment, including a Russian rifle dated 1901. This gives an indication of how the Republican Army in general suffered from a lack of up-to-date armaments, not to mention shortages of food, medical equipment, and proper uniforms. Photographs in the book show that the Brigaders dressed in a variety of jackets, when they had them, and trousers. Jump says at one point, "we had hardly any equipment. Most of us were bareheaded, dressed in shirts and trousers. Few had boots. Most of us wore sandals or rope-soled *alpargatas*. I doubt if there were four steel helmets in the whole company. We had no pouches, but carried our ammunition in our pockets or in bags tied to our belt".

Because he spoke Spanish Jump was frequently assigned to act as an interpreter. As he points out, few of the British Brigaders spoke any Spanish beyond a few basic words and, when he ran classes to teach the language, hardly anyone came to them. His language and journalistic skills also came in useful when he was told to take on administrative duties, such as paymaster, postman, and clerical worker keeping records of new arrivals, deaths, departures due to wounds or sickness, and similar matters. This may seem like the routines I referred to earlier, and not as interesting as what was taking place at the front, but Jump has a light touch that makes it relevant by tying it in with reports of what was happening generally in Spain. His facility with the language gave him greater contact with the local people, and he went to the nearby theatres and bars. He was consequently probably more aware than most Brigaders of how the Spanish people were managing to survive the privations of the war. There are tiny character sketches of some of the Spaniards he got to know.

The war finally came close to Jump when he was posted to the International Brigades preparing for the last great offensive by the Republican Army, the crossing of the Ebro and the assault on Franco's forces. He was in action during the attack on Gandesa and, while surviving unscathed, he saw several of his friends cut down by bombs and bullets. He notes that there was little, if any, air support provided for the soldiers on the ground, and that Franco's aircraft, often piloted by Germans and Italian, dominated the skies. Jump may have been lucky when it came to being killed or wounded during the fighting, but he fell victim to one of the other problems that beset soldiers and was diagnosed as suffering from yellow jaundice.

Sent back across the Ebro, he had spells in various hospitals before he was considered fit enough to return to duties. But by that time the decision had been taken by the Spanish Government to withdraw the International Brigades from Spain. If the Prime Minister, Negrin, hoped that this would persuade Franco to similarly dispose of the German and Italian forces supporting him, he was sadly mistaken. Russia had already virtually abandoned Republican Spain to its fate, and it would not be long before Franco easily swept to victory and began a policy of purges and reprisals.

Before that happened the Brigaders were brought together and prepared for their departure. Jump provides some vivid descriptions of slow-moving trains, long delays in decrepit stations, and arrival in a bombed-out Barcelona. The British contingent was finally shipped through France to Dieppe and eventually London. Different nationalities were not as lucky, and many Brigaders, unable to return to countries such as Germany and Italy, were interned in France.

Jump was honest enough to admit that he was frightened at the thought of being under fire. And, with this in mind, he had doubts when an announcement was made that two Scandinavians had been executed for desertion. They were automatically labelled as Trotskyists, the implication being that it was their political affiliations that influenced them to desert. Jump, though, "suspected that the condemned men were victims of their own fear. They had been terrified out of their lives and, unable to stand anymore, had deserted. I had been terrified, too, and knew what it felt like".

It was due to this, and similar occurrences, that he "came to the conclusion that I would never make a real soldier.......and I was only intellectuality an anti-fascist". He could never imagine himself shooting a Spanish conscript who had thrown away his uniform and gun and was attempting to flee. There are some other examples of the ways in which discipline was exercised in the Brigades, and not only in relation to battlefield circumstances. Anti-semitism, racism, drunkenness, sexual deviation, and catching venereal diseases, were all offences: "The atmosphere was, in fact, quite puritanical".

Jump married his Spanish fiancée when he returned to England, served in the British Army during the Second World War, and later became a teacher. He additionally wrote several books about Spain, and his *The Penguin Spanish Dictionary* was published in 1990, the year he died.

The Fighter Fell in Love is an engaging book, largely due to Jump's clear writing style, his humanity, and his sense of humour which allowed him to see the funny aspects of some strange situations. It was never published during his lifetime, and the current edition was assembled from two draft versions and diary entries by his son, Jim Jump. Placed throughout the book are several poems, some of them written in Spain, some later. I have a memory that a few were published in *Tribune* around the time I was writing for the paper in the 1960s and 1970s.

Paul Preston has contributed an informative Foreword, and there is a Preface by Jack Jones which was written for a planned 1987 edition of the book. Jones, one-time General Secretary of the Transport and General Workers Union, had fought in Spain and been wounded. Jim Jump writes about his father and mother and there are useful notes which clarify many of the references to individuals and places in the text.

THE FIGHTER FELL IN LOVE: A SPANISH CIVIL WAR MEMOIR

By James R. Jump

The Clapton Press, 213 pages. £9.99. ISBN 976-1-913693-05-3

PEEL ME A LOTUS

In 1954 the Australian writers, Charmian Clift and George Johnston, tired of the dreariness and drabness of post-war London, decided to move to the Mediterranean and a life in the sun on a Greek island. Their reasons were not just a matter of seeking warm weather and following a hedonistic lifestyle. Johnston, ten years older than Clift, had been a well-regarded war correspondent, and had published several books. And the couple had worked together on three novels. They reasoned that they could live a lot cheaper wherever they settled in the Mediterranean, and Johnston would be able to get down to the "serious" writing he wanted to do and not have to turn out pulp novels to earn money. Clift also had ambitions to produce something of value under her own name.

The couple spent a year or so on the island of Kalymnos, and Clift, who had a flair for what is often referred to as travel writing, produced a book called *Mermaid Singing*, published in 1956, about life there. The family (there were two daughters, one of them from Johnston's first marriage, a son, and Clift was pregnant) moved to Hydra in August, 1955. It will probably be evident from what I've outlined so far that, whatever plans Clift had in mind, she would find much of her time taken up with looking after the children and organising domestic arrangements, while Johnston applied himself to his writing. Despite these limitations, Clift wrote two novels while they were living on Hydra, as well as *Peel Me a Lotus*, which first appeared in print in 1959.

Polly Samson, in a useful introduction, refers to Johnston and Clift as "at the vanguard of what was soon to become a fabled bohemian community of artists and writers, of exiles and dreamers". But initially they were among a handful of non-Greeks resident on Hydra. The Australian painter Sidney Nolan was there, and is in Clift's book as Henry Trevena, and there was a writer she calls Sean Donovan who was based on Patrick Greer. His wife, Nancy Dignan (Lola in the book) provided illustrations for the first printing of *Peel Me a Lotus* which are also in the new edition. Donovan/Greer is shown as always struggling to get published. Clift is not unsympathetic to someone like him and says: "Every one of us, in his particular way, is a protestant against the rat race of modern commercialism.......Each of us has somehow managed to stumble off the treadmill, determined to do his own work in his own way".

It's interesting to read Clift's observations on the island and its native-born inhabitants. Described as "a mainly barren rock" by Samson, and certainly impoverished in terms of opportunities for employment, it had declined in importance as a trading centre. It did attract some visitors from the mainland during the summer months. But many of the houses were empty, so could be rented, or even bought, quite easily, and low-waged domestic help was available. The locals may not have been always fond of the loose social and moral ways of visitors, but there doesn't appear to have been extensive outright hostility.

It's also worth noting that at the time Clift is writing about there was an armed struggle taking place on Cyprus in an attempt to oust British troops stationed there. An organisation called EOKA was carrying out a campaign of guerrilla warfare which inevitably brought aggressive responses from the British. People on Hydra were naturally sympathetic towards the Cypriot causes, though apart from one or two minor incidents noted by Clift there were few overt hostile acts directed against non-Greeks on Hydra. Many of those who started to drift in were not British, in any case, so could not be held responsible for what was happening in Cyprus.

In a way it's possible to take what you want from *Peel Me a Lotus* and not expect it to shine a lot of light on the relationship between Clift and Johnston. She is certainly shown as being dissatisfied because she feels that she's held back by having to look after the children and see to general domestic demands. But there is not much evidence of what, if other accounts are reliable, was frequently a somewhat fractious situation often brought about by excessive drinking and extra-marital affairs. It was, perhaps, inevitable that, when people were pushed together in a confined area with not many other distractions, there are likely to be liaisons of varying degrees of intensity. There would be few opportunities to disguise or hide such affairs on a small island where gossip was a game that most people played. Clift, writing about the way the bohemians formed a little circle of like-minded people, described how it was: "Always the same conversation, yesterday, today, tomorrow, the same smart verbal catch-ball with obscure poets and philosophers, the same Freudian terms, the same 'frank' piggery, the same little shafts of malice and spite, the same derisive laughter".

Hydra may have had few expatriate writers and artists when Clift and Johnston landed there in 1955, but things would soon change. What would appear to have been a new breed of drifters began to call in at Hydra as they moved from place to place, rarely settling anywhere for very long, and using a desire to write or paint as an excuse for not working and sponging off those they thought likely to have money to give away. Bohemia has always been a playground for such types, but the late-1950s and early-1960s saw them multiplying in number.

Clift referred to them as "intellectual hoboes" and "transient bohemians" and noted how they had a fund of anecdotes about the places they'd been and the well-known writers and artists they'd met. They had read the reviews of the latest books and carried magazines like *Perspectives, Encounter,* and *Partisan Review*. I would guess that, a year or two later it might have been *Evergreen Review*. But only a handful had any real talent for painting a picture or writing a novel. Too many were like Sykes Horowitz, a would-be artist Clift names, who "hasn't really been able to get down to it in Europe". While waiting for inspiration to arrive he borrows money and drinks. It's amusing to note that they sometimes looked down on a writer like George Johnston because he wasn't experimental or avant-garde. And, as well as books under his own name, he wrote popular crime novels as Shane Martin. But they weren't averse to asking Clift and Johnston to lend them money or provide free meals.

If many of the newcomers had little money to spend they nonetheless usually drew attention to the places they stopped at for a time, and were soon followed by more-affluent types who pushed up the prices of property and inclined hotels, bars, and restaurants to increase their charges. A genuine bohemia can only exist where food, drink and accommodation are cheap, and so the productive writers and artists often move on to where, for a time at least, it's more economical to live.

Not every new arrival on Hydra lacked the talent or drive to create. The Canadian singer and poet, Leonard Cohen, turned up in 1960, and features prominently in Clift's book, as does Marianne Jensen, who had a deep relationship with Cohen and was celebrated in his songs and poems. Gregory Corso, one of the leading lights of the Beat movement, also appears to have put in an appearance. He was certainly in Greece in 1961. It would be possible to place him in the "transient bohemians" category, but though he seemed to survive mostly on handouts and other substitutes for working, he had collections of poetry to his name, a novel, and a selection of scattered writings. He had some genuine creative powers, even if many people found him hard to take at times. Anyone interested in following up on just who came to Hydra around the time Charmian Clift and George Johnston were there should have a look at *Half the Perfect World: Writers, Dreamers and Drifters on Hydra, 1955-1964* (Monash University Publishing, 2018) by Paul Genoni and Tanya Dalziell.

It may have been a sign of the growing popularity of Hydra that, in 1956, a Hollywood film crew descended on the island. The film in question was *Boy on a Dolphin*, which starred Alan Ladd and a young Sophia Loren. Clift's comments on the presence and activities of the various people involved in its making were less than enthusiastic. She acknowledged that some short-term economic benefits were felt by the islanders, but the long-term effect was to emphasise the increasing commercialisation of Hydra as a place for tourists to visit. Clift didn't openly end her book with a wistful lament for the Hydra of old and a hint that unwelcome changes were inevitable, but it's in the writing, nonetheless.

They did eventually leave Hydra in 1964 and returned to Australia and a parting of the ways. George Johnston worked on *Clean Straw for Nothing*, the second novel in a semi-autobiographical sequence that had started with *My Brother Jack*, published in 1964. *Clean Straw for Nothing* came out in 1969. A third part, *A Cartload of Clay*, though never completed, was posthumously published in 1971. Johnston had suffered from tuberculosis for many years and died in 1970. Charmian Clift worked as a journalist in Australia and published several books. She committed suicide in 1969, and some sources say that it was because she was worried that Johnston's *Clean Straw for Nothing* would lay bare her sexual indiscretions when the couple were living on Hydra.

Those who disapprove of the bohemian lifestyle will no doubt shake their heads knowingly, as they will when they learn that three of the four children in the Johnston family had what can be called sad endings. Gae, the daughter from Johnston's first marriage, died from a drugs overdose in 1988. Shane Johnston committed suicide in 1974. Martin Johnston, widely praised as a poet, was an alcoholic and died in 1990. Were their lives affected by their upbringings on Hydra? The other son, Jason, who was born on the island, seems to have survived the experience. And plenty of people commit suicide or succumb to drugs and alcohol without ever having been the children of bohemians.

I've briefly rounded off the Charmian Clift/George Johnston story, though *Peel Me a Lotus* can easily stand alone as a well-written and vivid account of a time and a place in the sun. Clift's skill at evoking the period is considerable, as are her quickly sketched but finely-observed portraits of both bohemians and the local community. But there's no denying that a degree of romanticism has now accrued to the characters of Charmian and George, with allusions made to similar ill-fated literary couples such as Ted Hughes and Sylvia Plath. A couple of recent novels, Tamar Hodges' *The Water and the*

Wine (Hookline Books, 2018) and Polly Samson's *A Theatre for Dreamers* (Bloomsbury, 2020) do show the friction that existed between Clift and Johnson, together with their heavy drinking and various affairs, so it isn't all made to seem easy-living and good fun. But the fact of their having been written, with surely more to follow, points to the near-legendary status that has grown up around them and their years on Hydra.

PEEL ME A LOTUS
By Charmian Clift
Muswell Press. 202 pages. £8.99. ISBN 978-1-83811-012-3

NINA HAMNETT

The fact that, as I write this review, an exhibition of Nina Hamnett's work has just opened at Charleston House, a location now famous for its Bloomsbury links, provides hope that, at last, attention might be paid to the paintings and sketches she produced. She wasn't just the "Queen of Bohemia", someone referred to in memoirs and histories of Fitzrovia and Soho in the 30s and 40s, and remarked on for her faded glory and unkempt appearance.

Hamnett was born in 1890 in Tenby and had what might be seen as a somewhat curious childhood. Her father was an army officer who was later dismissed from the service because of some financial irregularities. A tomboyish child, never prone to behaving conventionally or obeying orders, she was educated in various places and showed an aptitude for drawing. She attended Portsmouth School of Art, and the Dublin School of Art, but following her father's disgrace the family moved to London. She went to the London School of Art, often referred to as "Brangwyn's", due to the presence of the popular painter and professor, Frank Brangwyn. It was then that she began to truly display her drawing and painting skills and make friends and contacts among the artistic community. Of "Brangwyn's", she said: "Here at last was paradise. It was run as a French Academy". Alicia Foster notes that among the staff at the London School of Art was William Nicholson whose "influence at this early stage in Hamnett's career was particularly significant: he helped to shape Hamnett's own approach to still life".

Foster's account is primarily focused on Hamnett's work rather than what might be called her unstable private life. And that's as it should be in view of the fact that the exhibition it relates to is designed to promote the work. But it is difficult to separate the story of Hamnett the artist from that of Hamnett the bohemian. She went to Paris in 1912 (and again in 1914), met Gertrude Stein, and studied in the atelier of the Russian painter, Marie Vassilieff. She was not averse to joining in the café life, and her autobiography, *Laughing Torso* (originally published by Constable in 1932 and reprinted by Virago in 1984) is a colourful account of encounters with Modigliani, Kees Van Dongen, Ossip Zadkine, and many others. It might give an idea of her exuberant and uninhibited personality if I quote from her reminiscences about a visit to Van Dongen's studio when he had a Thursday open house: "One day they asked me to dance, so I took off all my clothes and danced in a black veil".

It was not all frivolity and loose-living, and Hamnett must have been alert to what was happening in Paris as Post-Impressionism, Fauvism, Cubism, and the work of individual artists who perhaps didn't fit easily into a definable category, came to her attention. Foster stresses that Hamnett had been aware of Post-Impressionist paintings before going to Paris, thanks to the exhibitions that Roger Fry organised in London. Several illustrations in Foster's book point to influences from Paris, though it needs to be remembered that she had already benefited from William Nicholson's lessons about creating successful still-life paintings in advance of visiting the French capital.

It could be that it was her skill as a portraitist that showed her at her best. There are several eye-catching portraits of Osbert Sitwell, Lady Constance Stewart-Robinson, and Horace Brodsky from the period prior to 1920. The point about them is that they are not simply photographic-style representations of their subjects. Instead, they attempt to capture some of the individual characteristics of the sitters. Foster, referring to the portrait of Brodsky, thinks it one of Hamnett's finest, and it "shows a figure doubly outside British norms of masculinity, as he was both Jewish and Australian……..He is a compact, dark presence in Hamnett's painting: his body seems too small for his head, which is as massy and sharp-planed as a carving, set against the stripes of strong colour behind him".

Hamnett produced work for the Omega Workshops over a number of years (she may be seen as a link between the Bloomsbury group and the Camden Town artists), painted murals for the Arthur Ruck House, helped edit *Coterie,* a short-lived little magazine of the period, provided drawings for Osbert Sitwell's *The People's Album of London Statues,* did some teaching, and exhibited and worked as a model in both Paris and London. She continued to achieve striking portraits. One, of the male ballet dancer, Rupert Doone, captures what has been described as his "Ariel-like beauty and mercurial temperament". But there's no doubt that she enjoyed the life of the cafés and bars, perhaps to the detriment of her talents as a painter. Most accounts of life among the artists and writers of 1920s Paris and London have a reference to Hamnett, noting that she mixed easily with the well-to-do, who no doubt found her amusing for her entertainment value, as well as with the bohemians.

But there may have been disturbing signs that all was not well. In 1931 Ethel Mannin published a novel called *Ragged Banners* (Penguin edition, 1940). There is a scene in it set in a pub clearly based on the Fitzroy Tavern, a favourite haunt of the bohemians of London's Fitzrovia. And one of the characters is a woman "with her glazed eyes, and her tawdry clothes, a ruin of a woman" who had once been famous in Paris. It was obviously a portrait of Hamnett, who, when she heard about it, threatened to give Mannin a black eye if she ever encountered her.

Some years earlier, probably around the mid-1920s, her one-time lover Roger Fry, who thought that she had failed to live up to her potential, saw her as "a coarse heavy middle-aged rouée". Fry had portrayed Hamnett in 1917 in what Denise Hooker says "was one of his most penetrating and successful works. In her dark polo-necked jumper and skirt, sleeves rolled up ready for work, she seems serious-minded, self-possessed and independent, very much of the breed of new woman". But it has to be said that a 1926 portrait by Jacob Kramer, on the cover of Hooker's biography of Hamnett, does tend to suggest a degree of coarsening and heaviness in her facial expression when compared to Fry's earlier painting.

Hamnett became a fixture around Fitzrovia and Soho, when the latter area and its pubs and clubs took over as the playground of the bohemians. It would take up too much space to list all the books she crops up in, but those dealing with the York Minster pub (usually known as The French) and the notorious drinking club, the Colony Room, mention her more than once. One of the most interesting publications in which she appears, albeit in fictional form, is Julius Horwitz's novel, *Can I Get There by Candlelight* (André Deutsch, 1964). Horwitz was an American serviceman stationed in Britain during the war years, and his novel, mostly set in Fitzrovia and Soho, is an engaging fictionalised account of some of his experiences. Hamnett appears as Nora, an artist who had spent time in Paris where she knew Modigliani, Picasso, Braque, and many others.

The narrator goes to her lodgings: "I like Nora's room. It has the look of the painters' rooms I knew in New York, those $16-a-month cold water flats on Hudson Street. The clean brushes, the squashed tubes of paint, the raw canvases, the piled-up books, the raw hanging paintings, hanging like newborn babies on display in a maternity ward, the stretchers, the empty wine bottles, all of it looks so god damn elegant". Nora/Hamnett isn't portrayed in a cruel way in *Can I Get There by Candlelight*, and is generally looked on in a nostalgically warm light, though some of her less-savoury habits are mentioned, along with her open sexuality. She had numerous lovers and liaisons, several with well-known people, many not. And another visit to her room significantly refers to a canvas on the easel that doesn't appear to have been touched recently.

Hamnett hadn't lost all her skills and when the second volume of autobiography, *Is She a Lady?* (Allan Wingate, 1955), was published it included a number of convincing drawings of young boys. But I wonder if she was painting (could she still afford the necessary materials?), or not getting much further than these preparatory sketches? A photograph taken in her room in 1954 shows her talking to the now-forgotten writer and editor Wrey Gardiner. It's noticeable that there are several bottles littered around the room. Nina Hamnett died in 1956 when she fell from the window of her flat and was impaled on the railings below. There were suggestions that she had committed suicide. She had been suffering from ill-health and had spent several months in hospital. But a verdict of accidental death was recorded by the coroner.

As I said at the start of this review, Alicia Foster's book doesn't have a great deal of information about what might be called the bohemian aspects of Hamnett's life. Her concern is to draw attention to her work as an artist. And she does that admirably. It's right that Hamnett's achievements as an artist should be acknowledged in what is the first retrospective of her work. I've added some details taken from other sources to round out the story – Hamnett's two books, Julius Horwitz's novel, and Denise Hooker's *Nina Hamnett: Queen of Bohemia* (Constable, 1986) – and Foster's book has some useful notes. It's attractively produced, and one of a series about women artists which includes volumes on Laura Knight, Eileen Agar and Marlowe Moss.

NINA HAMNETT
By Alicia Foster
Eiderdown Books. 60 pages. £10.99. ISBN 978-1-9160416-6-0

IN LOVE WITH HELL : DRINK IN THE LIVES AND WORK OF ELEVEN WRITERS

"Most writers are drinkers", according to Jimmie Charters, the barman who served up drinks to the likes of F. Scott Fitzgerald, Ernest Hemingway, Jean Rhys, Robert McAlmon, Nancy Cunard, and numerous others in Paris during the 1920s. Being a "drinker" can mean many things, and it doesn't necessarily imply that every writer in the land is likely to be a slave to the demon drink. But there's no denying that more than a few have been and an extensive list can be compiled of authors who had their lives and work affected by a liking for alcohol. By picking out eleven writers William Palmer is simply offering a selection from the many who could be candidates for inspection.

What causes writers to drink? The reasons are probably as numerous as the writers they might apply to. Palmer, looking at John Cheever, says that "Many writers have had indifferent school careers and a fairly dismal home life; perhaps imagination, like the mushroom, needs a dark, neglected area to grow in". And it does seem true that, if the lives of several of those pinned down on the pages of Palmer's book are anything to go by, they didn't exactly flourish in the classroom, and you couldn't say that their childhoods were models of happiness and enlightenment. Still, it's surprising what can provide the spur to creativity. It may be a price worth paying if the result is a finely-written story or a well-crafted poem. Cheever, "all of his life a haunted man, troubled by feelings of duality and bisexuality", in Palmer's words, once said of his writing: "It has given me money and renown, but I suspect that it may have something to do with my drinking habits. The excitement of alcohol and the excitement of fantasy are very similar".

It does need to be said that the drinking wouldn't be of interest if it wasn't for the writing it inspired, if it did, or the damage it caused to the quality of the work. Only a doctor, or family and friends in the direct line of fire from drunken incidents, might have been curious about Patrick Hamilton's intake of whisky, had he not been a writer: "His daily consumption can seldom have fallen far below the equivalent of three bottles". It's relevant to the reader in relation to Hamilton the novelist who, among other works, including highly-successful plays, wrote at least two novels that have retained their appeal – *Slaves of Solitude* and *Hangover Square*. The latter, with its brilliantly-accurate descriptions of pubs and their customers, might well be forever associated with Hamilton's name because of its title and his alcoholism. It's noteworthy that Hamilton's novels may additionally have attributes as social documents, in that the pubs and places and the atmospheres they describe are part of a lost world of simpler tastes and expectations.

Hamilton's novels are often set around pubs and drinking, so it could be argued that they reflect his own habits. But they can't be seen as directly autobiographical in the way that Jean Rhys's first four novels, and many of her short stories, were. A later novel, and it's the one she's best-known for, *Wide Sargasso Sea*, moved away from the facts of her own life. It brought her some late-fame and success. I have to admit to a preference for the earlier works, perhaps because the worlds they deal with – experiences as a chorus girl in London before the First World War, the expatriate bohemia of Paris in the 1920s – and the way they were written (in a clearcut, direct style) interest me more. It was in her early days that she began to drink and alcohol gripped her for the rest of her life. When she was older she was frequently at loggerheads with neighbours and was an abusive and sometimes violent drunk.

Was it the rackety nature of Rhys's life that drew her to drink as a kind of protection against men who used her, the seedy surroundings, and an inner loneliness? A combination of all three would be a powerful incentive to try to blot out the world or provide a temporary refuge. For the poet Elizabeth Bishop, the only other woman surveyed, Palmer suggests "she must have found in drink something other than a chemical or genetic imperative". He says she was "intensely shy" and "uncertain of her social position". Her childhood was certainly "broken", with her father dying when she was a baby, and her mother eventually committed to an asylum. She was shuttled around various relatives and sent to boarding schools. Palmer also thinks that initial uneasiness about her lesbianism might have had something to do with her drinking. If so, then "coming out" didn't resolve her difficulties with drink and she continued throughout her lifetime. But, as Palmer says, she never used the drinking in her life as a basis for her work: "When she drank self-destructively it was for reasons we can only guess at".

A reason for drinking in the case of Charles Jackson could be his repressed homosexuality. He's now only remembered as the author of *The Lost Weekend*, a novel regarded as one of the "classics" about the curse of alcoholism. Malcolm Lowry, who Palmer also investigates, and who wrote *Under the Volcano*, certainly thought that Jackson knew what he was talking about when he described the horrors of delirium tremens and incarceration in New York's Bellevue Hospital. Lowry had himself been there. The interesting thing about Jackson is that, according to Palmer, "his early childhood seems to have been happy and uneventful". But when he was twelve his father "deserted the family" and shortly after a sister and baby brother died in a car accident. There may also be hints at Jackson's unsettled sexuality in the story "Palm Sunday" in the collection, *The Sunnier Side and Other Stories*. Jackson published a number of novels and stories, but his reputation rests on *The Lost Weekend*.

In the same way, Malcolm Lowry is best-known for *Under the Volcano* even though he wrote other works, some of which only appeared after his death and, it's suggested, might have been better left unpublished. Lowry appears to have actually enjoyed being an alcoholic, and is quoted as saying, "I love hell. I can't wait to get back there". He did have periods of sobriety but they often ended when old friends and drinking companions turned up. There was an occasion in 1937 when Lowry and his wife Jan were living in Mexico, and he was "mostly sober" and working. Conrad Aiken – described by Jan as "that bottle-a-day bard" – came to visit, with the inevitable result that he and Lowry promptly embarked on a drinking spree. Jan recalled that her husband would drink anything – " tequila, mescal, whisky, gin, beer, rubbing alcohol, after-shave lotion, and hair-tonic". Was there a reason for his addiction to alcohol? Palmer records some indications of shyness and feelings of sexual inadequacy, but they don't seem a totally useful explanation.

What impelled Dylan Thomas to drink like he did? Did he, as an outsider of sorts, feel out-of-place and inhibited when in the company of established writers and intellectuals, and so compensate for it by getting drunk? Or could it be that the drunkenness provided an excuse for his failings in terms of petty thefts, unreliability, cadging, and much else? Or was there an awareness in Thomas's thinking that he had probably written many of his best poems when he was young? His reputation mostly rested on his performances on and off the platform by 1950 or so. Palmer thinks that Thomas probably drank less than the rest of the writers he examines, but he died younger than them. And his death wasn't really due to an over-extended drunken episode but more likely because of inept medical treatment.

Kingsley Amis detested Dylan Thomas, both as a person and a poet. By the time Amis was beginning to make a name for himself, both with his novel, *Lucky Jim,* and his poems, Thomas and many of his contemporaries were out-of-fashion. The 1950s were the years of The Movement poets and the so-called Angry Young Men novelists. The Soho bohemians of the 1940s were fading fast, and the university-educated taking over. Surrealists and the New Apocalypse poets were looked on with suspicion and common sense and plain speaking came to the fore. None of this explains why Amis, described as "a charming and extremely funny man" when he was a young academic in Swansea, turned into an alcoholic "capable of gross and unforgiveable behaviour". Palmer does say that he had a "sort of defensive shyness which could easily change to the offensive" when he was drunk. Many of his novels are located in pubs, as Palmer notes: "By 1986, drink flows like a river through *The Old Devils*".

"Writing is an agony mitigated by drink" said Anthony Burgess, which some might see as more of an excuse than anything. I'm not sure that it is, and when I look at his output (it included a fair amount of what would be considered hack work – Palmer says Burgess wrote around "350 reviews in two years for the *Yorkshire Post* alone") it may be that he needed the stimulus that drink provided to keep him going. There were novels, general journalism, broadcasts, film scripts, trips to London, and he additionally had musical involvements. When did he get time for the affair he was engaged in for four years prior to his alcoholic wife's death? Palmer asserts that Burgess's drinking "assumed more or less reasonable proportions" as he got older and he lived until he was seventy-six. Will his work survive? Palmer points to several of the novels that he considers have lasting value, and it may be that *A Clockwork Orange*, "his most famous and notorious book", will ensure some sort of recognition in years to come.

Someone who could be excused for considering that he had valid excuses for drinking was the Irish writer, Flann O'Brien, famous for *At Swim Two-Birds* and *The Third Policeman*, though the latter only found its way into print after O'Brien had passed on. Both were written before he was thirty, and though he was well-known for a newspaper column he wrote under the name Myles na Gopaleen, his books did not attract wide attention among general readers. A job in the Irish Civil Service, the routines of family life, and the restrictive and repressive nature of Irish society, with the Catholic Church dominating social and cultural activities, pushed O'Brien into the refuge of the pub, "a licensed and necessary relief". Here, for a time, at least, he could escape into the company of like-minded friends, such as Patrick Kavanagh and Brendan Behan, though it's mentioned that he "rarely joined in the general conversation". He drank steadily until it was time to go home. Generally, for O'Brien, it was a choice "between drinking and being bored to death".

Palmer is of the opinion that, if only one of Richard Yates's novels survives it will be *Revolutionary Road*. Perhaps so, but he wrote some other good books and short-stories. They weren't given the right kind of attention when they were published, and Yates was sometimes unfairly said to be covering the same ground as John Cheever, a fellow-alcoholic who looked at the lives of suburbanites and found them wanting. But Cheever had a greater "range of emotion and character: Yates's work was almost entirely based on his own life and he used family members and friends in his fiction, making little effort to disguise them, or his contempt for them". Yates had grown up in a household of drinkers, with his mother, a would-be sculptress, especially prone to taking to the bottle. Yates seems to have been an awkward youth and it could be that his drinking was an attempt to put himself at ease with other people. But he drank enough to find himself in the same place where Charles Jackson and Malcolm Lowry had been residents – the alcoholic wards of New York's Bellevue Hospital. Palmer doesn't think that Yates will ever be a popular writer, despite a revival of interest in his work in recent years. He's too often "grey and depressing".

In Love with Hell is a fascinating if sometimes frightening book. And yet, it's hard not to accept that, despite all the problems that alcohol brought, the writers mostly produced fairly substantial bodies of work and survived into surprisingly reasonable old age. Would they have written as well if they hadn't drunk? It's impossible to tell, and their work would almost certainly have been much different. A lot of the novels that Palmer refers to are still worth reading, and he does a good job of analysing them in an informative way and relating them to the alcoholism of their various writers. His book ought to interest anyone who likes to know about writers and their experiences. It's the work that's of key importance, of course, but the lives add to its appeal.

IN LOVE WITH HELL : DRINK IN THE LIVES AND WORK OF ELEVEN WRITERS
By William Palmer
Robinson. 262 pages. £20. ISBN 978-1-47214-501-7

UNBURY OUR DEAD WITH SONG

Let me say that, before I read this novel, I had no idea what "Tizita" is. It's a form of music from Ethiopia which expresses the history, dreams, ambitions and tragedies of the country and its people. Or that's what I understand it to be. But it goes beyond that and, as characters in the book frequently remind the narrator, it has something undefinable about it that can only be felt. This doesn't preclude anyone outside the Ethiopian experience from ever sharing the feelings expressed by Tizita. They are often universal in their application and, it is suggested, everyone has their own Tizita. Some comparisons are drawn between it and the blues. But perhaps it's useful to quote the description that is given in the novel:

"The Tizita was not just a popular traditional Ethiopian song: it was a song that was life itself. It had been sung for generations, through wars, marriages, deaths, divorces and childbirths. For musicians and listeners exiled in Kenya, the US and Europe, or trying to claim a home in Israel as Ethiopian Jews, the Tizita was like a national anthem to the soul, for better and worse".

Telling the story is a Kenyan journalist. John Thandi Manfredi. He works for a publication called *The National Inquisitor*, a tabloid that largely specialises in gossip, innuendo, exaggerations, and even lies if they help to sell the paper. Manfredi also has his own demons, in that his parents are part of the ruling elite in Nairobi and he's conscious of the fact, with his good education and comfortable life, he's been a beneficiary of the corruption his family may have been involved in.

There are Ethiopians living in Nairobi, and Manfredi visits a seedy club in a run-down area of the city and listens to four Tizita performers. Intrigued by their music, he determines to find out more about it by interviewing and writing about them: The Diva, The Taliban Man, The Corporal, and Miriam, who is the barmaid at the club. What happens as he carries out the interviews, and talks to other people to collect information, becomes, in effect, something of a potted history of Ethiopia, as well as a chronicle of individual lives. The Diva, for example, can attract large crowds to her well-organised concerts and comes across as flamboyant in her costumes and gestures, but when she appears in the club it is as Kidane and she offers a quieter personality as she works alongside other musicians to provide a convincing Tizita performance. She has to persuade a more-discerning audience to recognise the sincerity of her singing.

The Taliban Man, with his stock of "weed" and cocaine, seems destined for popularity and is careful to cultivate an image – "youth, looks and self-possession all rolled into one" - that will capture the crowd. As for The Corporal, he has a shady background, having served in the war against Eritrea and, if some accounts are to be believed, he had been a ruthless and even sadistic fighter. And there is Miriam, who makes it clear to Manfredi that he will never be able to appreciate Tizita unless he visits Ethiopia: "You cannot know a river by drinking its water from a glass".

The combination of the journalist's own story and those of the Tizita artists is tidily handled, and it shows how he is searching for answers to his own doubts, as well as trying to learn about Tizita. When he goes to a party he observes the young people there – the children of affluent parents and themselves well-educated and in successful careers – and comments: "I had never seen so much talent and promise in one room. Feeling less optimistic than I had yesterday, I could not help but wonder, through the fog of my unfolding brain, how much of this talent was going to eventually go to waste – overdoses, alcoholism, drug addiction, the occasional suicide and, even worse, being co-opted into corrupt governance".

There is much to be gained from reading this novel, not only in terms of its capable storytelling in which one can envisage not only the Tizita performers, but also many of the minor characters who crop up in the bars and on the streets. There are comments that provoke: "Bob Geldoff, and much later, Bono, had pulled a number on the world; they had redefined the image of a whole continent to one that was always holding a beggar's bowl – a black hand stretched out for blessings from a white hand – with the help from African leaders for whom suffering immediately translated into dollars and pounds".

And there is the music that is central to the story. Tizita takes the key role, but there are references to American blues artists, country and western singers, jazzmen, Michael Jackson, and more. Pianos, guitars, accordions, saxophones, and trumpets are there, but alongside them local instruments like the masenko (a one-string item played with a bow) and the krar, a "five or six-stringed bowl-shaped lyre". The music is often improvised in an atmosphere similar to that of jazz jam sessions.

There are examples of Tizita music easily available on YouTube, some of it by singers and musicians named in the novel. Of particular interest is the "plaintive and celebratory", song "Malaika", "composed and sung by Fadhili William, who was to die penniless in a tenement slum in New Jersey while others made millions off the song". It isn't exactly claimed to be Tizita and relates more to Manfredi's Kenyan upbringing. When I googled it, the Wikipedia entry said that William didn't compose "Malaika" and it was written in Swahili by the Tanzanian singer Adam Salim in 1945. Well, American blues likewise often had convoluted composer credits, and it's a lovely song whoever originated it.

UNBURY OUR DEAD WITH SONG
By Mukoma Wa Ngugi
Cassava Republic Press. 253 pages. £11.99. ISBN 978-1-911115-98-4

ON THE MESA : AN ANTHOLOGY OF BOLINAS WRITING

A few words of explanation may be needed before going any further with a review of this book. In 1971 City Lights Books published *On the Mesa: An Anthology of Bolinas Writing*, edited by Joel Weishaus, and with 128 pages of mostly poetry and some prose by around 17 writers who were then living in and around Bolinas, California. It has long been out-of-print and is now something of a collectors' item. For this new 50th Anniversary edition, the book has been expanded to 244 pages and has "more than 65 poems by 19 more authors than were in this geographical area around the time of its (original) publication". There is also a Preface by Ben Estes outlining how he has expanded the initial selection, and an Afterword by Lytle Shaw which provides what might be called a degree of historical background to how and why Bolinas had been a place for poets to gather.

It isn't clear how many of the 36 or so poets in the new collection were there at the same time, if they ever were. I suspect not. And the fifty year gap between the old and new anthologies surely suggests that there have been deaths and departures, and perhaps some of the people concerned were only short-term visitors. I'm reminded of those coastal art colonies, so prevalent in the late-19th century and up to the outbreak of the First World War. They often had a hard-core of permanent or semi-permanent artists in residence, but others came in on a short-term basis, especially during the summer months.

So, even if we said that there were 20 to 25 poets in Bolinas at any one time, they would only make up a small proportion of the inhabitants of the town. I'm not sure just how many people live there now. A glance at the Internet brings up figures that rise as high as 1,600. Were there that many in 1971? A passing reference by Lytle Shaw mentions 500. As for the place itself, it's an hour or so by car north of San Francisco and situated on the coast in beautiful surroundings. The locals don't encourage tourists, even to the extent that they have been said to destroy road signs pointing to Bolinas. There doesn't appear to be any indication about how they reacted in 1971 to an anthology which might have encouraged would-be poets to head for the town. Nor whether the new edition is likely to have any effect. A glance at entries on the internet for Bolinas doesn't bring up any mention of it now having a thriving community of poets as part of its appeal.

How relevant were the poets in terms of participating in the day-to-day activities and functioning of Bolinas? At some point in the future someone – a sociologist, a literary scholar – might well take on the job of investigating just what the poets did beyond writing poetry. Lytle Shaw says he was drawn to researching Bolinas "not just as an alternative community but as the only instance I could think of where a town was essentially governed by poets". And elsewhere, he says: "poets in Bolinas sought to create an ecologically sustainable town where anyone could be an agent of news-making".

It is slightly frustrating not to have detailed information about how long the experiments in a kind of "collective" living where "poetry was the organising feature of daily life in the town" continued, and if it still does in any constructive way. Ben Estes refers to Bolinas as "this very specific place in time (which) stands for a refuge for San Francisco Renaissance and Beat poets and prominent poets of the New York School and Black Mountain College all living and working together, in one place, for a brief period of time". Again, we need an in-depth social analysis to help us determine exactly what happened and for how long. I ought to add at this point that Kevin Opstedal's *Dreaming as One*, which can easily be found on the Internet, does provide a lengthy account of activity in Bolinas between 1967 and 1980. And *Beat Scene* 51 (Coventry, 2006) devoted most of its pages to an account by Opstedal and reminiscences by some of those who had lived there.

On the Mesa wasn't meant to offer an account of the social side of what the poets got up to in Bolinas, other than when it was reflected in the poems. And it was, which may be, when reading them now, both an advantage and a disadvantage. If you weren't there, but wish you had been, you might find them attractive. On the other hand, if you tend to the view that poets ought to be out and about in the wider community, then you may not express much of a response to poems which rely on an awareness of individuals mentioned, or experiences shared by a few friends, to make them meaningful. I too often had the impression that some of the poets had little or no interest in writing for anyone beyond their immediate circle. Bobbie Louise Hawkins in her poem, "Depths and Heights and Sweet Red Melons", records that "The bottom fell out of the market/over all the plains where melons/weren't worth the pickings", but has nothing to say about the situation other than that "Donald-Gene and me in overalls/got sick day after day walking/the rows eating watermelon hearts".

As with any anthology it's necessary to move around to find the best bits, those that have survived the passing of the years that inevitably take the edge off most poems. Sometimes it's the prose that has retained its vigour. The excerpts from Joe Brainard's journals are entertaining. They are admittedly as full of in-references as some of the poems, but seem able to carry them better, possibly because what we expect of a journal differs from what we want from a poem. I accept that some poems aren't meant to do more than entertain, but others frequently claim to achieve something beyond that and when they fail to do so, it's more noticeable than in jottings from a journal.

Am I being too critical? One commentator is quoted as claiming that the book contains "lost masterpieces" and specifically mentions Anne Waldman's "Spin Off", but I can find little in the poem that justifies such extravagant praise. It seems fragmentary and with little cohesion (not unlike other Bolinas poems), though I accept that without quoting it in full it's difficult to give substance to my criticism. And it has those little naming of names – Philip Whalen, Don Allen – that the knowing will recognise. It may have some attributes I can't see, but it isn't memorable. And a good poem ought to be, in one way or another.

What is also noticeable about the poems is that few of them show any regard for the world outside the immediate boundaries of the poets' lives. Yes, they observe certain concerns regarding the environment, but it's as if the small world they have created for themselves and their immediate families and friends suffices. Does this indicate that they had given up on the wider society, and they see little purpose in commenting on it? Some of the poets may well have had involvements with social and political matters, and determined not to let them creep into their poetry, but it's hard to believe that's the case. The biographical details I obtained about Bill Brown do indicate that, in his younger days, he had experiences as a sailor and a soldier in the Second World War. They're not in the poems and prose used in *On the Mesa*. He obviously preferred to write about the here and now as it was in his days in Bolinas, and slip in the names of friends in the community. But, to be fair, he had published a book about his war experiences, *The Way to the Uncle Sam Hotel*.

John Thorpe's "September", a prose piece, is interesting, both as a record of aspects of life in Bolinas past and present. It isn't great literature, but it is useful. Another prose piece, Max Crosley's "Epic Today", would probably be of value to a sociologist looking into the life of the community. Both Thorpe and Crosley mention problems dealing with Social Services, which might raise a question in some people's minds – the contradiction in dropping out of a supposedly corrupt society but depending on it for financial assistance.

Aram Saroyan's poem "Love" has charm, and Jim Carroll's "The Distances" is worth reading. Older readers may smile nostalgically when they read Diane di Prima's "Revolutionary Letters" and Richard Brautigan's oddball little musings. Fifty or so years can't help but make them seem forever located in a time and place (60s

San Francisco), but there are still moments of relevance in what di Prima says, and a kind of winsome charm in Brautigan's contributions. I suppose the same can be said for some of the other poems in the anthology, and there is a noticeable absence of the doom and gloom that other poets, not in the Bolinas community, seemed to rely on. It can lay one open to criticism if there is an intense concentration on the local, the immediate, and the personal, but there is no law that requires poets to engage with the wider world and its difficulties.

It was inevitable that the Bolinas group, commune, colony, call it what you will, would eventually splinter. Poets move on in search of new ideas. They also usually need to work at something or other outside poetry to earn a living. I doubt that many of them, in any case, intended to make Bolinas their permanent home. It's instructive to read the Kevin Opstedal account of the Bolinas adventure, *Dreaming as One*, and find out that drugs, sex and other problems contributed to the collapse of the dream. A history of utopian colonies will show that very few of them survived for any length of time.

Not only poets came to Bolinas. There were musicians, artists, and the inevitable hangers-on and drifters intrinsic to any bohemian scene. Alcohol and drugs played a part in the day-to-day life of many in the community. Clashes of personality, affairs, the unwillingness of some people to do more than follow their own interests, and economic pressures (grants and welfare payments were becoming harder to obtain), all played their part in thinning out the ranks of the Bolinas poets. In the end people had to move back into the mainstream in order to survive.

Had anything worthwhile been achieved in literary terms during the Bolinas years? Opinions will vary, and I don't think there was ever a particular method of writing that might be related to the area (poets arrived from San Francisco, New York, and elsewhere), but as well as the anthology there is a reasonably substantial bibliography of work by Bolinas writers attached to Kevin Opstedal's survey.

ON THE MESA : AN ANTHOLOGY OF BOLINAS WRITING
Edited by Ben Estes and Joel Weishaus
The Song Cave. 244 pages. $20. ISBN 978-1-7340351-7-9

ARVIN GARRISON

It has often been my contention that minor figures in the arts can provide a better picture of a period than more-successful writers, artists, and musicians. Their work reflects what was happening stylistically in its range of references. This can be seen as a limiting factor if they failed to move on, but it should not be a reason for neglecting what they did achieve, albeit in a small way.

It's doubtful if the name of guitarist Arvin Garrison will arouse much response, even among jazz historians and enthusiasts. If he's known at all, it's probably because of his presence in a group that Charlie Parker led on a 1946 recording session for Dial Records in Los Angeles. But Garrison, in his short career, had made something of a name for himself as a leading exponent of modern guitar soloing on the West Coast. The appearance of a 3-CD compilation of just about every known recording on which he appeared (or at least soloed) gives listeners an opportunity to judge his capabilities.

Garrison was born in Toledo, Ohio, in 1923. I'm not intending to provide a biographical account of Garrison's life. It's the music I'm mainly interested in. In any case, biographical details are not easy to come by. Reminiscences by his ex-wife, Vivien Garry, and friends, refer to him as being unworldly in the sense of not able to cope with the mundane facts of everyday life: "Garrison wasn't exactly a worldly man. Guitar simple might be more like it. Geography, politics, ball scores, even balancing a chequebook were beyond his comprehension. He was a mama's boy who never got around to leaving mom. She taught him how to read music and placed him at the centre of the universe around whom all things revolved. She took care of his daily affairs while Arv played along with his Django records from morning until night".

Vivien Garry had met Garrison in Toledo where he had been working with local groups, and determined to learn to play the double-bass so she could work with him. In due course they combined with a pianist named Bill Cummerow and formed the Vivien Garry Trio. As she later recalled: "Our repertoire included a lot of Nat Cole material. Wherever we played, the people loved us, so it wasn't that hard to get booked in Chicago, where we played at the Brass Rail. A lot of name jazz musicians were dropping by to hear this crazy trio with the chick bass player".

That reference to Nat Cole might intrigue those who only know him as the singer Nat 'King' Cole who had hit records in the 1950s and later. But in the mid and late-1940s he worked extensively with a trio that, at one time or another, had Oscar Moore and Irving Ashby playing guitar. Cole also took part in Jazz at the Philharmonic concerts and appeared on records with Illinois Jacquet, Lester Young, and others. With his trio he specialised in smooth renditions of popular songs, novelty numbers, and relaxed piano and guitar improvisations. He was popular in night clubs and on records.

Garrison and Garry, with a new pianist named Teddy Kaye, moved to New York and were hired to appear at Kelly's Stable, one of the small clubs along the fabled 52nd Street. It gave Garrison the opportunity to hear the new sounds of bebop as played by leading exponents of the style like Charlie Parker and Dizzy Gillespie. And the trio made its first recordings, two sides for Guild in June 1945. One of them, "Altitude", was an instrumental number which showed that the guitarist was rapidly developing an approach to soloing which reflected influences from Django Reinhardt, Oscar Moore, and Charlie Christian, but had its own individual manner of phrasing. The other track, "Relax Jack", was a composition by Garrison much in the style of Nat Cole or the Page Cavanaugh Trio, a popular group of the period. My recollections of hearing records by Cavanaugh are that it wasn't as interesting from a jazz point of view as the Cole and Garry groups, but it was commercially successful.

It was when Garrison and Garry moved to California that they began to achieve a measure of popularity, particularly around Los Angeles. In December, 1945, the trio, boosted to a quartet by the addition of Roy Hall on drums and with George Handy taking over from Teddy Kaye at the piano, recorded half-a-dozen tracks for Sarco, a small label based in the city. It's worth noting that, as opposed to Nat Cole, who was contracted to Capitol Records, and Page Cavanaugh, whose records were released on well-known labels like RCA and Columbia, Garry's trio seemed fated to have links to only small companies. As a consequence, their records probably had only limited distribution.

A notable fact about the Sarco session was the involvement of George Handy. A pianist and composer/arranger, he worked with the forward-looking Boyd Raeburn orchestra. It's not surprising that a couple of the compositions used by Garry's group were also in the Raeburn book. "Where You At?" was a novelty number in the hip format of the time, and "Tonsillectomy" was a medium-tempo instrumental feature. Garrison's guitar skills are in evidence on both.

It may have been Handy who was responsible for Garrison's presence at a recording date for the newly-established Dial label. Ross Russell, who owned the Tempo record shop in Hollywood, had decided to launch Dial as a platform for the new music, bebop. It's perhaps indicative of the period that Russell, who had written pulp fiction and served in the Merchant Marine during the war, hadn't initially decided whether to open a record shop or use the money to break into screenwriting. He later commented that he luckily made the right choice. Most of his contacts among the writers he knew in Hollywood were blacklisted when the House Un-American Activities Committee (HUAC) started its investigations into communist activity in the film capital in 1947.

The Dial date turned out to be chaotic, with only one number, "Diggin' Diz", being recorded. Russell's inexperience as a producer, and the problem of "a small army of hipsters", who had arrived with the musicians, getting in the way, limited what could be achieved. But it did show that Garrison was competent enough to be working alongside Charlie Parker and Dizzy Gillespie.

A second Dial session with Garrison in a rhythm-team backing Charlie Parker, Miles Davis, and tenorman Lucky Thompson was much more successful. Tracks such as "Yardbird Suite", "Ornithology", "A Night in Tunisia", and "Moose the Mooch" (the nickname of Bird's narcotics supplier In Los Angeles) are rightly seen as important items in the recorded evidence of Parker's visit to California. As for Garrison, he was completely at home with the "complexities of the new music" and "delivered some of his most nimble Reinhardt-influenced playing on record".

1946 was the key year in Garrison's career and his standing among the West Coast practitioners of bebop was further emphasised when he took part in a recording session under trumpeter Howard McGhee's name. Again, he was in good company. McGhee was one of the leading bebop trumpet players, tenor saxophone Teddy Edwards among the first in Los Angeles to pick up on the new sounds, and the talented but ill-fated pianist Dodo Marmarosa was admired by a wide range of musicians and critics. He worked well with the guitar-player in the rhythm-section. As for Garrison. he "let his solo playing breathe, utilising space as much as he employed fretted notes".

The appearances at recording sessions were, of course, in addition to the work Garrison was doing with the Vivian Garry Trio in clubs around Los Angeles. The group additionally participated In a number of broadcasts for the Armed Forces Radio Service (AFRS), one of which spotlights Garrison in the up-tempo "Mop Mop" and another with the group backing singer Frankie Laine. In the 1950s he became well-known for his versions of "High Noon", "Blowing Wild", and other film-related songs, but in the mid-1940s he was slowly establishing himself in the Los Angeles night-clubs.

The group also provided support on records by the little-known vocalist, Rickey Jordan, and the extrovert Leo Watson, best described as a scat-singer. He had some currency in the late-1930s and early-1940s, but his performances are hard to take today. Still, the records with the Garry Trio and singers do have spaces for solo guitar by Garrison and piano stylings by Wini Beatty. But his most-striking performances can be heard on some of the AFRS broadcasts, especially on a couple of versions of what was often referred to as the boppers' National Anthem, "How High the Moon", where his fleet improvising is impressive. The trio also gave a nod to its need to appeal to a wider audience than bebop enthusiasts when it performed the novelty number, "Rip Van Winkle", another George Handy tune that the Boyd Raeburn band recorded.

A 1947 return to New York found the Trio engaged at The Famous Door night-club and making an appearance on the "Saturday Night Swing Session" broadcast over radio station WNEW. There were good work-outs on "Lover man" and "Indiana", as well as the cute "The Three Bears", a song also used by Page Cavanaugh and, in Britain, by Ray Ellington, whose group became well-known for its contributions to The Goons radio shows in the 1950s. Ellington neatly blended modern jazz with humorous vocals. On the WNEW show, the Garry Trio can also be heard behind bop singer Babs Gonzales, though like Leo Watson he's an acquired taste. What may have seemed entertaining at the time comes across now as faintly embarrassing in its aim to be up-to-date and in the bebop mode.

It seems that not all was well with the group. Garry and Garrison were having difficulties in their personal relationship, and the guitarist was showing signs of epileptic seizures which affected the group's performances. Garry, looking back on their marriage, said that essentially all she had done was take his mother's place: "I fixed his soup and sandwiches twice a day the way she used to, arranged for all the hotel and travel accommodations, picked out all his clothes, and paid the bills". There were a few recordings in 1948, mostly featuring El Myers, the new singer and pianist with the group, but by mid-1948 Garry was in Los Angeles and Garrison was back in Toledo with his mother.

Little was heard about Garrison after 1948. He worked in clubs in Toledo in the early-1950s, but his problems with epilepsy were increasingly affecting him and by the mid-1950s he was in poor condition. Wini Beatty allowed him to sit in with the group she was leading at a club in Palm Springs in 1956, but had to ask him to leave the stand: "It was so pathetic. He couldn't play a lick. His hands were moving, but his coordination had gone". His one great obsession, the guitar apart, had been swimming and he died in 1960 after he had a seizure while in the water and drowned.

Was Arv Garrison a major musician? Probably not, but he was a very good one, and seen as having a lot to offer when at his best in the period between 1946 and 1948. Musicians admired his playing and well-regarded critics like Leonard Feather and Barry Ulanov spoke highly of his work. The potential was there, but it's impossible to know if it would have resulted in anything significant, even if he hadn't been held back by epilepsy. We simply have to listen to what he did produce in his short career and enjoy that.

NOTE

The basis for this essay was the 3-CD set, complete with a 76-page booklet full of facts and photos, issued by Fresh Sound Records of Barcelona (catalogue number FSR-1104). For anyone interested in placing Garrison in context, particularly when he was in California, I recommend *Central Avenue Sounds*, edited by Clora Bryant and others, published by University of California Press, 1998. He's not actually mentioned in this book, but it offers a vibrant picture of what was a colourful and often creative scene in which he was involved.

KEROUAC'S MILES : JACK KEROUAC AND THE MUSIC OF MILES DAVIS

Jack Kerouac was a jazz enthusiast. His novels contain numerous references to musicians and records, particularly those from a period stretching between 1935 and 1955. Yes, his interest in the music continued after 1955, but I'd suggest that essentially his tastes were formed in the twenty years indicated and stylistically didn't move much beyond them. What needs to be noted, too, is that there often wasn't a clear-cut division between jazz and the popular music of the day. Big-bands were active into the 1950s and many musicians made a living in them. The more-interesting bands featured a fair amount of jazz and gave space to prominent soloists. I recall seeing Lee Konitz with Stan Kenton's orchestra in Dublin in 1953.

Konitz was essentially a small-group improviser, but had taken a job with Kenton for financial reasons. There simply wasn't a decent living to be made performing on the jazz club circuit. Kenton's musicians were well-paid, his orchestra attracted large audiences, and the music it played was heavily inclined towards jazz. In 1953 it featured arrangements by Gerry Mulligan and Bill Holman, among others, and spotlighted soloists such as trumpeter Conte Candoli, trombonist Frank Rosolino, and tenor saxophonist Zoot Sims. Kerouac would have been familiar with their music.

He would also have known about Miles Davis, the trumpet player who came to the fore in the 1940s as a member of Charlie Parker's group. Davis arrived in New York in September, 1944, ostensibly to study at Juilliard School of Music, but essentially to involve himself in the bourgeoning bebop scene. That he did, to the extent of becoming one of its leading practitioners, is a matter of jazz history. But it's interesting to see how, in those early days, Davis went through the standard experience of most jazz musicians as he worked with the Benny Carter and Billy Eckstine bands, and took part in recording sessions where he was a member of groups backing the blues shouter and vaudeville performer Rubberlegs Williams and the singers Ann Hathaway and Earl Coleman. Short statements by Davis can be heard scattered around the records that were made, and on airshots by the Carter ensemble.

We don't know for sure when Kerouac first became aware of Davis, though it was more than likely when he worked with Charlie Parker in the New York clubs and appeared with him on records that were issued on the Savoy and Dial labels. Mike Andrews, whose aim in Kerouac's Miles is to find possible occasions when Kerouac may have been present at a Davis club date, directs us to the accounts of him going to the Three Deuces on 52nd Street and Minton's Playhouse in Harlem. He may well have come across Davis at both locations, but it's a question of speculation rather than fact. There were other clubs such as the Downbeat and the Spotlight on 52nd Street that Davis worked at with groups led by Coleman Hawkins and Dexter Gordon. Kerouac may have visited them. Incidentally, Andrews refers to "these sessions in the Village", but 52nd Street is not part of Greenwich Village.

Tracking both Kerouac's and Davis's movements through the years, Andrews doesn't ever manage to pinpoint an actual date where there is sufficient evidence to indicate that the two could have been in the same club at the same time. There are references to Davis in Kerouac's writings, and Andrews notes that a comment in The Beginnings of Bop would seem to suggest that he had seen and heard Davis in a club setting at one point. But where and when is unclear.

It's relevant to refer to the section where Andrews is keen to discuss the possible influence of Lee Konitz's playing on Kerouac. The alto player had been a member of the Miles Davis group that appeared at the Royal Roost in 1948 and recorded for Capitol in 1949 and 1950. The recordings signalled a departure from the frenetic nature of bebop and were labelled "The Birth of the Cool" because of their tightly arranged and more relaxed approach to the music. Konitz was an ideal choice for this kind of jazz. Kerouac would surely have heard the records, even if he didn't see the band during its brief Royal Roost engagement.

He may also have been aware of Konitz's work with the Claude Thornhill orchestra in 1947 when Gil Evans was one of Thornhill's arrangers. His solo on Thornhill's version of Charlie Parker's "Yardbird Suite" is worthy of note. Evans was later involved in the Birth of the Cool innovations, though it's incorrect to name him as the sole arranger. Gerry Mulligan contributed as much, if not more, to the sound of the group, and pianist John Lewis was also deeply involved in its development.

There are less references to Davis in Kerouac's writing as the 1950s progressed. But Davis's career had re-ignited in the late-1950s after what Andrews refers to as "a fairly awful early to mid-1950s". Davis himself was dismissive of some of the recordings from the early-1950s when heroin addiction was taking its toll, but they have a certain kind of appeal, perhaps because he was expressing how he felt through the music and there is a sadness in the playing which is noticeable. I still occasionally play my copies of "Blue Room" and "Whispering", recorded in 1951, and find their plaintiveness curiously attractive. And there's the pensive "My Old Flame". There may be an element of nostalgia present. I can remember the records first becoming available in Britain on Esquire 78s, and later on EPs and LPs.

I enjoyed reading Andrews' excursion into the likely or unlikely times when Kerouac and Davis might have been within sight of each other. His enthusiasm for the lives and achievements of both is infectious. He provides some useful information regarding relevant Davis recordings, along with the titles of appropriate Kerouac books.

Beat Scene Press books are available from 27 Court Leet, Binley Woods, Coventry, CV3 2JQ. Contact them for details of prices, etc.

KEROUAC'S MILES : JACK KEROUAC AND THE MUSIC OF MILES DAVIS

By Mike Andrews

Beat Scene Press Pocket Book Series

ROSS RUSSELL AND BEBOP

I recently re-read Ross Russell's novel, *The Sound*, certainly not for the first time and probably not for the last. It's not a literary classic, but the subject-matter and Russell's vibrant accounts of the characters and the milieu in which they operate always fascinates me. His descriptions of the music at the centre of the book make me want to get out the records from the period and listen to them again.

It's not surprising that Russell describes the music so well. He had played an important role in the early days of the bebop movement of the 1940s, not as a musician but as someone who helped draw attention to bop by starting a company to record Charlie Parker and other practitioners of the new sounds. Not many major record labels were interested in promoting bebop in the mid-1940s and it was left to Dial, Savoy, and other scattered small companies to take a chance with artists like Parker, Dexter Gordon, and Howard McGhee. There are stories about some of the small record labels that came and went in the 1940s, and their shady ways of operating, but without them there would have been fewer examples available of the changes taking place in jazz and popular music.

So who was Ross Russell? He was born in Los Angeles in 1909. In the 1930s he published pulp fiction in magazines, and was a great admirer of the work of Dashiell Hammett and Raymond Chandler. He served in the Merchant Marine during the Second World War In both the European and Pacific theatres. When the war ended he returned to Los Angeles and, being an enthusiastic jazz fan, decided to open a record shop. He was initially a collector of traditional-style jazz, but when he started to listen to the records by Charlie Parker that local hipsters ordered he became interested in bebop. Opening a record shop was probably a wise choice in more ways than one. Russell had considered trying to get into screenwriting in Hollywood, but later reminisced that, had he done so, he might have been caught up in the HUAC investigations into communism in the film industry. Most of his contacts in the studios were writers who were later blacklisted.

His next step was to form a record company, Dial, to record Charlie Parker who he had met and become friendly with. Parker was in Los Angeles with a group led by Dizzy Gillespie which had a booking at Billy Berg's Club in Hollywood. But he was proving to be somewhat unreliable due to his drug addiction and the fact that narcotics were not as easy to come by on the West Coast as they were in New York. Parker asked Russell to be his manager, and he also willingly signed an agreement to record for Dial. He was actually under contract to another company at the time.

I'm not intending to analyse the music that Parker produced for Dial. There were seven sessions, some recorded in Los Angeles, some in New York after Russell had moved there. Russell's own accounts – there were several – can be found in various places, the most accessible probably being in *Bird: The Legend of Charlie Parker*, edited by Bob Reisner. But one recording date does stand out, if not for the best reasons. In July, 1946, Parker went into the studio and came up with the music from the famous (or infamous) *Lover Man* session. He was in poor condition, due to being unable to obtain the necessary supply of heroin, and was barely able to play. Howard

McGhee, the trumpet player on the date, was a tower of strength, but even he, and the rhythm-section, could not cover up for Bird's dismal performance.

It has always been a matter of contention whether or not the four tracks that Parker managed to stumble through should have ever been released. But they were, much to his annoyance. Russell's intentions, beyond wanting to try to recover his losses, can be questioned, and they led to accusations of exploitation. Had he realised that there would be an audience for recorded evidence of a great jazzman breaking down? In the studio was a journalist associate of Russell's, a man called Elliot Grennard who wrote a short-story called "Sparrow's Last Jump" which was a lightly-fictionalised account of the events of that day. It was published in *Harper's Magazine* in 1947. He later recalled Russell saying that he'd "lost a thousand bucks" because of what had happened. At the end of the story the narrator makes the comment: "Yeah, Sparrow's last recording would sure make a collector's item. One buck, plus tax, is cheap enough for a record of a guy going nuts".

Russell had recorded other modern jazz musicians in California – Dexter Gordon, Wardell Gray, Dodo Marmarosa, - and besides making the final Parker records for Dial in New York in 1947, he produced a session with singer Earl Coleman backed by the brilliant trumpeter Fats Navarro and tenor saxophonist Don Lanphere. There may be an irony in the fact that Russell seemed keen to record Coleman. In 1947 when Parker brought the singer to a Dial session and insisted he should be recorded, Russell had remarked that he needed a singer like he needed a hole in his head. Bird's version of "This is Always", with a vocal by Coleman, turned out to be one of Dial's best-selling discs.

After 1948 Russell seems to have given up on jazz, at least from a recording point of view, and focused on contemporary classical scores, releasing records of the music of Schoenberg, Ernst Krenek, and others. In the 1950s he turned to documenting calypso music in the West Indies. I can't offer any critical comments on what he recorded, either classical or calypso, but it has been suggested that he offended Schoenberg in the same way that he'd upset Parker by issuing records of what the composer considered sub-standard performances.

Biographical information regarding what Russell did in the 1950s and after is fairly limited. At one time or another he lived in various countries, contributed articles to jazz magazines, taught jazz history courses at the University of California and elsewhere, and sold the Dial records catalogue, especially the Parker sides, to one or two different companies. The material was perhaps best preserved by Spotlite Records, based in the United Kingdom. Russell had kept most of the recorded tracks, including incomplete takes, so critics and ardent fans could study Parker's work in particular. He claimed that Parker was often at his best on the first take, even if the group as a whole didn't function as well as it did on later takes, so there was a good reason for issuing everything that survived. It was Parker's music that mattered most of all.

Russell also wrote several books, beginning with *The Sound*, a novel based in part on Parker's life and music. Published in 1961 it was generally well-received, in jazz circles at least, though some people did find the close attention paid to the drugs situation a little distracting. But somewhere (I can't pin down the source) I recall the writer Nat Hentoff saying of the 1940s: "That's the way it was, and only someone looking for serialisation in *Reader's Digest* would want to pretend otherwise".

The Sound is colourful and it's possible to see Russell's grounding in the pulp fiction of the 1930s at work in some of the writing. But there's no doubt that he knew the scene in terms of capturing the nature of the music. Early in the story Red Travers, a trumpet-player who is closely modelled on Charlie Parker, arrives in Los Angeles for a club engagement. He's accompanied by a saxophonist from New York, but the rhythm-section is comprised of local musicians, among them Bernie, a white pianist. He isn't too familiar with bebop, but has the musical training to follow what Travers is doing harmonically. His induction into the hot house atmosphere as Travers launches into a fast first number that initially confounds everyone apart from the saxophonist, is excitingly evoked by Russell. It always makes me want to listen to some authentic bebop whenever I read it. Which is, I think, a tribute to the quality of his writing when he's concerned to describe what is happening during a performance by Travers.

A second book by Russell gave an indication of his genuine knowledge and appreciation of jazz developments. *Jazz Style in*

Kansas City and the Southwest, published in 1971, was a close look at an area which, as the book claimed, "was the source for many of the musical ideas that have dominated jazz from the late thirties to the present and resulted in the bebop revolution and the foundation of modern jazz style". Tracing the music from its roots in "the blues, brass bands, and ragtime" Russell brings it to the 1930s when bands like those led by Andy Kirk, Count Basie and Jay McShann featured key soloists, including Howard McGhee, Lester Young, and Charlie Parker. What is particularly valuable about Russell's history is that it doesn't only document the activities and achievements of a few of the better-known names. Minor but interesting musicians like Buddy Anderson and John Jackson are given attention. Anderson, a trumpet player, "was the most advanced musician in the band (Jay McShann's) after Parker", and Jackson was an alto-saxophonist who, initially at least, sounded a little like Bird when both were working with McShann.

Russell's best-known book was *Bird Lives! The High Life and Hard Times of Charlie 'Yardbird' Parker,* published in 1972. Because of his involvements with Parker, and his experience of the Los Angeles jazz scene of the mid-1940s, Russell could obviously provide insights into the events relating to certain of Bird's activities. This particularly applied to information about the Dial recordings and the situations surrounding them. And his awareness of the lively scene in "Lotus Land", with its cast of hipsters, oddball characters, and enthusiastic musicians, added variety to his account. But questions were raised about some of the events and facts that Russell wrote about. He had talked to a great many musicians and others over the years, and it may have been that some of the information he gathered was more anecdotal than factual, and therefore not totally accurate. But it still occurs to me to think that there are things to be gained from Russell's Bird biography. He makes the music come alive in a way that later commentators on Parker, while academically correct, often failed to do.

Russell died in January, 2000. He had been working on a book about bebop with Red Rodney, but it was incomplete at the time of his death. He knew the worth of his collection of records, books, magazines, manuscripts, interviews, and much more, and in 1980 had sold his archives to the University of Texas. I think he was aware that his association with Parker and other bop musicians at a time when major musical developments were in process gave him a place in jazz history.

NOTES

1. *The Sound* by Ross Russell. Dutton, New York, 1961.

2. *Jazz Style in Kansas City and the South West* by Ross Russell. University of California Press, Berkeley, 1971.

3. *Bird Lives! The High Life and Hard Times of Charlie 'Yardbird' Parker* by Ross Russell. Quartet Books, London, 1973.

4. *Bird: The Legend of Charlie Parker* edited by Robert Reisner. Citadel Press, New York, 1962.

5. *The Bebop Revolution in Words and Music* edited by Dave Oliphant, Harry Ransome Humanities Research Centre, the University of Texas at Austin, 1994. This assembles some of the papers delivered at a symposium in 1992 and includes a particularly useful piece by Edward Komara on "The Dial Recordings of Charlie Parker". There is also a Keynote Address by Ross Russell which was delivered on his behalf when health problems prevented him from attending the symposium. It's informative about, among other things, the social and cultural scene in Los Angeles in the 1940s.

6. "Sparrow's Last Jump" by Elliott Grennard in *Jam Session* edited by Ralph J. Gleason. Peter Davies, London, 1958.

7. *Central Avenue Sounds: Jazz in Los Angeles* edited by Clora Bryant & others. University of California Press, Berkeley, 1998.

8. *Jazz West Coast: The Los Angeles Jazz Scene of the 1950s* by Robert Gordon. Quartet Books, London, 1986. Despite its title the book has a couple of useful chapters about jazz in Los Angeles in the 1940s

9. *West Coast Jazz: Modern Jazz in California 1945-1960* by Ted Gioia. University of California Press, Berkeley, 1998.

10. *Bebop: A Social and Musical History* by Scott DeVeaux. University of California Press, Berkeley, 1997.

Readers may be interested in my essay, "Bird Breaks Down" in *Beat Scene* 49, Coventry, Winter 2005/6, and in *Radicals, Beats and Beboppers*, Penniless Press, Warrington, 2011.

PICTURING A NATION :
THE ART AND LIFE OF A.H. FULLWOOD

In 2017 I went to the National Gallery in London to have a look at an exhibition entitled *Australia's Impressionists*. It covered the work of four artists – Tom Roberts. Arthur Streeton, Charles Conder and John Russell. With the exception of Conder, I knew nothing about them but the exhibition was an eye-opener in terms of introducing me to paintings by Roberts and Streeton. Both seemed to have absorbed some ideas from Europe but adapted them to producing canvases which were resolutely Australian in their content. They had not slavishly followed Impressionist techniques and, like some of the painters linked to the Newlyn School in Britain, had taken what was needed from French sources and used it within a home-grown context.

The catalogue accompanying the exhibition was informative and mentioned a few other Australian artists active towards the end of the nineteenth century and the early part of the twentieth. But the name of A.H. Fullwood certainly wasn't among them. And yet he had been a close friend of both Roberts and Streeton and had sketched alongside them on their trips into the bush. Plein air painting in Australia often took place in a setting where mates (a term employed by Gary Werskey, and which points to the primarily male membership of the groups) gathered round the campfire in the evening to compare notes and tell tales. Werskey refers to a 1991 exhibition, *Bohemians in the Bush: The Artists' Camps of Mosman,* which perhaps sums up the situation. From what he says in his book, Fullwood was a convivial type, as well as a talented artist, so it seems strange that he disappeared from the records of Australian art in later years.

He was born in 1863 in Birmingham, England, into a family engaged in the jewellery trade. He left school "possibly as early as 1876, (and) joined the family business as an apprentice jeweller". But his inclinations were towards becoming an artist and he enrolled at the Birmingham School of Landscape Art around 1879. When his father died in 1883, and the economics of the jewellery trade went into a downturn, Fullwood's mother took her son and two of her daughters to Australia. His skills had developed enough to enable him to quickly find employment in Sydney. Fine art was not then of great concern in Australia, and Fullwood's work involved "catalogues, illuminated addresses, and illustrations for the firm's publications". He could paint pictures in his own time, but the steady income needed to help support his mother and sisters would come from commercial activities.

He set up his own studio and advertised himself as "artist-illustrator" and ready to turn his hand to designing and illuminating. Art by him was soon appearing in the *Australian Town and Country Journal*. What probably brought him more notice was his work for the *Picturesque Atlas of Australasia*, a project designed to celebrate "the scenic beauties, civic virtues, and social progress of the nation". Well-produced and with "engraved illustrations from the pens and brushes of leading artists" the sections circulated widely, and brought attention to Fullwood's achievements. Illustrations in Weskey's book show him to have been a deft illustrator of landscapes but also able to turn out quick sketches of mines and similar settings. It strikes me that Fullwood's quite considerable contributions to the Picturesque Atlas should have ensured him a place in later surveys of Australian art, but perhaps the division too often made between fine and commercial art prevented a genuine acknowledgement of his talents?

That he was quite capable of producing paintings designed to appeal to collectors of fine art, and those in charge of private and public galleries, can be seen in the 1889 canvas, "Wet evening, George Street, Sydney", which captures well the overcast scene with its horse-drawn carriages and scurrying people. A somewhat sombre painting, it might suggest certain Impressionist influences. Being of the opinion that "impressionism" could be one of the most overworked words in the art dictionary, I'm more inclined to think that it draws its inspiration from late-19th century naturalist painting which, admittedly, had taken on some surface aspects of impressionism but retained a firm basis in direct representation. A lighter painting, "Sturt Street, Ballarat", clearly indicates this.

There are rural paintings by Fullwood which made me think of Daubigny and Bastien-Lepage, though it's difficult to determine how familiar he was with the work of these French artists. And one painting, "The Swing", put me in mind of the English artist, William Stott of Oldham, who had been influenced by Bastien-Lepage, among others. On the other hand, a canvas such as "Reflections" quite clearly has a direct link to late-19th century Parisian painting (if one didn't know otherwise it could easily be mistaken for a Paris street scene). One wonders just how much he knew about French art in general and impressionism in particular?

Fullwood seemed to have an established place as "one of Sydney's leading artists", and he was, largely thanks to his commercial work, comfortable from a financial point of view. But it may have held him back from achieving wider critical recognition. Werskey points to the fact that Tom Roberts and Arthur Streeton both concentrated on oil painting and on the whole kept clear of working as illustrators. But economic circumstances were to affect all artists in the 1890s and, for Fullwood, there was the added problem that photographs were increasingly being used by newspapers and magazines and so reduced his earnings as an illustrator.

By 1900 he had decided to try his luck in New York where there appeared to be opportunities for an illustrator. He failed to establish himself sufficiently in the art world there and moved to London. He had married earlier and had two sons, but his wife, Clyda, was showing increasing signs of mental instability possibly as a result of post-natal depression accentuated by worry about the financial problems that now began to affect Fullwood's career.

I mentioned earlier that Fullwood was a convivial type who enjoyed associating with old friends like Tom Roberts and Arthur Streeton, who were both in London, and new friends such as Alfred Munnings and Frank Brangwyn. He became a member of the Chelsea Arts Club and seems to have spent a fair amount of time there. Was he a heavy drinker? There are suggestions by Werskey that he may have had a liking for alcohol, though perhaps not to the point where he was an alcoholic. But the facts were that, despite some critical attention, he wasn't earning a great deal from painting, and had to find school fees for his sons, and the expense of keeping his wife in a private asylum. At one point he had to apply for relief from the Wandsworth Poor Law Guardians. There was also a strange episode when Fullwood, despite problems with his wife and sons, disappeared to Cape Town for several weeks. Werskey acknowledges that it's unknown what Fullwood's reasons for this action were.

He was "exhibiting everywhere – selling nowhere" and turned to designing postcards for the Raphael Tuck organisation. But Werskey suggests that he did make a living of sorts as "a producer of affordable fine art – small oils and watercolours, as well as pastels, monotypes, lithographs, and etchings", and that he relied on "boutique galleries" to sell his wares. When the war started in 1914 he enlisted in the Royal Army Medical Corps and worked at a hospital in London. He was 52 and needn't have joined up but gave his age as 42. When he was discharged from the army in 1917 he became a War Artist and went to the Western Front to draw and paint pictures of Australian soldiers in action and behind the lines.

Fullwood's youngest son had died in 1910. And his wife, Clyda, had passed away in an asylum in 1918. With the eldest boy, Geoffrey, now living in Australia, he must have felt isolated in London. He wasn't prospering as an artist, either. In addition, Frances Prudence, a woman he had formed an attachment to, had moved to Australia. It was not long before Fullwood himself would take the decision to return to Sydney, which he did in 1919. Once there, he had some successful exhibitions, sold pictures, and led a lifestyle which was, as Werskey puts it, "largely defined by his daily transit between his home, studio, and favourite drinking establishments". He did sometimes visit Frances, though it doesn't appear that she ever contemplated a settled arrangement with him. And it perhaps wasn't what he wanted, in any case,

Throughout the 1920s, Fullwood managed to support himself with artistic endeavours of one kind or another. He had exhibitions in private galleries and his work sold but not at high prices. He also mixed with younger artists who saw him as a survivor from "a bohemian yesteryear". There is a delightful caricature of Fullwood which shows him looking dapper and cheerful. He seems to have been popular among the younger artists and writers he mixed with. It's possibly significant that he chose to align himself with a group called the Black and White Artists' Society whose members were painter-etchers, and to relax in the Sydney Press Club. Did he network among the fine art practitioners in Sydney to any great degree? Possibly, though not enough to draw attention to his work outside the illustrative and commercial.

On the surface things might have looked reasonably tolerable, though his jaunty bohemianism may have simply been a cover for his uncertainties about the future. He was frequently impoverished, partly because he gave money away, especially to veterans of the Australian armed forces who had fallen on hard times. His health wasn't good, and towards the end of September, 1930, he was taken into hospital suffering from "acute lobar pneumonia". He died from heart failure on the 1st October, 1930.

It's possible to make suggestions about why Fullwood was forgotten so quickly after his death. He had spent almost twenty years absent from Australia between 1900 and 1919 which must have removed him from the public eye. And there were all those diversions away from gallery-art into areas of illustrating and designing. He was also probably a victim of changing tastes. Fresh ideas were creeping in from Europe and America in the 1920s, and by the 1930s were sufficiently established to provide for a new bohemia often with paintings of a radical nature, whether of an artistic or political persuasion and sometimes a combination of the two. I have a book, *Rebels and Precursors: The Revolutionary Years of Australian Art* by Richard Haese (Allen Lane, 1981), which looks at movements in the 1930s and 1940s. It's significant that established artists such as Tom Roberts and Arthur Streeton are mentioned more than a few times in the text, even if in a critical way which sees them as typical of an older, more-conservative tradition. But Fullwood doesn't even rate that sort of reference, nor any other. He just doesn't exist in the story.

One aspect of Werskey's account that struck me is the number of times he refers to a painting as "now lost". There is an irony in the fact that, provided the old newspaper and magazines still survive in a library somewhere, it might be possible to see a fair amount of the illustrative work that Fullwood did. But if a canvas is lost then it may be necessary to rely on a critic's description, assuming one exists, or a reproduction in a contemporary newspaper or magazine, again assuming one exists though it's likely be in black and white, for an idea of what the painting in question amounted to.

Picturing a Nation is a well-researched book that not only highlights the life and work of a neglected artist, but also throws light on the development of an artistic tradition in Australia. Looking at canvases like "Bad News" and "Solitude" inclines me to think that Fullwood was a very good painter.

PICTURING A NATION : THE ART AND LIFE OF A.H. FULLWOOD

By Gary Werskey

NewSouth Publishing (UK distributor – Eurospan). 340 pages. £28.95. ISBN 978-1-7422-36681

COLD WAR SECRETS : A VANISHED PROFESSOR, A SUSPECTED KILLER, AND HOOVER'S FBI

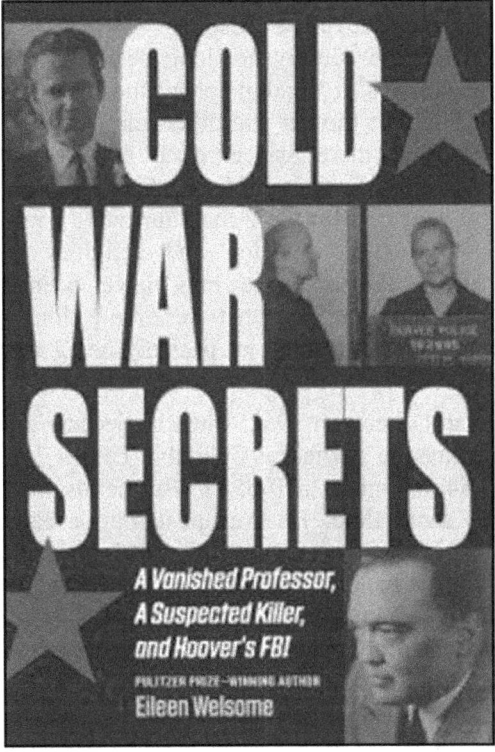

On the 15th March, 1969, Thomas Riha said good night to a friend he had been visiting, climbed into his car, and drove off. He had seemed apprehensive, the friend said later, and thought he had been followed to her house. She invited him to stay but he told her he needed to go home. He was never seen again. His disappearance was initially ascribed to his somewhat chaotic domestic circumstances, which revolved around messy divorce proceedings he was involved in, but the facts of his absence looked odd. He appeared to have gone without taking any clothes, and he hadn't told anyone that he was intending to be away for a few days. As the days and weeks passed he failed to get in touch with the university where he was an associate professor in the Slavic Studies Department.

Riha was employed by the University of Colorado at Boulder. He had been born in Prague in 1929, managed to survive the Nazi occupation of Czechoslovakia despite having two Jewish grandparents, and left the country not long before the Communist takeover in 1948. He was in London for a time, but moved to the United States in 1947. His mother and other relatives were living in California, so he went there and enrolled as a student at the University of California, Berkeley. He graduated in 1951 with a degree in political science. But there then appear to be a couple of years where details of his location and activities are scarce. According to Eileen Welsome:"He may have been travelling, working some non-academic job that he didn't think important enough to put down on his résumé, or possibly being trained as an intelligence agent".

He next appeared in December, 1952, when he became a naturalised citizen. Welsome says he studied at Columbia University's Russian Institute in 1953/54 and again in 1955/56. But he also served in the army around the same time. He was posted to a Psychological Warfare Centre in North Carolina, but if the testimony of one of his fellow-soldiers is to be believed, did little of any consequence while there. Riha spoke five languages, "including flawless Russian", but it doesn't appear that the army put his skills to any great use.

A master's degree from Berkeley, and a Ph.D in Russian history from Harvard followed. In 1958 he was an exchange student at Moscow University. He had been warned not to try to enter Czechoslovakia while on his way to Russia, but ignored the advice and flew to Prague from Paris. Welsome says that Riha's file in the StB (Czech secret service) archives shows that he had been charged with leaving the country "without permission" in 1947, so should have been arrested when he entered Czechoslovakia. He was instead given a room at the Flora Hotel in Prague, "an arrangement that suggests the Communist government knew he was coming and had authorised his visit".

He was subject to surveillance while in Prague, but soon moved on to Moscow after visiting Vienna, Copenhagen, and Helsinki. While in Russia Riha "was allowed to travel freely" and to meet a variety of people. He eventually returned to America, and a year or so later was contacted by FBI agents who wanted to know about his experiences in Russia. The Bureau already had a file on him and were aware, through mail interception, that he had received Soviet "propaganda" publications as early as 1954. These could, of course, have been purely for study purposes. He seems to have assured the agents that nothing he had done in Czechoslovakia or Russia could be construed as detrimental to the interests of the United States. What he didn't tell the FBI was that he had been offered a professorship in Bratislava, coupled with the promise of the return of some family property in Prague that had been seized by the State, if he stayed in Czechoslovakia.

In 1960 Riha obtained a teaching post at the University of Chicago, where he "developed an innovative course on Russian civilisation based upon the histories of three cities – Moscow, Kiev, and Leningrad". He spent a year at the University of Marburg in Germany, during which time he visited Moscow and Leningrad. Curiously, however, when he was back in Chicago, and his name was put forward for an exchange programme with Czech academics, he was denied entry on the grounds that some of their nominees had been turned down by the Americans.

It was probably in Chicago that Riha first met Galya Tannenbaum, a strange lady who was to play a significant part in the events surrounding his disappearance in 1969. She had an affair with Leo Tanenbaum, a Chicago businessman and political cartoonist who was a member of the American Communist Party. Prior to that she had been briefly married to a graphic artist named Charles Russell Scimo, and had served a prison sentence for "obtaining money by false pretences".

A whole book could be written about Galya. She was a liar and fantasist who claimed to be an FBI agent and to have a high position in the INS (Immigration and Naturalisation Service), among other security-related organisations. It would seem that, during her relationship with Tanenbaum, she was providing information to the FBI about American communists. It was hardly likely to have been of any great value. The Party was a shell of what it once had been and was riddled with informers. And the FBI knew from another informant in Tanenbaum's design studio that Galya could not be relied on to tell the truth. It was Galya who added the extra "n" to her name and later claimed that Tanenbaum had fathered a child she had.

In 1967 Riha moved to Boulder where he had been offered "a tenure-track job" in the history department at the University of Colorado. At first, everything seemed to be going well. Riha got along with his colleagues and was popular with students. The nature of his relationship with Galya in Chicago doesn't seem to have been a particularly close one, but they renewed their acquaintanceship when she turned up in Boulder in 1968. There was another problem, too. Riha had entered into a quickly-arranged marriage to a young woman named Hana who he had met in New York. From observations by those who knew him, it didn't strike them as a marriage likely to last long, and it didn't. The marriage took place in October, 1968, and quickly fell apart. Hana had separated from Riha by the time he disappeared in March, 1969, and claimed that he and Galya had tried to kill her so that they could collect on a large insurance policy he had insisted Hana agree to when they married.

Reading Welsome's book it is obvious that some people took Galya's claims of high-level contacts in official circles seriously. There were suggestions that Riha was wary of her, perhaps because she knew something he didn't want others to know. She had turned up at the wedding reception and lured Riha away from his bride and guests for a long conversation. And Galya was present in the Riha household on the night when Hana, afraid for her life, climbed out of a window and ran to neighbours for protection. Police who were called to the scene detected a strong smell of ether in the room Hana had escaped from. Telling the people who had helped Hana not to interfere, Riha said that Galya was a colonel in military intelligence and was armed with a pistol.

When Riha didn't turn up at an academic symposium he was supposed to attend, and couldn't be located at home, it was at first assumed he'd gone away for a few days because of the situation with Hana. But as his absence lengthened enquiries began about his possible whereabouts. Local police didn't seem particularly interested in pursuing the matter once they'd made a preliminary investigation of the circumstances. It was a domestic dispute, as far as they were concerned. And when the FBI and the CIA were contacted they claimed they knew nothing about the case. Welsome's investigations have unearthed the fact that both agencies were aware of events as early as April, 1969. And had files on Riha dating back to the early-1950s.

It's impossible not to think that there was something odd about the response of the authorities to people asking about Riha's disappearance. Several times the answer came back that he was alive and well and living in Brooklyn. And there were hints that he might be living in Czechoslovakia. Welsome notes that more than one person probing into the Riha case was told "You don't want to know" or advised "not to be interested" or "I suggest you drop it". Fred Gillies, a reporter for the Denver Post, who on and off over a ten-year period looked into the case, encountered some evasion from local police. Welsome says that he remarked just before he died, "There was so much espionage".

So what did happen to Riha? It wasn't long after he went missing that Galya, claiming he had left some blank cheques and his credit cards with her, took charge of Riha's estate. She told people that he had authorised her to "dispose of his assets". She claimed that she was owed seven thousand dollars she had loaned Riha when he bought his house in Boulder. And she sold the house and his car. It had been parked in Boulder, which was strange if he was supposed to have left quickly to get away from his wife. It was noticeable that any money that accrued as Riha's house and belongings were disposed of was paid into Galya's account. Welsome calculates that Galya received "roughly seventy thousand in today's dollars from Riha's estate by using his credit cards, siphoning off his savings, cashing his royalty cheques, and from monies obtained through the sale of his home, his car, and his artwork".

Did she murder Riha? She was not at any time accused of committing the crime, though Welsome makes a convincing case for her being responsible and for the killing of two other people not connected to the Riha mystery. A sequence of misspellings of words she used in paperwork relating to all three victims convinced Welsome that, with other evidence, Galya must have been guilty. But she was never actually charged with any of the murders, and was convicted of forging signatures on cheques and a false will. Because of medical reports that described her fantasies as dangerous, and diagnosed her as a sociopath and/or psychopath, she was committed to the Colorado State Hospital. She somehow managed to smuggle cyanide into the ward she was placed on and committed suicide on March 5th, 1971. Cyanide was the cause of death for two of the people she killed, but Thomas Riha's body has never been found so it's only possible to hazard guesses as to how he died.

There may be some people who will have doubts about whether or not he was murdered. Or did he somehow make his way to Czechoslovakia and spend the rest of his life there? It's not likely, given that the security archives in Prague were opened up when communism collapsed in 1989. There surely would have been some traces of his existence among the files and other documents. It is curious, though, how the FBI and CIA continued to play down their possible involvement in the case. Welsome, an experienced investigative reporter, obtained many documents under the Freedom of Information Act. They were, as usual, heavily redacted, but she could often work out what was being referred to. None of it appears to indicate that Riha was other than one of Galya's victims.

Cold War Secrets is a fascinating book, thoroughly researched and well-written. It not only delves into Thomas Riha's disappearance and death, but also sheds light on the mood in the United States in the 1950s and 1960s. There is a large cast of characters, ranging from academics to secret agents, to members of the Communist Party, criminals, local policemen, and more. They are often interesting in their own right, for one reason another, and Welsome does more than just use them to provide colour for her narrative. She makes them and the whole confused situation come alive.

COLD WAR SECRETS : A VANISHED PROFESSOR, A SUSPECTED KILLER, AND HOOVER'S FBI

By Eileen Welsome

Kent State University Press (UK distributor – Eurospan). 266 pages. £24.50. ISBN 978-1-606-354254

ALSTON ANDERSON : DANCE OF THE INFIDELS

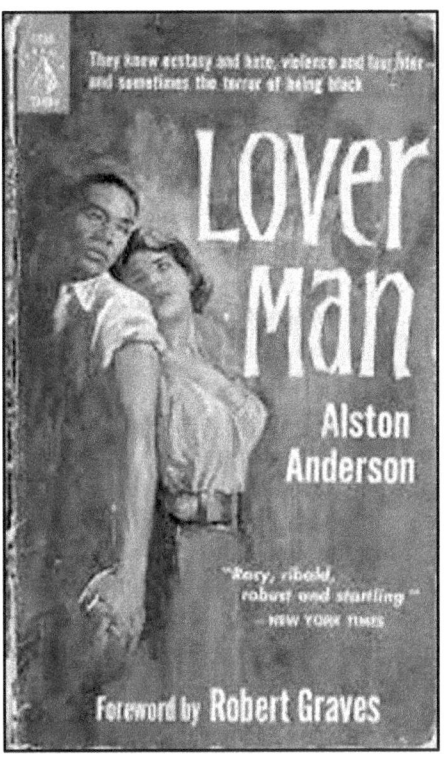

I have a small book on my shelves by Alston Anderson, a now-forgotten black writer. It's a collection of short stories entitled *Lover Man* and was published in 1961 by Pan Books, though it had previously appeared in hardback from Cassell in 1959. And it had the advantage of a fairly long, favourable introduction by Robert Graves. I bought my copy of the paperback in 1961 and have re-read the stories several times since then. One of them, "Dance of the Infidels", I've probably read a dozen times, if not more. I'll explain why later, but it might help if I first of all say something about Alston Anderson himself. It will not take long. Very little is known about him.

He was born in Panama, though his parents were Jamaican, Working back from his age (84) when he died in 2008 I'd say his date of birth must have been around 1924. He went to school in Kingston, Jamaica, and moved to the United States when he was fourteen. A long story, "Schooldays in North Carolina", is about the two years he spent at the Mary Potter-Redstone Albion Academy. It includes a few references which relate to some of his extra-curricular interests. He talks about listening to the radio with friends: "If we were lucky we would get Glenn Miller or Tommy Dorsey or Artie Shaw, and if we were real lucky we would get Earl Hines or Count Basie or Erskine Hawkins". And he fantasises about being "a star soloist like Lester Young or Chu Berry, and when it came for my solo I'd ease myself out of the orchestra, like Lester Young does, and walk up to the microphone and hold my sax way off to the side".

He studied at the North Carolina College in Durham from 1940 to 1943, when he was drafted into the army. There is an army story in *Lover Man*, but Graves points out that it isn't autobiographical. It's set in Germany at the war's end, and it would appear that Anderson actually spent nearly three years in a unit based in the Persian Gulf. When discharged from the army he returned to North Carolina College and graduated in 1947. He later spent some time studying philosophy at Columbia University in New York, and then moved on to the Sorbonne in Paris where Graves says he "specialised in eighteenth-century German metaphysics". But he also mixed with other expatriates like Terry Southern and the Canadian Mordecai Richler, soaked up the bohemian atmosphere of the Left Bank, and read Dostoyevsky, Joyce, Kafka, and Faulkner. And began to write himself.

It's difficult to know just when he was in Paris and for how long. I've looked at a couple of books which are about American and other writers in the French capital in the 1950s –James Campbell's *Paris Interzone* and Michael Fabre's *From Harlem to Paris* – but neither makes any mention of him. And none of the stories in *Lover Man* take place in Paris. He was at Yaddo art colony at some stage in 1955, and in New York where he wrote the stories that comprised *Lover Man*. They were revised in Majorca, where Anderson lived in the late-1950s.

His friendship with Graves appears to have ended in 1962 when the older writer said he was "tired of your drinking and doping" and the fact that Anderson wasn't settling down to work. It's after this that the account of his life is hazy. Anderson returned to the United States, and had a novel, *All God's Children* about slavery in the Southern States, published by Bobbs-Merrill in 1965. This was probably the book that was published by New English Library in England in 1968 with the title *The Slave*. But there is nothing to suggest that he had any more books in print after 1968, nor what he did to earn a living. His obituary says he died in poverty, no-one came forward to claim the body, and he was buried in potter's field, New York.

There are a few other facts that are known about Anderson. He had a short story published in the *New Yorker*, some of his stories from *Lover Man* crop up in anthologies of black writers and collections of jazz writing, and an obituary in the *New York Times* described him as a poet and jazz critic, as well as a novelist and short-story writer. Where did he publish his poetry and jazz criticism? He and Terry Southern interviewed the novelist Nelson Algren for a 1955 issue of the *Paris Review*. There were reports that his stay at Yaddo had been terminated because of his behaviour and the fact he had been mixing with disreputable characters. They were presumably from outside Yaddo and not among the other residents? It might be worth mentioning, too, that, as a veteran, his body was eventually disinterred and given a decent burial under a scheme that tracked down and provided graves for ex-servicemen who had died in impoverished circumstances.

The stories in *Lover Man* are mostly about life in North Carolina and illustrate Anderson's capacity to offer fresh views probably resulting from the fact that he hadn't grown up there and as a consequence saw things in a different light. The racial element is present, of course, though not necessarily as a dominant factor. But it's not my intention to say anything about these stories in this context.

The story that had a particular attraction for me when I first read the book is called "Dance of the Infidels" and is about a young man's encounter with bebop and its dark side. As the narrator says: "I used to listen to jazz all the day and most the night. I'd go to bed with it and wake up with it. Look like nobody else in town was as crazy about it as me: they all said I was music happy. But that was ok by me. They live their life and I live my own",

He often goes to a little café in the town (in North Carolina?) where he lives and if there's a bebop record on the jukebox he'll put his "ear right up against the speaker and listen. That way all I could hear in the whole wide world was music, and that was fine with me". One day he notices a stranger doing exactly the same so goes over and tells him he has the record and others like it at home. The man is called Ronnie and he's in town from New York. He's a piano player and particularly likes to listen to Bud Powell, the premier bop pianist.

They go to the narrator's apartment and listen together to Powell, Dizzy Gillespie, Charlie Parker, J.J. Johnson, and others. I'd guess that the meeting is happening around 1948 or 1949. The title of the story is taken from a 1949 recording by Bud Powell and trumpeter Fats Navarro. They're drinking and the visitor produces some reefers and introduces the young man to his first experience of marijuana. He gets high and can hear the records in a way that he never has before: "It was just like I'd heard them for the first time. I mean really heard them".

When Ronnie returns to New York he promises to send the young man some marijuana, which he does. After a while, though, the narrator's letters aren't answered, so he decides to go to the city to see if he can locate Ronnie. He discovers the world of the Dewey Square Hotel, the Savoy Ballroom, and Minton's Playhouse. He eventually meets Ronnie and finds that he is a heroin addict and not capable of performing as a musician. He watches him having a fix and then leaves, saying they'll meet tomorrow. The story ends there. It's bleak, but effective in its evocation of a certain period and its habits that, like it or not, seemed to be a part of bebop. There were probably numerous people similar to Ronnie, sometimes with musical skills, sometimes not, who became addicted to the music and its attendant way of life.

"Dance of the Infidels" has always seemed to me one of the few authentic fictional accounts of the bebop milieu. Had Anderson experienced something similar to what his young narrator, like him not long out of the army, describes? His writing certainly makes me think of the music he refers to. And want to listen to it in preference to most other sounds. The stories in *Lover Man* are generally still worth reading, but it's the one I've described that I'll keep on returning to as I do with the music.

SPANISH REPUBLICANS AND THE SECOND WORLD WAR: REPUBLIC ACROSS THE MOUNTAINS

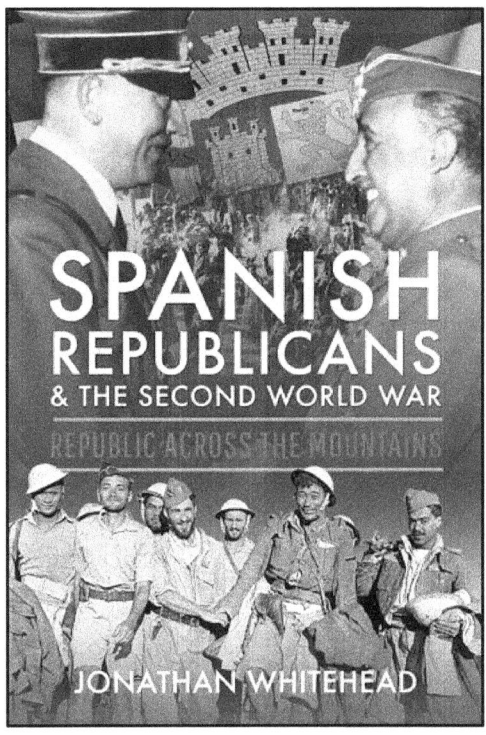

Anyone interested in reading about the Spanish Civil War can choose from a range of books, both old and new, which look at different aspects of the conflict and encompass just about everything from general histories to personal memoirs. The International Brigades, for example, have been written about in more ways than one. And programmes on TV have provided visual portraits of events and personalities, sometimes to the point where the glamour surrounding the celebrities visiting the war-zone seems more important than what was happening to the poorly-armed troops (many of them volunteers and without military training) holding the line against Franco's better-equipped army.

There are also the sad scenes as the Republic collapsed and thousands of refugees, both soldiers and civilians, poured into France and internment. I have on my desk a collection of poems by Philip Levine. The book is called *The Names of the Lost* and both the front and back covers have a photograph of a long column of Republican soldiers, disarmed and carrying everything they have managed to salvage, being led into what was essentially captivity by a French gendarme. To be fair, the French government had opened the border to allow the refugees to enter, but it was overwhelmed by the numbers involved and had no time to prepare for their arrival. Living conditions in the makeshift camps that were set up were at best rudimentary, at worst primitive.

What happened to the people pushed into what Jonathan Whitehead refers to as concentration camps? The luckier ones were rescued by friends, or found other ways to get out, and either left France or dispersed around the country. The unlucky ones waited to see what would happen, knowing that a war with Germany was almost inevitable. Men from the International Brigades who had gone to Spain from countries like Germany and Italy were particularly concerned. They couldn't return to their homelands. One option open to them, and to Spanish Republicans, was to enlist in the French Foreign Legion. And when France fell, and some forms of opposition to the occupiers began to emerge, it was possible to join a Resistance group. Spanish Republicans may, in fact, have played a leading role in the early days of the Resistance. There was also the opportunity to become a member of the Free French Army in North Africa.

It's probably true to say that little has been written about the role of Spanish Republicans in the Second World War. Passing references have mentioned them, and documentaries about the liberation of Paris in 1944 sometimes bring in the fact that the lead vehicles in General Leclerc's Second Armoured Division were manned by veterans of the Spanish Civil War. De Gaulle, anxious to create a myth of the Parisians themselves ridding the city of Germans was always keen to play down the involvement of other nationalities, just as he was to minimise the role of communists in the Resistance. This isn't to suggest that the Spaniards who fought with the Resistance, or served with regular army units, were necessarily communists. Anarchists, for example, were also prominent. But it's difficult to determine what individual fighters in any context saw as their political affiliations. Suffice to say that all of them looked to a time when they could participate in returning to Spain to overthrow Franco and re-establish a Spanish Republic.

Whitehead provides some details of the numbers involved in various organisations. Around three thousand joined the Foreign Legion, and "their most significant involvement in the Second World War was their role in operations in Norway which were truncated by the German attack on the Low Countries and France". Roughly the same number opted for the *Régiments de Marche de Voluntaires Étrangers* (RMVE), special units formed to provide support for other elements of the French Army. There were also fifty-five thousand in the *Compagnies de Travailleurs Étrangers* (CTE), "unarmed work battalions" which were sent to the Maginot Line, and to "the Swiss border, to the south coast area adjacent to the Italian frontier and to the north coast area near Dunkirk". They were employed on the upkeep of existing military installations, digging anti-tank trenches, and similar work. It's also relevant to note that approximately four thousand other refugees had been released from the camps to work on the land when French agricultural workers were called up.

Whitehead's account of the early days of the war suggests that: "An unknown number of Spanish recruits in CTE 118 which had been assigned to the British Expeditionary Force (BEF) fought in the rearguard as hundreds of thousands of Allied troops massed on the beaches of Dunkirk. Approximately thirty Spaniards were later rescued alongside French troops in the final hours of Operation Dynamo".And he tells other stories about Spaniards involved in the fighting as the German onslaught continued. One small group attached to the Manchester Regiment when told that only British troops were being evacuated managed to obtain British uniforms and mingle with soldiers being evacuated at St Nazaire. They arrived in Plymouth and "were eventually recruited into the No. 1 (Spanish) Company of the Royal Pioneer Corps". It's more than probable that had they been captured by the Germans they would have been sent to the Mauthasen concentration camp where many thousands of Spanish Republicans were held.

Those Spaniards who remained in France were quick to form "solidarity networks" that were, Whitehead says, "the precursors of resistance units". He additionally points to "the first recorded action of Spanish resistance workers ......in the winter of 1940/41, a sabotage team in central France partially destroyed a railway bridge at Saint-Brice-sur-Vienne". The news soon spread to other Spaniards, many of whom were being forced by the Germans to work on the Atlantic Wall and the submarine bases at Brest and La Rochelle". Many were also employed in the Channel Islands building bunkers and an underground military hospital.

Some Spanish Republicans who had found their way to the Soviet Union served in the Russian Army (estimates of the numbers involved range from eight hundred to fourteen hundred), and others joined up with partisan groups who fought guerrilla actions against the Nazis. In the Middle East, Spanish troops were part of the Allied forces in Lebanon and Syria. And it's said that of the three thousand five hundred men who put up a stout defence at Bir Hakeim in North Africa, one thousand were Spanish.

In North Africa General Leclerc was now in charge of the 2nd Armoured Division which included Spaniards. It was what Whitehead describes as a "light armoured division, and was equipped by the US Army with Sherman tanks, half-tracks, armoured cars, bazookas and anti-tank weapons". It seems that a number of men deserted from the Foreign Legion and joined Leclerc's regiment. Whitehead gives an account of the 9th Company of the 3rd battalion which "was made up almost exclusively of Spanish soldiers". Its commander was French and, in later years, he claimed that he was there partly because he spoke Spanish but also because other officers were "afraid" of the Spaniards: "They lacked military spirit, some were even 'anti-military', but they were magnificent soldiers, brave and battle-hardened warriors". And other French officers said: "They never retreated. They never gave up an inch of land they had taken. They always went first".

Not all Spaniards fought with the French, and Whitehead has accounts of several who served with British forces. Justo Balerdi had started with the Foreign Legion in Africa, but deserted when the Vichy government came to power. He joined the Queen's Royal Regiment, trained as a commando and saw action on the Greek island of Castellorizo. He fought in the Desert War "with various army groups", and then was taken into the Special Air Service. He was dropped into France behind enemy lines and teamed up with the Maquis to carry out acts of sabotage. He next moved onto Northern Italy, again working with partisans to disrupt German lines of communication. He was killed in a raid on a German supply depot.

Another Spaniard, José Maria Irala, went in with the paratroopers and was killed in the Arnhem operation.

It had been confidently expected by many Republicans that, once Germany was defeated, the Allies would turn their attention to Spain. Franco had resisted attempts to bring Spain into the war on the side of the Germans and Italians, and had taken care to deter Hitler from using Spain as a springboard to attack Gibraltar. It quickly became obvious that neither Britain nor America had any real interest in overthrowing Franco. The politics of post-war Europe were complex, and even before the war came to a close there were plans to limit the influence of communists when countries began to recover. Italy and France had strong communist parties, and it may have been thought that aiding or even just encouraging Spanish Republicans to invade Spain might lead to a hard left-leaning government there. Clement Attlee had visited Spain during the Civil War and been photographed giving the clenched fist salute with members of the International Brigades but, faced with the political situation that applied ten years later, he and his staunchly anti-communist Foreign Secretary, Ernest Bevin, made it clear that intervention in Spain was not part of their post-war agenda.

Left to their own devices some Spaniards did attempt an invasion, though others considered it a foolhardy plan with few hopes of success. The force that crossed the border in late-1945 was lightly armed, and though it met with little initial opposition it was clear that, once Franco began to move troops and artillery into the area, it would only be a matter of time before the invaders would be pushed back. There was, too, the problem that the civilian population showed hardly any enthusiasm for another civil war. Franco's army and police had exerted too tight a control for a rising to succeed. Some guerrilla activity continued into the late-1940s but achieved only limited objectives.

Whitehead looks at the role of the Communist Party in Spain in the aftermath of the Second World War. Driven underground, it seemed to spend much of its time engaging in bitter in-fighting, with expulsions and assassinations being the order of the day. It had lost credibility because of the fact that, when thousands were driven into exile in France, and often carried on the anti-fascist fight, many of the Party leaders had escaped to Moscow and survived the war.

I think it's worth noting that Whitehead devotes some space to the Spaniards who fought alongside German soldiers in Russia. They were an element in Franco's plan to placate Hitler while ensuring that Spain would not participate directly in the war. Around twenty thousand volunteers seem to have served on the Russian front at one time or another. They were noted for their bravery.

Spanish Republicans and the Second World War is a useful addition to the library of books about the Spanish Civil War and its consequences. It balances the broad outline of what happened with the activities of individual men and women who were determined to carry on the fight to overthrow fascism, no matter that circumstances often seemed to be against them. It's clearly written, has extensive notes and a bibliography. It tells an ultimately unhappy story in terms of dreams of freeing Spain from tyranny being dashed when Britain and America backed away from intervening. But it is inspiring in drawing attention to the very real sacrifices that were made by people who nursed those dreams through years of exile and war.

SPANISH REPUBLICANS AND THE SECOND WORLD WAR: REPUBLIC ACROSS THE MOUNTAINS

By Jonathan Whitehead

Pen & Sword Books. 304 pages. £25. ISBN 978-1-39900-451-0

AMERICAN SHERLOCKS : STORIES FROM THE GOLDEN AGE OF THE AMERICAN DETECTIVE

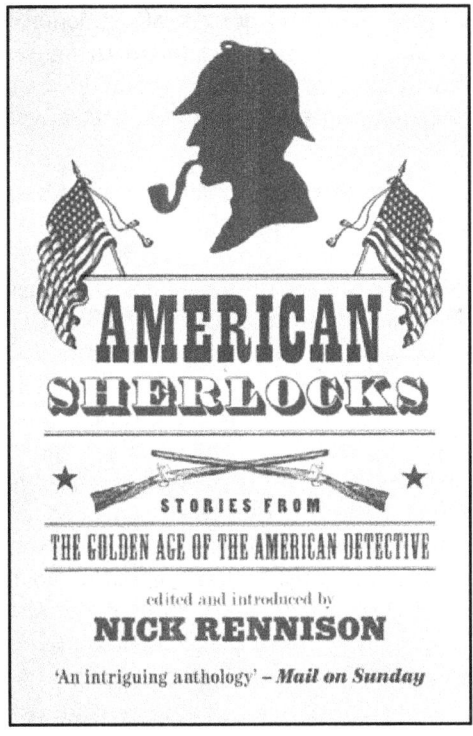

For those of us who delight in the discovery of old detective stories, especially those from the Victorian and Edwardian periods, the appearance of another anthology edited by Nick Rennison can only be welcomed. Following on from *The Rivals of Sherlock Holmes* (2008), *Supernatural Sherlocks* (2017), *More Rivals of Sherlock Holmes* (2019), and *Sherlock's Sisters* (2020), his new collection, *American Sherlocks*, provides another sampling of the adventures of a variety of detectives investigating murders, mysterious disappearances, robberies, and other misdemeanours.

As the title indicates, American authors of pulp fiction are on display. As in Britain, there were numerous magazines catering for readers who weren't looking for high-grade literature and instead wanted stories that were easy-to-read, tickled the imagination a little, but didn't demand too much in terms of complex characters and situations. They often did require the reader to suspend disbelief as the detectives unravelled sometimes bizarre methods of committing crimes, and in doing so displayed powers of deduction beyond the capacity of most people. It seemed a standard theme that ordinary professional policemen fumbled in the dark while those practising, in one way or another as amateur sleuths or private detectives, could see the light at the end of the tunnel.

One of the earliest American detective series was built around Nick Carter. a character created by John R Coryell for a serial in the *New York Weekly* in 1886. Rennison's notes about how Nick Carter survived well into the late-twentieth century are fascinating. As he says, "There have been literally thousands of Nick Carter stories, nearly all of them the work of the mostly unidentified writers who followed Coryell". And the portrait of Carter was altered to meet changing tastes as he developed from "a dime novel hero to Sherlockian consulting detective to hardboiled private eye…….and was even relaunched as a James Bond-style secret agent" in the 1960s. The story that Rennison uses was published in 1914 and involves an attractive actress, a mad doctor, a prison breakout, hypnotism, and much rascally behaviour. It's notable for a conclusion which involves several pages revolving around a detailed description of a fight between Carter, accompanied by an assistant, and a gang of miscreants.

It might give an indication of the widespread fame of the Carter stories, and the audience they catered for, if I mention that, in another story, Clinton H Stagg's "The Flying Death", a young boy who is a kind of protégé of the "problemist", as the detective is called, is said to see Carter as one of his fictional heroes. Thornley Colton, the detective, is blind, a fact that, as with Max Carados in the stories by the English author, Ernest Bramah, heightens his other senses. Combined with his analytical intelligence this enables him to come up with solutions to crimes that have baffled other people. In "The Flying Death" he deduces how a pistol can be fired without anyone being physically near it to pull the trigger, or having attached a cord to do it. I have to admit that my disbelief really did kick in with this piece. It's in this story, too, that the sneering villain, explaining how he carried out his crime, says that "there's Indian blood in me, mixed with the Irish", as if it explains how he could be so clever and so devious. Racial stereotypes were often a feature of writing at this time, and not only in pulp fiction.

It's possible to see them at work in the use of "wop" in more than one story to refer to Italians. Jacques Futrelle's "The Problem of the Opera Box" sees an Italian exacting vengeance with a knife, a weapon favoured by Latins and the like, but disdained by sturdy Anglo-Saxons. Or in Rodrigues Ottolengui's "Mr Barnes and Mr Mitchel" where there is a reference to a "sneaking Mexican". The story concerns a rare jewel, the Montezuma Emerald, the theft of such items being a fairly standard ploy in detective fiction. George Barton's "Adventure of the Cleopatra Necklace", for example, has his detective, Bromley Barnes, tracking down the item in question. I was intrigued by Rennison's notes about Ottolengui who "devoted most of his energies to his career as a dentist", but also wrote four novels and a number of short stories. He pioneered "the use of x-rays in orthodontics" and edited a dental journal, and when he died in 1937 the obituaries focused more on those facts than on his fiction. Which is, perhaps, understandable. Unlike now, little serious attention was then paid to crime fiction, especially of the popular variety.

The racial stereotyping would upset people today, and certainly incline publishers to persuade their authors to delete any signs of it from their work. And what would be the reaction to some of the scenes in Arthur B Reeves' *"The Azure Ring"*, where his hero, Craig Kennedy, described as "the scientific detective", blithely uses a cat and a couple of white mice in his experiments to determine the lethal nature of a substance he suspects has been used to kill a young couple? To prove his point the animals die. I suppose it's only fair to say that Kennedy, to reach his final conclusion regarding the quantity of the material required to kill a human, is prepared to subject himself to the test. He does so with a near-fatal result. But I can imagine animal lovers being concerned about the cat and mice, and possibly suggesting that the man had voluntarily used himself as a guinea pig, knowing full well the risks involved, whereas the animals had no choice in the matter.

Reeves is the one writer with two stories in the book, the other story being "The Mystery of the Stolen Da Vinci", with the female detective, Clare Kendall, on the hunt for a painting said to be "the companion piece to *Mona Lisa*, painted about the same time". The thieves turn out to be a couple of foreigners, again Italians, which could cause some people to think that, bearing in mind where the picture was painted, it was just being removed from the possession of a vulgar millionaire, and returned to its rightful home. But I doubt that the thieves were patriots who had that in mind. Rennison points out that the story was written around the time that the *Mona Lisa* had been stolen from the Louvre, so had some contemporary relevance. It's also worth noting that the detective makes use of a telegraphone, a device which works along the lines of a tape recorder. It was an actual machine, invented by Valdemar Poulsen, known as the "Danish Edison".

The contemporary crops up in Anthony M Rud's "The Affair at Steffen Shoals", which lets us see how Jigger Masters and his friend foil some spies who are passing secrets to the Germans. The story was presumably written during the period – 1917/18 – when the United States was involved in the First World War. The secrets are to do with plans for a new kind of gas that can be used with terrifying effect and must not be allowed to fall into enemy hands. Masters manages to outwit the spy and his gang and help sink a German submarine into the bargain. It's interesting in the way that it relates to the fact that there were numerous pro-German sympathisers in the United States owing to the large numbers of immigrants from that country.

Rennison mentions that old, supposedly humorous detective tales tend not to survive too well, but I did find Carolyn Wells's "Christabel's Crystal" quite entertaining as a gentle send-up of the Sherlock Homes–style story. Its female narrator, Elinor Frost, admits to not being familiar with different brands of cigar ash which, she says, are often key clues when attempting to identify who has been present in a room. There's also an English aristocrat who, like Holmes, can pinpoint someone's background from a quick glance at his complexion or his clothes. It's mildly amusing, which is more than can be said for the laboured humour of Ellis Parker Butler's "Philo Gubb's Greatest Case", where Philo, a paper-hanger by profession, and a keen amateur detective, adopts a number of disguises that fool no-one. It's easy to see how it would have appealed at the time in the context of a casually-read magazine, but it has dated badly.

Carolyn Wells is one of only two women writers in *American Sherlocks*, the other being Anna Katharine Green. Her detective, Violent Strange, is a well-heeled young woman who moves in high society circles in New York, but also accepts assignments from a detective agency, though she's fussy about which investigations she'll accept. She's reluctant to take on the case of "The Second Bullet", but eventually agrees to meet the grieving widow whose husband and child have died in a mysterious shooting incident. There's a somewhat implausible ending to the story, but Green's writing is competent enough to keep the narrative moving and perhaps persuade the reader that it could have happened that way.

I think "competent writing" might well be the correct way to describe the better-told stories. None attain the heights of great literature, but they often have a drive and energy that moves the narrative along in a convincing manner. Hugh Cosgrove Weir's "Cinderella's Slipper" spotlights his engaging heroine, Madelyn Mack, who is known to chew cola berries to stimulate her thinking when the situation requires intense wakefulness and concentration. I had come across this story earlier, in Hugh Greene's *The American Rivals of Sherlock Holmes* (Penguin, 1978), but it's good to have it in print again. The writing is crisp and clean, with few wasted words.

A writer I've never encountered before is Samuel Gardenhire, "a Missouri-born lawyer who turned to writing fiction in middle-age". He produced eight stories, one of which, "The Park Slope Mystery", has his sleuth, Ledroit Conners, looking into a bizarre shooting in a highly-respectable household. I know that questions have sometimes been raised about Sherlock Holmes's attitude towards women, but what are we to make of Conners who says, "I endeavour to avoid women". His friend says "I glanced again at his pictures, where sylph and siren, Venus in nature with Venus à la mode showed every phase of beauty to the eye". Conners, noting his friend's action, says: "These do not count. You recall the temptation of St Anthony? I hold discipline to be good for a man. These I may love – none other".

Whatever their qualities in terms of the writing, the stories in *American Sherlocks* always have an entertainment value. And Rennison's introduction and notes add to the appeal of a book like this. Who can resist reading about Charles Felton Pidgin, who created Quincy Adams Sawyer, "a professional private investigator, clearly influenced by Sherlock Holmes". Pidgin himself turned his hand towards various activities – a statistician, a writer of musical comedies for the stage, and an inventor, plus writing "more than a dozen novels". His story, "The Affair of Lamson's Cook", has a neat twist in the tail.

Even if we only look at the late-Victorian and Edwardian years, there must be hundreds of detective stories buried in now-forgotten magazines and newspapers. Many of them may not deserve to be dug out and reprinted. But some can still interest and intrigue as their sleuths, both men and women, endeavour to hold the forces of evil at bay. Let's hope that Nick Rennison will come up with more examples.

AMERICAN SHERLOCKS : STORIES FROM THE GOLDEN AGE OF THE AMERICAN DETECTIVE

Edited by Nick Rennison

No Exit Press. 333 pages. £9.99. ISBN 978-85730-439-1

THE LAST BOHEMIAN : AUGUSTUS JOHN
Lady Lever Art Gallery, Port Sunlight. 18th May, 2021 to 30th August, 2021

There was a time when Augustus John was seen as one of the leading artists in Britain. He was also looked on as something of a bad boy in terms of his personal behaviour. It went beyond the mere flamboyant and gave him a reputation for sexual adventuring with just about every lady he met. An anecdote says that, when walking down the street where he lived, he always patted every child he encountered on the head because he could well have been its father. It strikes me that some of the reluctance to deal with him today may stem from an understandable objection which frowns on women being exploited by those who can exert some sort of control over them. John's status as an acclaimed painter, coupled with his personal charisma, no doubt enabled him to turn on the charm to his advantage.

But should his alleged failings as a person be allowed to affect our admiration for his skills as an artist? I don't think John was an innovator, but he was a splendid draughtsman and an accomplished painter. Henry Tonks, himself noted for his drawings, thought highly of John's work when he was a student at The Slade. And the examples on show in the small, but satisfying exhibition at the Lady Lever Art Gallery point to the confident way in which he sketched his subjects and put something of their personalities into his portraits. He perhaps extended this achievement even more in his paintings, as for example one of the poet, Dylan Thomas, whose seeming baby-faced innocence can't hide the turbulence in his life and poetry. It might be worth noting that Caitlin Thomas, as she later became, had been one of John's many lovers when she modelled for him.

A major part of the exhibition revolves around the period when John taught at the art school in Liverpool in the early-1900s. It was a time when he extended his interest in the life-style of the Romani people, or gypsies, as he referred to them. Their near-bohemian wanderings no doubt appealed to his sensibilities. His own tendency to gypsy-like proclivities may have been tempered at times by the fact that he was married and his wife, Ida, gave birth to five sons. She can be seen in the exhibition, as can Dorothy "Dorelia" McNeill, John's mistress in their *ménage-à-troi,* who had four children by him.

There are portraits in the exhibition, and it was in this field that John achieved his prominence. It's said that he never flattered his sitters, with the result that some of them were less than satisfied with the finished product. And it may have been that his later work fell short of his previous high standards. His biographer Michael Holroyd, thinks so and comments on his heavy drinking, and a critic said that "the painterly brilliance of his early work degenerated into flashiness and bombast".

The range of paintings and drawings on display in Port Sunlight doesn't allow us to generalise about a decline in John's work over the years. But it does provide evidence of how talented and promising he must have seemed when he was younger. There is, perhaps, some irony involved in that his sister, Gwen, who was overshadowed by Augustus, has in recent years been re-discovered, and is now possibly better-known than him. Her quiet, low-key paintings seem to reflect the subdued personality seen in one or two photographs in the exhibition. But her brother understood that, while his work had "technical mastery", hers had "interior feeling and expressiveness".

Augustus John's bohemian capers are an obvious explanation of why he was often in the news, but it's his best work as an artist that we should now pay more attention to.

**THE SPANISH CIVIL WAR AT SEA:
DARK AND DANGEROUS WATERS**

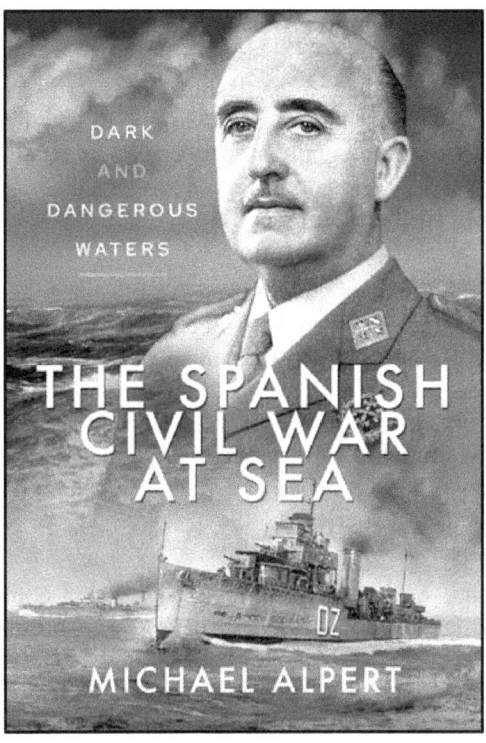

I've noted before that the Spanish Civil War has attracted attention from numerous writers. Most, whether writing fact or fiction, have focused on the war on land, and, to varying degrees, in the air. Little has been written about what happened at sea, though the physical location of Spain, and the supposed embargo on other countries supplying war materials, meant that shipping had an important part to play in keeping both sides provided with the essentials required to enable them to carry on functioning. Non-intervention was something of a farce in that Germany and Italy regularly supplied men and weapons to the Insurgents (I'm using Michael Alpert's term for Franco's forces) while Russia did the same for the Republicans.

When Franco and his supporters launched their insurrection in July, 1936, the Republic's navy was in what might be called a run-down condition. There had been an attempt to build up the fleet after it suffered heavy losses in the Spanish-American War of 1898, but little had been achieved in forming a truly modern naval force. By 1936 many of the ships were outdated in terms of their equipment. In theory the Government had a battleship, three cruisers, thirteen destroyers, twelve submarines, and a variety of smaller vessels, including torpedo boats, a gunboat and coastguard cutters, at its disposal. In practice it would soon become obvious that not all of the officers and crews of these ships could be relied on to support the Republic.

The situation in the Spanish Navy appears to have been that a sharp class distinction existed between the officers and the rest. Alpert puts it this way: "As for the men, the Spanish navy was not a happy service. There was mutual antipathy and suspicion between officers of the General Corps or *Cuerpo General,* who commanded the ships, and the specialist branches of engineers and gunnery, both among officers and the various branches and ranks of petty officers". No matter how skilled or experienced they were, petty officers could never become officers.

On the other hand, Alpert suggests that "Significant communist or revolutionary cells do not seem to have been present in the navy……Nor was there a history of indiscipline in the navy even during the social and industrial agitation in Spain in the months since the electoral victory of the Popular Front in February 1936". But sailors' committees were formed "and their purpose was to observe the officers and to nip a possible officers' uprising in the bud". It would soon become obvious that, when they could, the great majority of officers would ally themselves with Franco and, given the opportunity, place their ships in insurgent hands. It was largely due to one man, a warrant officer and telegrapher named Benjamin Balboa, based in the navy's communications centre, that some plots by officers were foiled. He kept In touch with radio operators on ships at sea and alerted them to attempts by officers to put in at ports controlled by the insurgents.

Mutinies among the crews spread on most of the ships that did stay loyal to the Republic. It was probably a sign of the existing antagonism that 350 officers were killed, usually by being thrown overboard. We know from other accounts that the Spanish Civil War was often a particularly brutal episode, with old enmities and class resentments coming to the fore. Anarchist sympathies were strong in Spain, and a hatred of all forms of authority, whether in the shape of religion or class, led to many outrages. It needs to be said that the Insurgents, for their part, could be just as savage when repressing any kind of radical activity.

The majority of ships remained under Republican command, but there were major problems facing them. Some of the more suitable ports had been occupied by the Insurgents, so questions of re-fuelling and similar matters were important. Republican ships were denied fuel in Tangiers, then under international control, ostensibly because the Control Commission feared that Franco might send aircraft to bomb the ships. But the port was full of French, Portuguese, Italian, and British warships, and their commanders were fearful of the effects of having mutinous sailors alongside their own crews. Alpert refers to a report that the Republican fleet "was under the direction of a Soviet led by a warrant officer". The absence of officers on the ships disturbed observers from other countries. Alpert also says that Shell refused to provide fuel for the Spanish ships because they were controlled by mutineers. And Shell's interests would probably have been more aligned towards the Insurgents than to a radical Republican government.

The position regarding officers who appeared to have remained loyal to the Republic was never very clear. The submarines were especially affected by doubts about their effectiveness because of a seeming lack of enthusiasm on the part of their commanders to carry out orders. And it was a fact that the removal of so many officers due to either desertion to the Insurgents or death at the hands of mutinous sailors, caused major Republican concerns. With men being promoted to the rank of officer at short notice, and with little practical experience in the overall running of a ship, not to mention the sailors' committees questioning and sometimes countermanding orders, putting to sea could be a risky enterprise.

The Insurgents did take over some ships, including a battleship, four cruisers, a destroyer, three minelayers, and some smaller vessels. They also established a number of armed trawlers to stop merchant ships heading for Republican ports. And they had the advantage of experienced officers and disciplined crews, though they sometimes had to train men quickly to take over from sailors who refused to fight for Franco. It's also significant to note that the presence of Italian and German ships played a major part in the operations of the Insurgent navy. They had reasons for being there, not just because Mussolini and Hitler wanted to support a fellow-dictator, which is what Franco would become with their assistance, but for strategic purposes. The Italians, for example, were keen to present a challenge to the dominance of the Royal Navy in the Mediterranean.

I mentioned earlier that moving goods into Spain, whether of a military or non-military nature, had to be done largely by sea. The land access through France was closed most of the time due to the Non-Intervention policy of the French Government. Some supplies could be landed in Portugal, whose dictator, Salazar, was sympathetic to the Insurgents and would then allow them to be moved into Spain. But this was not an option available to the Republicans. Most of what they needed had to arrive by sea, and was transported by merchant ships, many of which were British, or at least registered as such to enable them to fly the British flag and be protected by the Royal Navy in certain circumstances. This didn't stop them being torpedoed by Italian submarines or bombed by Insurgent aircraft frequently manned by German or Italian pilots. It isn't necessary for me to give a ship-by-ship account of all the attacks and incidents involving merchant ships – sometimes they were stopped so their cargoes could be examined to see if they were carrying war materials – but Alpert provides an informative selection of relevant stories.

It's often alleged that the role of the Communist Party, and particularly of Russians present in Spain, was a determining factor in the decisions made by countries like Britain and France in relation to the Republic. It might seem obvious now that Hitler and Mussolini were using Spain as a form of testing ground, not only for their armed forces, but also to determine how other nations would react. And to hopefully have Spain on their side when a showdown with the British and French came. As it happened, Franco kept Spain out of the Second World War. But at the time the possibility of a Republican victory leading to a communist Spain seemed the greater danger to politicians and business leaders in Britain and France. Their turning a blind eye to Germany and Italy openly intervening can be explained in this way. Russia, of course, was also intervening by providing arms and ammunition, together with some "advisers", to the Republic, but that was condemned.

With regard to the Russians who arrived in Spain, it's useful to note the comments of Nikolair Kuznetsov on the lack of qualified officers in Republican ships. He had a low opinion of their "insufficient and out-of-date training" and the navy generally was "not even minimally ready for a naval war". What appeared to have caused him much consternation, however, were the on-board sailors' committees: "For Kuznetsov, the lack of organisation, leadership, and firm direction, added to anarchistic indiscipline, rendered ineffective the efforts of petty officers and officers". The inefficiency among the crews was also found in the dockyards where ships being repaired could be held up for months. Some blame for this was attributed to sabotage, and management sympathy for the Insurgents.

There were no major confrontations between the two fleets. Alpert sums up the situation at one point: "Thus, by spring 1937, the tone of the naval war off the Spanish coast had been established. The Insurgents would strive even more to prevent merchant ships bringing arms to Republican Spain, and the Republicans would continue to escort vessels on their way to Republican ports. Neither fleet would show much enthusiasm for an encounter which might endanger their navies 'in being'".

This didn't mean that individual ships weren't sunk or badly damaged. The Insurgent battleship, *Espana,* struck a mine (seemingly one laid by the Insurgents themselves in a blockade operation off Santander) and sank. Luckily, most of the crew survived. But when the Insurgent cruiser, *Baleares,* was torpedoed by Republican destroyers, 790 of her crew died. And an Insurgent transport ship, the *Castillo de Olite*, hit by shore batteries near Cartagena, went down with 1,477 men. In the Republican fleet, the battleship, *Jaime Primero,* which was in dock for repairs following an air attack, was lost when an explosion in a powder magazine killed 179 men and rendered it unfit for further service. There was also the loss of the destroyer, *José Luis Diez*, and several submarines, some of which may have been deliberately scuttled by their officers who were secretly pro-Franco and reluctant to follow Republican orders.

When the end came the Republican fleet left Cartagena and sailed to Algiers where it was ordered to proceed to Bizerta. The ships were eventually handed over to the Insurgents when France recognised the

Franco government. Some of the sailors went into exile, others opted to return to Spain. Franco wasn't content to have won, he needed to exact revenge, and Alpert reports that "192 officers appeared before courts-martial, of whom 80 were acquitted and 112 found guilty. Ten death sentences were imposed, of which two were commuted". Some other officers were sentenced to life imprisonment. And he adds, "As for other ranks, 153 death sentences were handed down of which 115 were carried out".

The Spanish Civil War at Sea is an important book, providing as it does a useful account of what happened off the coast of Spain. It was often a story of relatively small-scale actions involving individual Insurgent and Republican ships, Royal Navy, German, and Italian warships, and numerous merchant ships. Michael Alpert supplies a brisk, detailed history of events between 1936 and 1939.

THE SPANISH CIVIL WAR AT SEA: DARK AND DANGEROUS WATERS

By Michael Alpert

Pen & Sword Books. 288 pages. £25. ISBN 978-1-52676-436-2

ART ALONG THE SOUTH COAST

JOHN NASH : THE LANDSCAPE OF LOVE AND SOLACE
Towner Gallery, Eastbourne, 18th May, 2021 to 26th September, 2021

SEASIDE MODERN : ART AND LIFE ON THE BEACH
Hastings Contemporary, Hastings, 27th May, 2021 to 31st October, 2021

DOWN FROM LONDON : SPENCER GORE AND FRIENDS
Brighton Museum & Art Gallery, Brighton, 18th May, 2021 to December, 2021

The main attraction on the South Coast at the moment is undoubtedly the big exhibition of the work of John Nash. But this should not be allowed to draw attention away from two other fascinating shows which, in fact, can be seen to have links of one kind or another to the Nash. What we are dealing with in all three is primarily English art (I'm deliberately using "English" as opposed to "British") in roughly the first fifty years of the Twentieth century. Nash did continue painting into the 1970s, though his key works had probably been produced earlier.

Born in 1893 he showed an early aptitude for drawing, but never had any formal training, unlike his older brother, Paul, who went on to establish a reputation as a well-known British artist. It has often been said that John was always overshadowed by Paul as the latter was acclaimed as a war artist and, in the 1930s, played a part in the British Surrealist movement. John himself had been a war artist before the end of the First World War, but prior to that had been an infantryman in the trenches. He had directly experienced what war was really like. His painting, "Over the Top", has nothing heroic about it. The soldiers walking wearily towards the enemy seem almost resigned to their fate.

Nash had been active before 1914 and a member of the New English Art Club. Among his contemporaries were Harold Gilman, Charles Ginner, Robert Bevan, and Spencer Gore, and one or two of them have a corner in the exhibition to indicate their involvement in the Cumberland Market Group, to which Nash belonged for a short period. But I have the feeling that groups and movements were never really to his taste. He seems to have gone his own way most of the time, though he had individual friends, such as Eric Ravilious and Edward Bawden, who shared his liking for rural life and landscapes. There are quite a few Nash landscapes to be seen in Eastbourne, and they are all a delight to look at, though I did occasionally feel that a blandness of composition sometimes seemed to creep in.

What I did find especially impressive were Nash's woodcut engravings and his work as a botanical artist. He illustrated issues of *The Countryman* and provided colour lithographs for various books. His drawings point to his extensive knowledge of flowers and plants. His work was varied, however, and he would sometimes take a break from country matters and paint a dockside scene in Colchester or somewhere similar. But he was a countryman at heart and the exhibition emphasises this fact. Nash may not have been an innovator, nor did he paint any truly major pictures, but he was consistently skilled at what he did. And this well-mounted and informatively-documented exhibition – the largest in over fifty years – is a fine tribute to an artist who deserves to be remembered.

John Nash isn't represented in the exhibition at the Hastings Contemporary, but brother Paul is there several times. The general theme is how, in the interwar years, the English took to the seaside for their day trips and holidays, and artists likewise decided that what could be seen on the shoreline was suitable for painting. There are photographs of families and it's noticeable how formally dressed they are for relaxing on the sands. Advertising indicates how rail companies sought to encourage people to travel to the seaside. And artists like Fortunino Matania and Laura Knight were employed to create designs for posters that would point to the excitement and glamour to be found in Southport and elsewhere. Matania's version of Southport suggests that it's all sunshine and pretty girls in bathing suits. It's a different world to the one provided by L.S. Lowry's *July, the Seaside*. Ordinary mums and dads with kids in tow or building sandcastles seem to be prominent. And, for another version of holiday fun, there's a delightful William Roberts' painting with his familiar tubular figures cavorting on the beach.

Other artists were busy capturing different aspects of the coast. Barbara Hepworth's abstract sculpture and Eileen Agar's surrealistic photograph of a beached tree are examples of what the imagination can do. Eric Ravilious and John Piper with a combination of colour and form extend the realistic into the curious. There's also a suggestion of a darker side to the coast in John Minton's pen and ink drawing, *On the Quay, Cornwall*, with a lone male figure posed by some small boats and an odd-looking bird almost beneath his feet. One of the pleasures of this exhibition is that some of the artists – Mary Adshead and Edgar Ainsworth, for example - are relatively little-known. Ainsworth's pen and ink drawing of Blackpool in 1945 captures its crowded and noisy good-humour.

Brighton, like Blackpool, attracted people out for a good time, but the exhibition there isn't concerned to register anything to do with that fact. In 1913 Spencer Gore, a forward-looking young artist and a member of the Camden Town Group, organised an *Exhibition of English Post-Impressionists, Cubists and Others* at the Brighton Public Art Galleries. The current exhibition doesn't attempt to recreate the earlier one, but it does aim to commemorate it in some ways. Gore's friends from Camden Town– Harold Gilman, Robert Bevan, Charles Ginner - are present, and just as he broke the rules in 1913 by including women (they weren't allowed to be members of the Camden Town Group), we can now see paintings by Sylvia Gosse, Thérèse Lessor ,and one or two other women artists.

I have a great fondness for the Camden Town painters, and Charles Ginner in particular. His precision is impressive (he trained as an architect) but his paintings are not just displays of technique and it never becomes overwhelming when combined with his astute handling of colour. There is a fine balance in his work that enables it to convince in a quiet way.

As for Gore himself, he tragically died at the early age of 36 as a result of developing pneumonia due to painting outdoors in bad weather. He had seemed destined to become a leading modern painter, influenced by Cezanne and André Derain,, and with encouragement from Walter Sickert, but has perhaps often tended to be overlooked when people talk about the Camden Town Group. It didn't last long and it might have been interesting to see what Gore would have done had he lived and gone on to different things. Would he have joined with others to form a new group? It seems that Wyndham Lewis spoke favourably about his work in the Vorticist magazine, *Blast*, but would Gore have moved that way rather than staying with the largely domestic and urban concerns favoured by Sickert?

It's a small exhibition in Brighton – around forty works on display – but a very positive one in terms of illustrating how attractive much Camden Town painting can be. It's not that any of the artists were great painters, but they were often very good ones. They had absorbed lessons from France but at the same time maintained a clear English sensibility when it came to subject-matter and how best to represent it in paintings. I've noticed how any exhibition of work by the Camden Town group, or the Cumberland Market artists, and the Fitzroy group – the same people were in and out of all of them – will usually attract a decent-sized crowd. It's understandable. With their often bright colours, and scenes of streets and market-places, or interiors with figures in a variety of situations, the paintings are pleasing to consider.

THE BELLE ÉPOQUE :
A CULTURAL HISTORY, PARIS AND BEYOND

The Belle Époque? Paris, the Moulin Rouge, the Can-Can, men in top-hats, Toulouse-Lautrec and Bohemia, paintings of pretty girls in long dresses on busy streets or in crowded salons by Jean Béraud, and society portraits by Giovanni Boldini. I could carry on pulling images out of the mass swirling around in my head at the mention of the Belle Époque. But what caused them to be there?

It's a question that Dominique Kalifa explores in this book. As he points out, the term Belle Époque was not used by anyone at the time. Which was when? After considering various options, he settles on the period between 1900 and 1914, though it's perhaps possible to push the starting date back by a few years. But 1900 is the key to an understanding of what Belle Époque came to mean as it faded into memory. It represented the change from one century to the next, but more than that it seemed to suggest a time when peace, progress and prosperity appeared to be prominent.

It wasn't quite like that, of course, but people wanted to imagine that it was. Nostalgia is a powerful force and it's easy to feel it for something that we didn't directly experience. But it is necessary to point out that those years between 1900 and 1914 did see "a prodigious cultural flowering that made Paris the incontestable capital of world art and letters, which in this period witnessed a sort of paroxysm of the audacious, of experimentation and aesthetic inventiveness".

So, in the case of the Belle Époque, why was there a need to celebrate an imagined past? And when did the celebrating start? Kalifa makes it clear that it wasn't in the 1920s. It might be thought that, following the end of the First World War, there would be a rush to reactivate the "golden years" that supposedly existed prior to 1914. But it seems not. There was a resurgence of fine living as cafés and restaurants flourished and energies were devoted to having a good time. The Twenties in Paris created their own Belle Époque, as foreigners flooded in (think of all those American expatriates writing poems and novels and the many more who were just there for business or pleasure) and there was plenty of money around.

There were other things going on, but on the whole we prefer to read about the bright side of life. And no-one felt the urge to look back fondly on the Paris of 1900. Perhaps a few people did, and Kalifa cites a newspaper survey which complained that there were now "too many automobiles, too many buses, too many tarred roads, not to mention all these metro-building sites that are disfiguring the urban landscape". But for many the trauma of the Great War helped displace thoughts of pre-war Paris from their minds. It was enough that they could now enjoy the Paris that had come to life after 1918. The Moulin Rouge had burned down in 1915 and a new one opened up in the early 1920s. But, Kalifa says, "not the slightest nostalgia was expressed in the new shows, which looked unhesitatingly to the present", with influences from America to the fore. And, after all, anyone of a certain age in the Twenties knew that pre-1914 wasn't all sweetness and light. Kalifa points to Louis-Ferdinand Céline's *Death on the Instalment Plan* and its depiction of Paris around 1900 as a "dirty, ignoble, infected place, peopled with failures, traversed by the 'numberless legions of thirst' ".

It was in the early-1930s that The Belle Époque made an appearance as a description of an era: "While the world horizon was darkening, the longing for the past grew and its tone changed......Backward-looking memoirs, novels, and songs multiplied, while the sensations of 1900 were being adapted for stage or screen". And Kalifa asserts that it was only around 1940 that it "came definitively to designate what for a dozen years had been known as the '1900 era' ". 1940 may seem to be a curious date to use. The Germans were marching through Paris by then, and life in France became a matter of survival. Why would anyone be thinking of an imagined past? But, why not? It could, perhaps, be a form of sustenance, a belief in a French culture that would survive occupation.

For some in Paris it may also have been an opportunistic move to focus on the imagined Paris of 1900: "The *'vie parisienne'* came back into its own, particularly because economic demand was high from both Occupation troops and privileged spectators and consumers.....At the end of 1940, more than 100 cinemas, 25 theatres, 14 music halls, and 21 cabarets in Paris were fully functioning". Kalifa refers to the way in which the idea of the Belle Époque was used to entertain Germans who had its mythological setting in mind, but was also "mobilised for good profits in a 'very French vein' at all the capital's theatres and *café-concerts*".

It was obvious that France as a nation experienced a loss of prestige after 1945 as the economy struggled to recover, and French colonies in Indo-China and Algeria fought to obtain their freedom. In the arts, too, the French suffered a diminution in their standing as the focus in painting shifted to New York, and the notion of the avant-garde having its headquarters in the French capital became defunct. Taken together, these factors might explain why "mobilizing the Belle Époque could signify a return to the age of cultural influence, the age of innocence, the age of France". It made people feel good to think that there had been a time when what Paris did today, the rest of the Western world did tomorrow.

Memoirs and general histories poured off the presses, and "From 1945 to the end of the 1950s more than, 60 French films in the '1900 spirit' came to the screens". Needless to say, the working-classes "do not count for much" in these films, other than that they pop up as servants, soldiers, cab-drivers, laundresses, and the like. But then workers were hardly in evidence in paintings dating from the original period. And memoirs were mostly written by the middle-class about their own class.

There were changes in the 1960s, particularly after the events of 1968. Young historians and others began to look at where the workers stood in the overall scheme of the Belle Époque : "This shift owes much to ideological movements that brought to the fore ideas impregnated with critical theory and with political and social radicalism". Obviously, it must have been known before the radicals came along that the years between 1900 and 1914 were not simply devoted to frivolities and frolics on the part of a small selection of Parisian society. There were deep social problems, such as poverty, alcoholism, syphilis, and industrial strife, that should not be ignored. But they often were overlooked in books, magazine articles, exhibitions, and films that purported to present an accurate account of the Belle Époque.

This may have been because their creators had to base their views on those they could find in books by people who had lived through 1900 and beyond, on paintings and photographs from the period, and similar material. New commentators wanted to challenge this approach. But how successful were they outside the universities and general intellectual circles? Popular forms, such as films, music, and many books aim to appeal to a wider audience. It's a fact that a film, book, or exhibition of an imagined Belle Époque of well-dressed couples dining in expensive restaurants, or parading their finery in shops and streets, is likely to attract a larger audience than anything taking a downbeat look at an era. Working-class deprivation, diseases, mine disasters, strikes, etc. are not glamorous.

The Belle Époque is inevitably always associated with Paris, but Kalifa widens his survey to show how, in the 1970s, there was a trend towards activity in the provinces which can be related to the nostalgia for an idealised past. In a sense, various cities, towns, districts, started their own celebrations of a Belle Époque with local festivals and exhibitions. A few years ago I was in Auvers one Sunday when the town was awash with bunting and flags. As I came down the hill from the cemetery where Vincent Van Gogh was buried I could hear music played on a street organ or some such instrument, and I could see at the bottom of the hill a couple dressed in costumes from 1900 or so dancing in the style of that period. The buildings alongside the road are old, there were no cars or pedestrians in contemporary clothes, simply the sounds and sights of an earlier era. And for a brief moment I was swept with nostalgia, despite not being French nor having any experience of the supposed Belle Époque.

Publishers sprang up to cater for the interest in the past. Collections of old photographs appeared and postcards from years ago became collectors' items. This fascination with facets of earlier years hasn't been limited to France. Kalifa sums it up well when he says of the Belle Époque: "In general, the term remained focused on the turn from the nineteenth to the twentieth century and still evoked forms of social and cultural life, but now 'Belle Époque' seemed more and more to escape the history of France alone. It also tended to escape history altogether and become a sort of cultural label with a rather broad significance. The commercial motive, partly decontextualized, soon was to satisfy the passion for the 'retro' and then for the 'vintage' that gripped many societies".

It's interesting to note Kalifa's comments on the number of novels that have been published in recent decades which are set in the Belle Époque or thereabouts. In particular he mentions the series of twelve published under the name of Claude Izner. They are crime stories with titles like *The Montmartre Investigation, The Père Lachaise Mystery, The Marais Assassin*, and involve the activities of a young bookseller and amateur detective as he unravels mysteries around Paris. I've only read the six translated into English, but have thoroughly enjoyed each one. They successfully re-create the mood and appearance of Paris in 1900. Or so I believe

Claude Izner is actually the pen-name of two sisters who are bouquinistes along the Seine. They know their city and its history, and many real-life characters appear in the novels. Do they cater to the nostalgic? Perhaps. Kalifa says: "Nostalgia is not history - it reconstructs or recollects more than it explains – but nor is it programmed falsification. It organises memory, stimulates the imagination, and may also lift the veil here and there on forgotten figures or disdained realities".

The Belle Époque is a thoroughly fascinating book with much to stimulate the imagination into reflecting on the past and how we view it. Dominique Kalifa ranges over a wide variety of subjects – literature, film, social history – and raises numerous questions about the seeming need for an idea of a "vague (almost mythic) era of happiness and shared fulfilment". This isn't just limited to a specific place (Paris) or a specific time (1900), and appears to apply almost world-wide and in any period. It would easily be possible to bring up many examples from within the British Isles, ranging through books, television programmes, films, art exhibitions, and much more. I sometimes hear people talking about the 1960s and wonder if they're referring to the same era that I lived through. But it does occur to me that, while many people will have in their minds certain ideas about the time of a Belle Époque they either experienced or wished they had, there is only one date, 1900, that can be identified with The Belle Époque that everybody knows.

Kalifa's research is thorough, and his book has ample notes and a useful bibliography.

THE BELLE ÉPOQUE : A CULTURAL HISTORY, PARIS AND BEYOND
By Dominique Kalifa (translated by Susan Emanuel)
Columbia University Press. 252 pages. £25. ISBN 978-0-231-20219-

HUMANKIND : RUSKIN SPEAR, CLASS, CULTURE AND ART IN 20TH CENTURY BRITAIN

Have you seen a Ruskin Spear painting recently? At one time they seemed to be everywhere, if not in galleries then reproduced in the pages of popular newspapers such as the the *Daily Mail,* the *Daily Express,* and the *London Evening Standard*. The "posh" papers tended to ignore him, or at best grudgingly acknowledge his skill with topics of cheerful vulgarity. Tanya Harrod quotes the then well-known critic Eric Newton saying, in 1946: "Great art cannot survive the full process of democratisation. It is essentially aristocratic. It requires to be removed from the world of half-pints and dart-boards". It's uncertain whether or not this was a barb directed particularly at Ruskin Spear, but it could well have been. He wasn't a limited artist, in terms of his subject-matter, but he did paint many pictures with pub settings.

Spear was born in 1911 in Hammersmith. His father was a coach painter, his mother a housewife. He had four sisters, all of them older than him, and it's suggested that they made a fuss of Spear to the extent that he was spoiled and often expected women to provide support of one kind or another during his lifetime. He was afflicted with polio when he was a child and it left him with a "gammy" leg which caused him to have to walk with the support of a stick. But his childhood also saw him learning to play the piano. This was to stand him in good stead in later life when he could always earn money performing with jazz groups and local dance-bands.

In 1926 Spear won a scholarship to Hammersmith School of Art. The teaching there was "rigorous", and long hours involved "drawing from casts and learning anatomy and perspective". He became friendly with Carel Weight, a fellow-student. Spear's skills were quickly noted, and he was allowed to enrol in the life drawing class when he was sixteen. He was only part-time at Hammersmith between 1929 and 1931, and earned money to get by with "Freelance commercial work including lettering, wall decoration, window-display, cut-outs, etc", not to mention playing the piano in pubs and other places. In 1931 he won a scholarship to the Royal College of Art (RCA). There's a painting of his father, dating from 1932, which points to his proficiency, and what can be seen as the influence of Walter Sickert.

The Principal of the Royal College of Art was William Rothenstein who, Spear later recalled, was "about the best influence a young painter could have had at that time". It was also while he was at RCA that he met Mary Hill, who he was to marry in 1935. It's worth quoting, at this stage, Harrod's comments on Spear's attitudes and ambitions : "His approach was entirely remote from the interwar move to abstraction among older artists…..This lack of interest in abstraction went hand-over-hand with Spear's desire to show at the Royal Academy Summer Exhibition, achieving this in 1932 while still a student". Spear believed that the Royal Academy was a "meritocratic institution" and the Summer Exhibitions provided an opportunity for anyone with talent to have their work accepted and appreciated by a wide public and not just an elite of critics and wealthy buyers.

Spear never became an overtly political artist but joined the Artists International Association (AIA) which, in the 1930s, was a left-wing organisation. A couple of Spear's works were included in *AIA : The Story of the Artists International Association, 1933-1953* produced for the touring exhibition of the same name which I recall seeing in Bradford in 1983. One of them, 'We Can Take It', dates from 1942, and its picture of a group of young children standing beneath the slogan chalked on a wall points to Spear's ambivalence about the war. He was a pacifist and supported the Peace Pledge Union which was formed in the 1930s. His commitment was still evident in 1963, when CND activity was often in the news, and his paintings, 'The Peace Ship' and 'Ban the Bomb', are evidence of it. They are not first-rate paintings, but serve their purpose as propaganda. Spear was known to the authorities for his views, and MI5 maintained a file on him.

He was not a communist, but in 1957 he went to Moscow with Paul Hogarth and Derrick Greaves for the exhibition, *Looking at People*. which, Hogarth later said, seemed to be an example of "how realist art could be accessible while possessing a sound aesthetic base". The trip was monitored by MI5, Hogarth having been, until 1957, an active member of the Communist Party, and in Spain with the International Brigades. Harrod is of the opinion that Spear's canvases were not always appreciated: "In Soviet terms Spear's imagery might have appeared grotesque – the unattractive couple in 'Success Story' and the colourful distortions of 'The Candidate' were remote from realism as defined in Soviet Russia". It could have been that Football Pools winners, celebrities, and competition prizes of cars, were too much of a British obsession to mean a great deal to Russian viewers of the paintings in 1957. Life was still restricted in many ways in the Soviet Union.

In Britain Spear's satire was often aimed at non-figurative artists. He mocked Henry Moore's large sculptures, and did a painting of the American artist Barnett Newman standing in front of one of his colour field paintings (the kind with a "zip" down one side to break up the monotony of an otherwise single-colour canvas). He even lampooned William Walton's Symphony No 1 by showing a group listening to it on a radio with their hands over their ears. To Spear it was "pretentious or incomprehensible art".

Spear taught at the Royal College of Art between 1948 and 1975, and opinions about his teaching methods and attitudes towards students seem to have varied, if the interviews that Harrod had with several people are anything to go by. He appears to have approved of those like David Hockney, Peter Blake, and John Bratby, who were firmly committed to figurative painting, but was less generous with anyone who showed an interest in abstraction and other approaches to creating works of art.

Roger Coleman described Spear as "a bully. Conceited, frightful. He seemed to want to make you feel as small as possible". And Bruce Lacey said that "Ruskin Spear would love to reduce a female student to tears". But Sandra Blow, who had been taught by Spear at St Martin's, thought him "very encouraging to me and because of Ruskin, I had enough confidence to go on with it". Harrod points out that Blow was then "painting in a fashion Spear would have favoured, laying in a dark ground with lighter and darker tones on top". It's not known what he would have thought of her later work when she moved into abstraction.

Despite his teaching commitments Spear continued to produce his own paintings on a regular basis. I think they may have been variable in quality and interest, and that was particularly true of the portraits. Some were done for Spear's own satisfaction, others were commissioned. And a few caused controversy because of the way in which they portrayed the persons concerned. His 1957 painting of Winston Churchill was one such example. It's certainly identifiable as Churchill, but "the dark triangular gash of a mouth" which drew attention did not please everyone, including Churchill himself. Churchill's contemporaries were not impressed. Clement Attlee thought the painting "a disgusting caricature", and Jo Grimond described it as "appalling".

Other portraits, like those of Professor David Chadwick, The Right Reverend Henry Albert Wilson, and Mary Cavendish, Duchess of Devonshire are professionally realised, but do not offer much more to a viewer unacquainted with the subjects. One would hardly pause to look at them if they were hung in a college corridor or similar location. On the other hand the striking portrayal of the actor Harry Locke, in costume for the role of Sir Justice Sqeezum in *Lock Up Your Daughters,* can't help but attract attention. But it's perhaps unfair to compare it to the more-formal portraits referred to earlier. And it's perhaps right to draw a distinction when looking at the portraits of people Spear came across in the pubs and on the streets of Hammersmith. A certain amount of exaggeration, even caricature. can creep into those, though it's not done with malicious intent.

Spear could see that, even if the people weren't famous or powerful, they had character and were individuals.

It's worth noting that Spear, like Sickert had done in the Thirties, sometimes used photographs as a basis for his portraits. This was especially true when he was dealing with public figures. The 1959 "Catching the Night Train" used a photograph of Princess Margaret, fashionably dressed and leading several dogs, about to board the train for Balmoral, and was "deemed offensive when hung at the Royal Academy in 1960". Harrod doesn't see it in that light and describes it as "probably the best post-war painting of any member of the Royal Family, Lucian Freud's small 2001 head of HM the Queen notwithstanding", and "it gives us the vulnerability, intermittent charm and volatility of Princess Margaret in her late twenties".

It's the variousness of Spear's work that appeals, in the sense that he easily switched from portraits, both serious and satirical, to pub and street scenes, and to landscapes, though not of a rural type. The seaside crept in a few times, often showing it as a playground for people from London. "Waves on a Beach" from 1965 is typical as children retreat from the water chasing them towards their mother. Its tonal quality is reminiscent of Sickert. From the same year, "Brighton Beach, East Sussex, depicts "isolated holiday-makers stranded on hot pebbles". Harrod remarks that Spear "was one of the few twentieth century British artists to document an era in which a holiday was part idyll, part ordeal".

Having a liking for industrial landscapes I looked at "Margam Works, Port Talbot (1956), with pleasure. And, of course, it has Spear way from his usual Hammersmith haunts. These are represented in the delightful "Summer Street Scene" (1950), with its close relationship to the work of the Camden Town painters, and "Ravenscourt Park Station" (1950) which seems simple in its composition, but cleverly balances the different aspects of the scene – a wall, a bridge, the street, and a single figure in the foreground. Referring back to the artists of the Camden Town School I couldn't help thinking of them again when I viewed "The Tea Shop", a 1946/47 canvas which has all the characteristics of Spear's forerunners.

There are some other paintings which caught my eye. "Snow Scene" (1946), and especially the lovely "The Riverside" (1946) show Spear In a sensitive and delicate mood, and away from the bright lights and the noise of pubs and dance-halls. This is not to condemn his pictures of those places. His "The Swing Band" (date unknown) took me back to the days of the 1950s when, as a young jazz and big-band enthusiast, I eagerly awaited the visits by touring bands to the local dance-halls.

There are a couple of self-portraits which indicate a decline in Spear's general health and, possibly, his mental state. In 1972 he looks robust and confident, and the painting has a good pictorial appeal. By 1982 he's "a much sadder, more doubtful man" and the overall composition is less interesting. Spear had always liked to drink, and Harrod notes that by the late-1980s he had started "drinking around mid-morning" and would get through "well over a bottle of whisky a day". Was he conscious of the fact that in the 1980s younger artists were attracting attention? There was an exhibition called *The Forgotten Fifties* that I saw in Sheffield in 1984, and Spear was included in it. But he remained active and his 1989 picture, "After the Hanging", featured some of his Royal Academy companions enjoying their meal with plenty of wine in evidence on the table. He died in 1990.

Tanya Harrod has produced a well-researched and beautifully-illustrated book about Ruskin Spear the artist, but isn't afraid to look at his sometimes negative aspects as a person. His wife, Mary, often had a lot to put up with, and seems to have tolerated his peccadillos with a great deal of patience and understanding. Is it too much to hope that the appearance of *Humankind* will spur some critics and art historians into a re-appraisal of his work, and a curator or two into mounting exhibitions? I have a feeling they would prove to be a popular draw. There's an old song from 1937 (though it only achieved some popularity around 1949 when the Andrews Sisters recorded it) that Spear the pianist might have known – "I Can Dream, Can't I ?".

HUMANKIND : RUSKIN SPEAR, CLASS, CULTURE AND ART IN 20TH CENTURY BRITAIN
By Tanya Harrod
Thames & Hudson. 277 pages. £35. ISBN 978-0-500-97119-2

THE SIEGE THAT CHANGED THE WORLD
PARIS 1870-1871

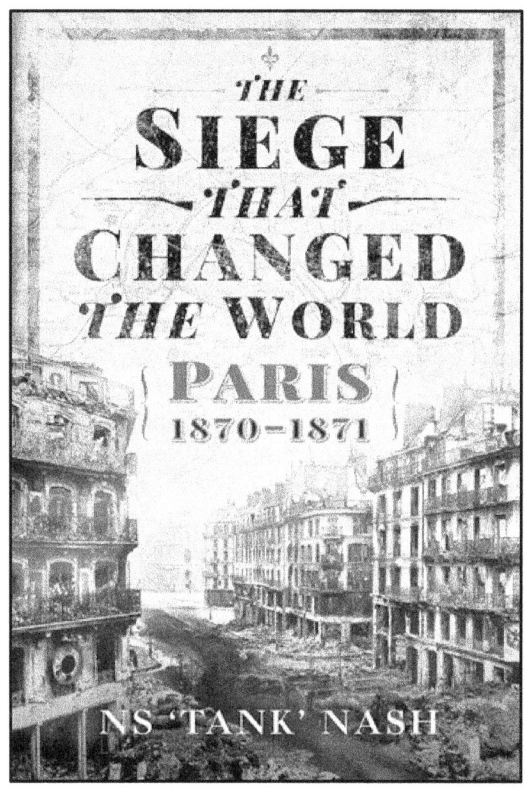

For many people the Siege of Paris may simply be a story of people hunting down cats and rats for food, and dining, if they were lucky and could afford it, on meat from the elephants and other animals in the Zoo. It is, of course, a much more complicated issue than that, and the Siege was just one aspect of a longer and bloodier encounter that involved Frenchmen fighting Germans and, ultimately, Frenchmen fighting each other.

It all started in July, 1870, when Louis Napoleon, Emperor of France, decided to declare war on Prussia, then the most powerful of the German states and, under Bismarck's guidance, working to bring together all the various principalities into one to form what became known as Germany. The reasons for France's truculence might be best summed up by saying they included French alarm at the rise of a unified German nation, French fears about the possible ascendancy to the throne of Spain by a Prussian prince, and a degree of arrogance on the part of the French. They assumed that, as the major European country, they had the political authority and military might that would assure them of a quick and decisive victory. The defeat of the Austrians in 1866 ought to have alerted France to the fact that it might not be all that easy to take on the Prussians and their allies. But it doesn't appear to have done so.

Once the war started it became apparent that there were severe shortcomings in the French military forces. Commitments in Algeria and elsewhere meant that the number of experienced troops that could be put into the field was restricted. There were large numbers of reservists and the Garde Nationale (GN), but their training was not of the highest quality and they were not equipped for extended periods of active service. By contrast the Prussians could muster a large army of regulars and well-trained reservists. It was also a fact that the Prussians were better prepared in terms of the support services they could provide to the front-line soldiers. Reading N.S. Nash's accounts of the often-chaotic French systems for supplying ammunition, clothing, food, and medical aid, it seems obvious that little serious attention had been paid to such matters. For example, no-one appears to have taken note of what had happened during the Crimean War when soldiers were wounded or fell ill due to disease and unsanitary conditions.

There were other factors, such as the calibre of the officer corps in the two armies. Nash says, "France's generals were all second-rate; they had established their reputations in colonial conflicts, such as those in Algeria. These generals had not confronted a modern European army since the Crimean War (1853-56) and the brief and unpopular foray against Italy in 1859". On the other hand, the "education, training and commitment of soldiers in the Prussian Army was, in all respects, superior to that of the French". And in Moltke it had a "military thinker who deduced that the key to military success was efficient planning, administrative excellence and total discipline". His creation of a "General Staff" led the way in the idea of "a body of professional officers with disparate skills and experience who, when trained, would provide cohesive, timely and accurate advice to their commander". The French military attaché in Berlin reported these developments, but his superiors didn't bother to take note of them.

Once the fighting started in earnest there were minor French successes, but the final outcome was never in doubt. Metz was besieged and, when the French Army was defeated at Sedan and the Emperor captured, it was only a matter of time before the Prussians reached Paris. Nash notes that in the French army "Bad behaviour was rampant. One officer commented, 'Our troops need severe discipline, far too many are *pillards* (looters) or *trainards* (stragglers), they sneak out of camp and have begun to defy their NCOs, complaining that they lack orders, food, wine or ammunition'.

The effect of the Prussian successes on the population of Paris was devastating. Opposition to Louis Napoleon that had always been there, but suppressed, came to the fore. A Republic was declared and figures on the extreme Left of the political spectrum began to assert themselves. The GN, in particular, was a source of disaffection. There were hopes that the Prussian siege would be short-lived. Not all of France had collapsed and there were substantial numbers of troops theoretically available to be in a position to move towards Paris, break the siege, and link up with the army there.

However, within the city the forces available to Major-General Trochu "were a mixture ranging from the professionally competent to the untrained, ill-disciplined, and criminal". Trochu, incidentally, had in 1867 written a book which took a highly-critical look at the French Army and in which he referred to, among other things, "chronic ill-discipline, unrestricted drinking and abysmal training standards". It wasn't popular with the establishment, military and civilian, and, as a kind of punishment, brought about his "removal from the War Office and further employment on half pay".

A curious situation had developed in that the authorities in Paris had made overtures towards peace negotiations with the Prussians, but not everyone in France generally felt that they were entitled to speak on their behalf. As noted earlier, there were sufficient troops available in the country to face up to the enemy and perhaps even defeat them. In the city, meanwhile, food and fuel became scarce, with the poor feeling the effects most of all. The rich, and others with access to restaurants where meals could still be obtained at a price, managed to eat reasonably well, even if they might have been surprised at what they were eating,

There were attempts to conduct sorties against the Prussians, but they tended to collapse because of bad organisation and an overall lack of equipment. In November 1870 a major French attack on the besiegers failed partly because the plans were known to the Prussians. They had been circulating in the city for days before the sortie. In addition, despite the weather being bad, the troops were ordered not to take their blankets with them: "The decision not to take blankets was seen for its absurdity as freezing French soldiers huddled together in the darkness dreading the morn". When it came it brought chaos as the French struggled to retreat into Paris. A British journalist, Tommy Bowles, observed what happened: "Every moment the mob increased, and with every moment the panic became greater and the struggle to get through fiercer. They fought with each other.... Trampled even on their wounded comrades....It was not an army that was retreating. It was not even a respectable mob".

As conditions in Paris continued to deteriorate, it became clear that, despite occasional small victories, the French armies in the country generally would not be capable of beating the Prussians. Some sort of armistice would have to be agreed. A defeat at Le Mans in January, 1871, perhaps summed up the parlous state of the French Army: "The French losses were huge: 6200 killed and wounded, 18,000 captured, but, critically, 20,000 deserted". And when, a few days later, there was another disastrous sortie from Paris, conducted, Nash says, by the Army "with its extraordinary capacity for calamity and fiasco", an armistice became inevitable. When negotiations started it was obvious that the Prussians were not inclined to be generous in the terms they demanded. They wanted the territory of Alsace and a large part of Lorraine to be ceded to Germany, reparations of 200 million francs, and some other conditions relating to disarming the GN and similar military matters. And they insisted on parading in triumph through Paris.

The signing of the Armistice, and the terms it stipulated, brought matters to a head in Paris. It had been agreed that the GN would be allowed to keep its arms, and they were, on the face of it, a potent force for opposing the new French government that came into being following national elections in February. That government, headed by Adolph Thiers, had moved to Versailles and was busy forming a strong military force, not to oppose the Prussians but to deal with the revolutionary elements in Paris who had seized the reins of power and declared the Commune. The siege of Paris would continue with the French Army ringing the city, while the Prussians stood to one side and provided some assistance by blocking possible supply and escape routes into and out of the Paris.

The story of the short-lived Paris Commune has been told in detail in other books, and Nash doesn't attempt to do more than provide a limited outline of events. But he does get across the mixture of high ideals and low behaviour that characterised the two months when the Commune existed. It has been romanticised in some ways, especially by those with Left-wing sympathies, but anyone looking at the facts dispassionately must surely accept that the whole venture was doomed to failure from its inception. A national government could not, as Thiers made clear, allow any part of the country, and particularly its capital, to effectively secede. It had to assert its authority. And that would necessarily be by the use of military force.

The leaders of the Commune may have felt confident that the GN could form a strong-enough force to oppose the Versailles troops, but if they did they were deluding themselves. The GN were badly-trained, poorly led, and not inclined to function in a disciplined manner. When the Army moved into Paris in May, 1871, they did so through unguarded gates. I'm necessarily summarising but though there were courageous actions by some of the defenders, and die-hard elements fought to the end, many members of the GN disposed of their guns and uniforms and disappeared in an attempt to escape the retribution that the Army brought. Prisoners were usually shot. Nash is not in favour of the brutal way the Commune was suppressed, though he does question the figures that have often been quoted in relation to the number of Communards (and sometimes their families), killed. He thinks that 25,000 or thereabouts is far too high, and refers to research by Professor Robert Tombs which suggested that "the death toll was 5,700 to 7,400".

Did the Siege of Paris change the world? The Franco-Prussian War certainly shifted the balance of power in Europe. France lost its role as the dominant country and the new Germany which came into existence at the time took on a wider significance. There were certainly people in Britain who viewed the rise of Germany as a major European country with some alarm.

In military terms the war highlighted a number of important aspects. Nash says that it was the first European "Railway War" and demonstrated that "logistic superiority, in purely material terms, is irrelevant unless there are the means of transport and distribution". The Germans used their railway network to greater effect. He refers to Rommel who commented: "An adequate supply system ......the essential condition for any army to be able to stand successfully the strains of battle. Before the fighting proper, the battle is fought and decided by the Quartermaster". As Nash notes, many of those in command of the French Army did not seem to acknowledge "the tedious but vital business of supply". There were, too, lessons to be learned about the decline in the usefulness and importance of cavalry, the need to avoid massed infantry attacks as machine-guns were developed (sadly, this lesson hadn't sunk in by 1914), and the effective use of artillery.

The Siege That Changed the World is a brisk account of events leading up to the Siege, the Siege itself, and what happened when the Commune flourished for a brief spell. There are plenty of notes, appropriate illustrations, and a useful bibliography.

THE SIEGE THAT CHANGED THE WORLD : PARIS 1870-1871

By N.S. 'Tank' Nash

Pen & Sword Books. 294 pages. £25. ISBN 978-1-52679-029-3

THE NATIONAL GALLERY MASTERPIECE TOUR : DEGAS'S *HÉLÈNE ROUART IN HER FATHER'S STUDY*

Gallery Oldham 18th September, 2021 to 8th January, 2022

Masterpiece – "A piece of work worthy of a master. One's greatest achievement". Looking at the Degas painting that is the centrepiece of this small but fascinating exhibition, I found myself wondering if the word "masterpiece" really applies in its case? The painting is interesting in some respects, but it doesn't strike me as showing Degas at his best. And the interest lies more in what the painting contains (i.e. its subject-matter) than in any purely painterly qualities. They, to my mind, have an unfinished aspect I found disconcerting.

Hélène Rouart was the daughter of Henri Rouart, an industrialist, art collector, and Impressionist artist who was a friend of Edgar Degas. The location of the painting is significant in that it places Hélène behind Henri's empty chair, denoting that, although he's not physically there, he's still present in spirit. This view is enforced by the documents on his desk, some Egyptian artefacts in the background, and, to one side of Hélène, paintings by Corot and Millet. Henri's treasured possessions are a key factor in the painting, and perhaps she can be seen as one of them.

I can understand why the painting has caught the attention of art historians and biographers. It relates to a minor figure in the Impressionist movement who was closely involved with Degas. What's seen on the canvas provides a basis for documentation and speculation, both factors being relevant to historians and biographers.

We know who the woman is in the Degas painting. But what of other portraits of women? The famous might easily be identified but there are numerous paintings where the women are anonymous. They may have been professional or part-time models, and few records survive of who they were. Gallery Oldham has selected a number of portraits from its permanent collection and used them to accompany the Degas on display. And the staff there have, to their credit, attempted to track down some details about the women in the paintings.

Knowing the names doesn't necessarily guarantee that the paintings will be accomplished or of real lasting value. Luckily, some have both qualities in evidence. Harold Harvey's *My Kitchen* is attractive, and one of the women in it is probably his wife, the artist Gertrude Boddimar. By contrast, Patti Mayor's bleak but striking *Mill Girl with a Shawl* doesn't offer any clues to the identity of the model. She probably was one of those "who toil without a name/and pass into the night".

Joseph Southall's colourful *Along the Shore* catches the eye, and Thomas Mostyn's romanticised but appealing *A Fisherman's Daughter* possibly had a student from a local Devon college for a model. I've just taken a sample from the works in the gallery, and most are from early last century, but there are some contemporary paintings on display and, among them, Peter Davis's *Stay Safe, Mum* stands out. Painted in 2020, amid concerns about Covid, it's impressive in the way it catches the character of the person concerned. I certainly preferred looking at it than at the nineteenth century painting, *Circe Offering the Cup to Ulysses*, by J.W. Waterhouse. A different idea of how women were perceived by some male artists – as temptresses and "idols of perversity", as one writer put it – is well in evidence there.

I enjoyed this exhibition as a whole and not just because it is built around a famous name. The Degas painting is worth seeing, but there are other good things nearby.

THE POET AND THE PUBLISHER: THE CASE OF ALEXANDER POPE, ESQ., OF TWICKENHAM VERSUS EDMUND CURLL, BOOKSELLER IN GRUB STREET

London in the early years of the eighteenth century. The Glorious Revolution of 1688 had seen William of Orange bring a Dutch army to England to overthrow the Catholic–inclined James the Second. James's daughter, Anne, was now Queen and Protestantism was the established religion. Catholics were looked on with suspicion and deprived of certain civil rights that everyone else took for granted. There were still fears that the exiled James Stuart (son of James the Second), the "Old Pretender" as he was called, could lead a French-backed uprising which would challenge the new government.

It was a turbulent time and conspiracy theories abounded. And it wasn't only in the political world that rivalries existed. Poets and publishers readily fell out and clashed with each other in ways that make contemporary literary spats look like mere bad-tempered exchanges at a tea-party. The arguments were often as much about personalities as they were about politics or poetry, though a combination of all three could make the fire blaze more brightly.

One of the more-famous feuds was that between Alexander Pope and Edmund Curll. It's most likely remembered now for Pope's part in it. He was, even at the time when he was locked in combat with Curll, widely-known and respected for his poetry and his translations of Homer's *Iliad* and the *Odyssey*. Edmund Curll, on the other hand, probably owes his fame, if that's the right word, to the fact of the long-running war with Pope. Curll was never one to give up easily.

A bookseller, publisher, and occasional versifier, he might otherwise have been just one of the many "dunces" satirised in Pope's epic *The Dunciad*, which mocked a whole gallery of hack writers, booksellers, printers, publishers, and others. They were all seen as having a place in Grub Street, even if they weren't necessarily based there. It was an actual street, but the name had become synonymous with the activities of all the struggling and often starving authors who, usually for a price, would produce a poem or a pamphlet to order. It might champion a cause, or lampoon a rival of whoever had paid for it. And be hawked around the town in bookshops or on the streets.

Why did the disputes between Pope and Curll develop? It may be necessary to consider both the copyright laws, or lack of their firm application, and the character of Edmund Curll. Pat Rogers says that he had a reputation as "a rascally publisher who had spent his career dodging prosecutions for various scandalous breaches of the law". There is no doubt about the fact that Curll blithely ignored copyright when it suited him, and cheerfully published poems and other works without seeking permission from the authors.

Pope wasn't the only one who suffered at his hands (Jonathan Swift, Matthew Prior, and John Gay, composer of *The Beggar's Opera,* were also victims), and Curll wasn't the only publisher practising deception of one sort or another. In the case of Pope and Curll it is necessary to add that there was something of a political aspect to it. Pope was a Catholic and suspected of having sympathies for the Jacobite cause. Curll was a supporter of the Hanoverian monarchy

(George the First had come to the throne when Queen Anne died), and wasn't averse to smearing Pope with references to his religious affiliations and alleged political leanings. The very name Pope led to hints of Popish plots and the like.

I'm not being precise when I place the start of the friction in 1714. These matters rarely have a simple explanation. However, Pope was increasingly annoyed by various attacks on him in publications that Curll was involved with. A work by Charles Gildon, *A New Rehearsal,* contained a scene where "an easily identifiable young poet" suggests that a lack of knowledge of Greek was not a hindrance to translating Homer, an obvious comment on Pope's alleged shortcomings in that line. On the face of it someone called John Roberts was the publisher, but Pope "undoubtedly believed Curll was the responsible party". And Gildon was one of "a small army of professional authors…….who slaved away for Curll". There appears to have been any number of hack writers who, for one reason or another, were more than happy to snipe at Pope. Leaving politics and money aside, was it just envy of an established poet who made money from his writing? Or a way of attracting attention by attacking someone famous?

In 1715 there was an attempt by the "Old Pretender" to invade England and re-establish the Stuart monarchy. The rebels reached Preston, but were then defeated and dispersed. It gave Curll an opportunity to attack people like Lord Lansdowne and Sir William Windham, Jacobite activists and friends of Pope. His Achilles Heel was that he "could not deny that he was a Catholic, or that many of his closest friends were loyal adherents of the faith and maintained contact with their co-religionists in hated France".

A year or so later Curll published what were known as the *Court Poems* and attributed them to Pope. They had, in fact, been written by Lady Wortley Montagu, then a friend of the poet. It was bad enough that Curll would happily publish Pope's work without his permission, but to claim that he was the author of poems he had no hand in was a step too far. As Rogers puts it: "From now open hostilities were declared". Pope's revenge took the form of an emetic slipped into Curll's glass of sack when they encountered each other in a London tavern. He then followed up by publishing a pamphlet which "turned the methods of Grub Street back against their usual perpetrators".

In it Pope took great delight in describing the colour of Curll's vomit, and a "plentiful foetid Stool" which drove everyone else out of the room when he arrived home. All this while Curll, convinced he was dying, made his Will in which he confessed to his past sins in relation to publishing unlawful and sometimes obscene material. It was known that Curll traded in pornography. Like others of his kind when challenged by the authorities he would claim that publishing such works had a socially-useful application by enlightening people to the dangers of deviant sexual practices. Pope's pamphlet quickly circulated among the London poets and journalists and the ridicule he experienced no doubt prompted Curll to continue even more energetically with his campaign against the poet.

It would be impossible for me to outline all the carryings-on over the years as Curll continued to make money by somehow obtaining material by Pope and making it available to the public. He caused him particular distress when he published "*A Roman Catholick Version* of the First Psalm; for the Use of a Young Lady", a poem by Pope that, Rogers asserts, Curll somehow stole. He describes it as "a skilful but blasphemous parody of scripture...... Pope supplies a close line-by-line burlesque, sometimes citing phrases from the original to turn them to obscene purposes". It was clearly not an item that Pope wanted to see in print, especially at a time when anti-Catholic feeling was running high. Rogers says that it being widely circulated "was to cause him lifelong distress". But for Curll it was one of his "greatest hits", and he reprinted it several times.

A key work by Pope in relation to his standing in the London literary world was *The Dunciad* (1728) which, Rogers states, "was more than a work of literature". It was meant to shock, and its impact was felt for "more than a generation". There are books that can be usefully read in connection with it. Rogers' own *Grub Street: Studies in a Subculture* (Methuen, London, 1972) is one that immediately comes to mind, and *Grub Street Stripped Bare: The scandalous lives and pornographic works by the original Grub St. writers* by Philip Pinkus (Constable, London, 1968) is given a favourable mention by Rogers in his bibliography.

Curll had a place in *The Dunciad* alongside numerous other "dunces" (of which there was a "confederacy") and he, like many of them, responded to Pope by publishing pamphlets and assorted items challenging what he had said. Rogers provides a provocative account of the skirmishes that erupted when *The Dunciad* first appeared and continued as later editions were revised and expanded. There is a kind of irony involved when one considers that, had it not been for *The Dunciad*, most of the people mentioned in it would have been completely forgotten, or at least known only to scholars pursuing research into the "subculture" of Grub Street. Would John Dunton and Ned Ward be remembered otherwise?

Curll's continuing clashes with Pope no doubt assured him of a place in literary history. But he may also have left a mark because of his problems with the authorities. Pope in a tongue-in-cheek- footnote in *The Dunciad* says that Curll was not only famous among the writers he exploited, but was also "taken notice of by the *State,* the *Church*, and the *Law*, and received particular marks of distinction from each".

There were several examples of Curll publishing books and pamphlets that led to investigation and prosecution. He was sentenced to "a stint of one hour in the pillory at Charing Cross", when he was convicted of bringing out John Ker's *Memoirs*. Ker was a one-time Government spy, and it was thought that what he had to say might reflect badly on some powerful people. At the same time Curll was also convicted of handling obscene publications. Unlike unlucky people who were pelted with garbage, and sometimes badly injured while pilloried, Curll seems to have been treated almost as a hero, and when released was carried away to a public house by an enthusiastic crowd.

In another case Curll fell foul of the authorities when he brought out a pamphlet by Robert Loggin, a young man who worked for the Customs service. He alleged there was fraudulent activity in its operations. When hauled before the commissioners who represented this branch of government revenue, Curll came up with a "grovelling" apology. But, as Rogers remarks of a different occasion when he was in trouble, "No one surpassed Curll in appearing to grovel while advancing his own interests. Uriah Heep could have learned from him".

The war between Pope and Curll perhaps reached its peak when the bookseller contrived to distribute *Mr Pope's Literary Correspondence*, a selection of letters to a variety of the poet's friends and acquaintants. It's intriguing to read Rogers' detailed account of how the letters came into Curll's possession, and to take note of the suggestion that Pope himself may have had a hand in facilitating their delivery to the bookseller. His aim was for Curll to be caught handling possibly purloined material and breaking copyright law by publishing it without permission.

Rogers says that "The Chancery case of Pope v. Curll was heard in the summer of 1741", and he stresses its importance in relation to establishing rules about "copyright in personal letters". The court found in Pope's favour, and Curll was ordered to stop advertising the book for sale. But no order was made "for the physical destruction of the book". Whether "he ceased to sell it is quite another matter". There were no major clashes between Pope and Curll following the court case and Pope died in 1744, and so just missed the failed 1745 attempt by the "Young Pretender" to regain the throne for the Stuarts and Catholicism. Curll died in 1747.

The Poet and the Publisher is a splendidly detailed work of scholarship that is highly entertaining to read. It isn't necessary to be an expert in eighteenth century literature or politics to follow its well-written story of personal rivalries, skulduggery and shady dealings. Pat Rogers uses contemporary documents, some of them previously unpublished, to great effect. And he demonstrates how a level of personal abuse was often a part of literary arguments. Poor Pope was singled out due to his physical appearance, a result of childhood illnesses. History has tended to treat him kindly, because of his skills as a poet, though it has been suggested that, as a person, he was capable of "double-dealing". And some have seen Curll as a "lovable rogue", despite the damage he probably did in terms of denying writers their rightful earnings and attempting to destroy their reputations. Whatever their true characters the narrative of the feuding, with its background of political intrigue and corruption, princes and pretenders, coffee house cliques, and rogues, rascals, and hacks, is never less than fascinating.

THE POET AND THE PUBLISHER: THE CASE OF ALEXANDER POPE, ESQ., OF TWICKENHAM VERSUS EDMUND CURLL, BOOKSELLER IN GRUB STREET

By Pat Rogers

Reaktion Books. 470 pages. £25. ISBN 978-1-78914-416-1

UNKNOWN NO MORE: RECOVERING SANORA BABB

At some point in the early-1960s I was in Collett's Bookshop on Charing Cross Road and bought an anthology called *The American Century: 34 Short Stories by 34 American Authors*. It was edited by Maxim Lieber and published by Seven Seas Books in 1960 from what was then East Berlin. Its left-wing leanings were plain to see. Lieber had been a literary agent in New York, but when the Alger Hiss/Whittaker Chambers confrontations hit the headlines in the late-1940s he was accused of being a Soviet spy and fled to Poland. And many of the writers in the anthology were identifiable as having left-wing inclinations. A few – Albert Maltz, Alvah Bessie, Philip Stevenson – had been caught up in the anti-communist purges in Hollywood, and others – Jack Conroy, Nelson Algren, Ben Field – had written radical novels.

A name that stood out was that of Sanora Babb. I knew little about her beyond the notes in the anthology, and those in *Cross Section 1945* (L.B. Fischer, New York, 1945) that I'd come across in a second-hand bookshop and which had a story by Babb. Again, the liberal/left-wing leanings of the editor, Edwin Seaver and many of the contributors were in evidence. All this was long before the Internet and I didn't follow up on finding out more about Babb, though I came across references to her in books by Alan Wald and others. There was a story in *Writers in Revolt : The Anvil Anthology 1933-1940* (Lawrence Hill, Westport,1973) reprinted from a 1934 issue of Jack Conroy's magazine, *The Anvil*. Curiously, she was omitted from what is otherwise an excellent collection, *Writing Red: An Anthology of American Women Writers 1930-1940,* edited by Charlotte Nekola and Paula Rabinowitz (Feminist Press, New York, 1987).

More recent years have seen a revival of Interest in Babb and reprints of most of her work. So, who was she? She was born in 1907 in Oklahoma and grew up there and in Colorado where the family moved to when she was seven. They lived with Babb's grandfather in a one-room dug-out. Her father, a failed farmer, was a professional gambler. Babb's early education seems to have been sporadic, though she did eventually leave school with qualifications, taught at a one-room schoolhouse, and obtained a job on a local newspaper. It's worth noting that "Babb's grandfather took the *Appeal to Reason*, a weekly socialist newspaper out of Kansas".

By 1929 she was living in Los Angeles, where she experienced "poverty and often homelessness" while writing poems and stories that were published in magazines and newspapers, especially those with a left-wing policy. The collection, *The Dark Earth and Selected Prose from the Great Depression* (Muse Ink Press, Old Greenwich, 2021) has material from the 1930s, with publications such as *The Anvil, New Masses, Outlander*, and *The Midland* credited. It's doubtful that she earned much from these magazines and she took various jobs, including one "writing copy for the Warner Brothers radio station KFWB".

She was also mixing with many young writers such as Tillie Olsen, Carlos Bulosan, William Saroyan, John Howard Lawson, and Ray Bradbury. Saroyan and Bradbury both became successful fiction writers, Lawson was a playwright, screenwriter and, as a leading communist in Hollywood, later one of the Hollywood Ten. Olson struggled to balance writing with family and political involvements. Bulosan was a Filipino-American who was encouraged to write by Babb and her sister, Dorothy. His *American Is in the Heart* (Penguin Books, New York, 2019) is a classic account of what it was like to be drawn to American ideals but come up against the violence and prejudice that immigrants experienced. The account of working in the fields and factories of Southern California parallels some of Babb's stories of the harsh practices that applied in such occupations. Attempts to form unions and strike for better pay and conditions could result in injuries and even deaths as local police, vigilante groups and hired thugs attacked strikers and their families.

Babb's "immersion in the milieu of diversely radical and untamed artists and writers who were pulled to the Communist-led John Reed Clubs in the early 1930s" quickened her commitment to communism as a possible solution to the social, economic, and political problems then evident in America and the world at large. In 1935 she attended the First American Writers Congress in New York, an event organised by the League of American Writers, a Communist "front" organisation. She would have heard speeches by, among others, Malcolm Cowley, Waldo Frank, James T. Farrell, John Dos Passos, Meridel Le Sueur and Kenneth Burke.

And there was Jack Conroy talking about "The Worker as Writer" and offering the opinion that "To me a strike bulletin or an impassioned leaflet are of more moment than three hundred prettily and faultlessly written pages about the private woes of a gigolo or the biological ferment of a society dame as useful to society as the buck brush that infests Missouri cow pastures and takes all the sustenance out of the soil". A fictional account of the Conference can be found in Farrell's novel, *Yet Other Waters* (Vanguard Press, New York, 1952), where Conroy is satirised as a somewhat blustering and not very intelligent novelist and activist.

A trip to Russia in 1936 persuaded Babb to take a positive view of communist achievements. She claimed that no restrictions were placed on her movements and she was allowed to talk freely to the people she met. In "Dr Fera of Moscow", a piece published in the left-wing magazine *The Clipper* in 1941, she wrote about the fact that "In Russia, women were competing equally with men in every field of work. I rode on a train completely run by women. I talked to a 22-year-old woman engineer who was directing a crew of a hundred men in the construction of a bridge. I visited the home of a collective-farm woman, who, freed of the drudgery of housework and baby-raising by co-operative effort and the amazing social care of children, had in middle-age become an expert in horticulture". She also wrote about Dr Fera, a peasant girl who, after many misadventures, was encouraged to train to become a doctor.

In 1938 she took the plunge and joined the American Communist Party. It was also the year that she volunteered to work in one of the California Migrant Camps set up to try to provide basic forms of sanitation and housing for at least some of the families who had fled from the great dust storms in the Midwest. Many of them had lost everything as the drought, winds, and storms destroyed their farms. Interestingly, the Camp she worked at was the one under the supervision of Tom Collins, and it was also visited by John Steinbeck when he was writing *The Grapes of Wrath,* his powerful story of the plight of the "Okies", the name given to the migrants. Babb herself wrote about them in her novel, *Whose Names Are Unknown*, which was initially intended for publication by a major New York house, but was dropped when Steinbeck's book appeared and became a popular success. The would-be publishers of Babb's book did not think there would be a viable market for another novel on the same subject.

Babb worked for T*he Clipper* and *The California Quarterly*, both radical magazines, continued to write, and helped run a restaurant with her husband, the noted Chinese-American Hollywood cameraman, James Wong Howe. When the anti-communist purges started in the film capital in the late-1940s and early-1950s, Babb immediately fell under suspicion. As a Communist Party member and contributor to left-wing publications, her name and activities would have been known to the FBI and HUAC. She moved to Mexico around 1950 in order to draw attention away from Howe. Quite a few Americans found it convenient to spend time in Mexico as HUAC widened its investigations and the mood in America turned to one of hostility towards anything that smacked of Un-Americanism. What that meant precisely could depend on circumstances, and it was used as a weapon against the unconventional not only in politics but also in the arts and even personal behaviour.

Like many people, Babb drifted away from the Communist Party in the early- 1950s. She had become disillusioned by the levels of conformity and control, and even earlier, in 1946, she had expressed support for Albert Maltz when he was condemned by Party hardliners for suggesting that writers should be free to choose their own topics and how to write about them. She continued to write and publish poems and short fiction in a variety of magazines. And there were extended works such as *An Owl on Every Post* (Muse Ink Press, 2012) and *The Lost Traveler* (Muse Ink Press, 2013). Her 1930s novel, *Whose Names are Unknown*, continued to be hidden away until renewed interest in her work caused it to be "discovered" and finally published by the University of Oklahoma Press in 2004.

It perhaps could be said of Babb's work as a whole that she essentially located most of it in the period prior to 1950. Her childhood in the Mid-West and her experiences in the 1930s seem to me to encompass many of her stories, memoirs, and longer works. *Whose Names are Unknown* is in two parts, the first of which deals with hard times in the Oklahoma Panhandle, and the second with the struggle to survive in California. The "Okies" (not all of them from Oklahoma) follow the fruit and other harvests, often residing temporarily in company shacks and forced to shop at company stores. When they try to organise and strike for better wages and conditions they're harassed by police and company guards, and evicted. There is a vivid description of a union activist being falsely accused of getting "fresh" with a local's wife and subjected to a beating by vigilantes.

The same sense of violent oppression is evident in "The Terror", an account of a secret night-time visit to striking miners in New Mexico which originally appeared in a 1935 issue of *International Literature,* published in Moscow. It has recently been included in *The Dark Earth and Selected Prose from the Great Depression*. This is an excellent selection of fiction and reportage from a range of magazines. A story, "A Good Straight Game", seems to have its basis in the activities of Babb's father as the male character, despite previous promises, succumbs to the lure of a game of cards. Another,

"The Old One", from *The Midland* in 1933, tells of the sudden death of an old man and how the neighbours come together for his funeral.

The non-fictional items include a piece about the way in which those working as "extras" in Hollywood struggle to survive in the face of low wages and fierce competition for the available work. But should anyone think that all of Babb's writing focused on social and political matters, they might have a look at the story, "Femme Fatale" which, to my mind, would not seem out of place in a collection of *New Yorker* short fiction from the Forties and Fifties. It was actually published in *Masses & Mainstream*, a communist journal, in 1954. They might also look at the stories in *Cry of the Tinamou* (Muse Ink Press, 2021), some of which appeared in widely circulated publications like *Seventeen* and *The Saturday Evening Post.*

Unknown No More is a collection of essays looking at different aspects of Babb's writing. I haven't wanted to single out individual pieces because they all seem to me of value in terms of drawing attention to an under-rated writer. I am tempted to refer to Christine Hill Smith's "The Radical Voice of Sandra Babb" because it reflects my own interest in what Babb did. But that would be unfair to the other contributors and to Babb who clearly wanted her writing to encompass more than the specific world of left-wing politics and proceedings. She seems to me a writer well worth reviving.

UNKNOWN NO MORE: RECOVERING SANORA BABB

Edited by Joanne Dearcopp and Christine Hill Smith

University of Oklahoma Press. 209 pages. £21.50. ISBN 978-0-8061-6936-1

HAROLD ROSENBERG : A CRITIC'S LIFE

The days of the New York Intellectuals seem very distant. It's perhaps difficult for younger people to understand why what Mary McCarthy said about Lillian Hellman attracted so much attention, or why magazines like *Partisan Review, Commentary,* and *Encounter* were essential reading. And the furore that erupted when it turned out that the CIA had been funding various publications. Not to mention the way in which that organisation backed the notion that a movement such as Abstract Expressionism represented Western ideas of freedom of thought and expression against the state-controlled artistic productions of Russia and the Eastern Bloc countries.

And why did Harold Rosenberg and Clement Greenberg fall out? It admittedly wasn't hard to do in the hot-house atmosphere of the New York intellectual world, where personalities competed and personal relationships often quickly soured. But the Rosenberg/Greenberg saga represented more than a simple matter of a clash of egos. Their different ideas about developments in art appeared to have significant relevance in post-1945 culture.

Harold Rosenberg was born in 1906. His father was a tailor who "loved to read and to write verse in Hebrew in his spare time". Little seems to be known about his mother. When he was young Rosenberg suffered a "debilitating bone infection that left his right leg permanently immobilised, and he needed a cane to walk for the rest of his life". He attended CCNY in 1923/24, and "graduated from Brooklyn Law School with a LL.B in 1927. He never practised law, and in fact had little interest in a career in that or any other commercial or business line.

In a way his "real" education began around 1928 when he met Harry Roskolenko on the steps of the New York Public Library. Roskolenko later recalled that the conversations he had with Rosenberg were "a crucial part of their intellectual development". And he added that the whole scene was lively and stimulating: "Everyone was there....from Kenneth Burke to Sidney Hook, philosophers, critics, grammarians, Marxists, Trotskyists, Stalinists, technocrats, vegetarians, free lovers – everybody with a talking and reading Mission". It's worth noting that Roskolenko himself was later identified with the Trotskyists in the United States. A poet, journalist, and novelist, his books are well worth searching for. The memoir of growing up in the Jewish ghetto on New York's Lower East Side, *When I was Last on Cherry Street,* is lively and informative.

Rosenberg's progression through the 1930s was fairly typical of a young, bohemian poet and intellectual at the time. He contributed to little magazines such as *Pagany, Poetry,* and *Blues,* the latter started by Parker Tyler and Charles Henri Ford. And he was involved in founding a short-lived publication, *The New Act: A Literary Review.* He was also reading Marx avidly, and had a loose association with the American Communist Party (he sometimes contributed to *New Masses*, the Party's cultural journal), though he was never a member and became known for his critical evaluations of Party policies and activities.

He had ambitions to be an artist, and was employed on murals for the Public Works of Art Project (PWAP) where he was assigned as an assistant to Willem de Kooning, and met Lee Krasner. He was eventually transferred to the Federal Writers Project (FWP) and worked on *American Stuff*, which essentially featured material from many of the writers (including Roskolenko, Weldon Kees, and Kenneth Rexroth) who had joined the Project, usually because it provided a small but steady wage at a time when many people were struggling to stay alive. Rosenberg continued to write for little magazines like *Partisan Review* and *New Masses* and to meet some of the people who became well-known in New York intellectual circles in the 1940s and 1950s – Lionel Abel, Philip Rahv, William Philips, and Meyer Schapiro.

Rosenberg's interests were changing and he drifted away from poetry and became more involved in writing about art. He joined the editorial board of *Art Front*, a magazine with a firmly left-wing approach to its subject. Among the topics Rosenberg tussled with was "How to reconcile political engagement with aesthetic commitment". It was something that often brought him into conflict with the communists associated with the magazine. But it was also during this period that his problems with Clement Greenberg seem to have seriously got under way. Both men had written erudite essays warning against the "menace of popular culture", and thought "that artists and writers had to form their own communities to retain their individuality and resist conformity". As the years developed, however, they differed about how to define and interpret developments in art. Rosenberg essentially thought that paintings had to be seen in their social as well as artistic context, whereas Greenberg might be said to have generally taken a more purely-aesthetic view of them.

They didn't necessarily differ in their awareness of how what came to be known as Abstract Expressionism developed, though Rosenberg's idea of the canvas as "an arena in which to act " (The canvas was "no longer a surface on which to paint a picture, but a surface on which to record an event") didn't appeal to Greenberg. He was more inclined to have a formalist approach to the way in which paint had been applied to a canvas. It's easy to see how he later promoted colour field artists and their work. Rosenberg's term for what was happening was "Action Painting" and he said, "The human being is nothing else but the situation in which he is acting".

Debra Brickett Balkan says of the artists: "As painting liberated itself from the figure, their Marxist politics became internalised as 'personal revolt'…..these artists became engaged in the enactment of what Rosenberg called 'private myths', or the revelation of their interior lives". The problem with a term such as "action painting" may have been that the word "action" is inevitably associated with movement, and as a consequence became linked to Jackson Pollock's highly-visual method of drip-painting. I doubt that many people had Action Painting in mind when they looked at canvases by Willem de Kooning, Robert Motherwell, and Franz Kline.

It might be useful to register that the critic Robert Coates had earlier described what painters like Pollock, Kline and de Kooning were doing as "Abstract Expressionism", and the artist Robert Motherwell preferred to refer to the "New York School" and thought that it represented "less an aesthetic style than a state of mind". I think it would now be generally acknowledged that Abstract Expressionism is the term mostly used in relation to what someone like Pollock produced, though Action Paining might well sum it up better.

Rosenberg's disability meant that he wasn't conscripted, but he did join the Office of War Information (OWI) and served on the War Advertising Council, which was, after 1945, "renamed the Advertising Council and became a national consortium of leading ad agencies, broadcasting outlets, and print media". His work in this line didn't go down well with many of his old comrades on the Left. Sidney Hook, for example, said that Rosenberg was involved in "celebrating the virtues of American business and at the same time was a 'closet revolutionist' or 'parlour social nihilist' attacking everyone else for selling out". And he added that Rosenberg was "a shameless political opportunist". I don't suppose these arguments mean much now, but they are interesting to read about in the context of the 1930s and 1940s. Hook's comments may have been brought about by Rosenberg's dismissal of those people who had gone into academia, as Hook had done. But in retrospect, it's relevant to look at Hook's later involvements with CIA organisations, and Rosenberg's own eventual entry into academic employment. Both can be said to have compromised in their different ways.

Whatever Rosenberg did to earn a living he didn't give up on his artistic interests. He mixed with artists, and in 1948 co-operated with Robert Motherwell on a one-shot little magazine called *possibilities*. Motherwell at the time was heavily involved with his large, influential book, *The Dada Painters and Poets*, and Rosenberg more or less took over the editorial role of the magazine. There was soon a disagreement between them. Rosenberg also managed to fall out with Mark Rothko. It was during this period that Lionel Abel, who met up again with Rosenberg in Paris, remarked, "It is the same old story, only older and less interesting. He can scarcely talk about any subject without blowing his horn, and all of his ideas sound like advertising slogans – for what?". The contempt that many intellectuals had, and probably still have, for those who work in advertising is well-known. But it would be interesting to look at some lists of poets and artists who have had stints, and sometimes careers, with advertising agencies. I can think of one friend, in particular, who produced excellent, well-received poetry while paying the bills by working in advertising.

Rosenberg was a regular presence at "The Club", the meeting place for the new painters in which they held discussions and invited critics, poets, and others to give talks. In Balken's words: "The Club was a remarkable gathering place, known for its erudite talks and as a place to assemble, gossip, and take part in shop talk......It was avowedly non-partisan, a place where politics was left at the door, and no single aesthetic credo dominated". Rosenberg said that it was alight with "exuberance".

It might be thought that Rosenberg's left-wing associations would have invited attention from the FBI and HUAC as anti-communist feeling built up in the late-1940s and early-1950s. It does seem that the FBI had a file on him, but he was never called to appear before HUAC. It may have been that his record of anti-Communist Party statements in the 1930s, and the fact of his being criticised by the Party for some of his activities, had been noted by the authorities. His work began to be published in *Commentary*, a right-wing Jewish publication, and he was hired to teach at the New School for Social Research. In 1959 his significant collection of essays, *The Tradition of the New,* was published. This isn't the place to go into an analysis or discussion about its contents, other than to say that, though art criticism might have taken pride-of-place, Rosenberg also engaged in surveys of "poetics, Marxism, and cultural politics".

A couple of years before the appearance of *The Tradition of the New* a short story by Leslie Fiedler entitled "Nude Croquet" had been published in *Esquire*. It was a sharp satirical look at some old 30s radicals ("they share a Marxist past, the only glue that remains of their sagging friendships") who come together for a party and proceed to fall out as personalities clash and they drag up old arguments and enmities. Balken says that Rosenberg "is represented by the character Howard Place, an abstract painter who is about to represent the United States at the Venice Biennale. Place is overly sure-footed about his professional success, yet envious of his friends with younger wives". There is an oblique reference here to Rosenberg's long-standing and long-suffering wife, May Natalie Tabak, who somehow tolerated his womanising and a string of affairs. As Balken puts it: "He thought his bohemianism freed him from monogamy. He would travel through life with multiple partners, but he would never leave his marriage".

Rosenberg had substituted for Robert Coates as the art critic of the *New Yorker* for a short period, and in 1967 was offered the post on a full-time basis. It gave him increased status in the New York art world, the *New Yorker* having a wide circulation. As another example of his now-rising reputation he was invited to teach at the University of Chicago (his friend Saul Bellow probably helped to get him there) where he had the post of a Professor of Social Thought. It was a curious move for a man who earlier had inclined to the view that a university was not, in Balken's words "the way to advance intellectual life". Some may have seen him as part of the academic establishment, but it wasn't how many in that establishment viewed him. She points out that Rosenberg's presence at the university wasn't always welcomed: "Unlike the Committee on Social Thought, where he was sought after and valued, the older art history faculty members were threatened by his public stature….They wrote off Rosenberg's pedagogy as 'too anecdotal', not grounded in connoisseurship and commitment to archival detail".

Harold Rosenberg died in 1978. A couple of his colleagues at Chicago wrote short stories about him. Richard Stern's "Double Charley", and Saul Bellow's "What Kind of Day Did You Have?" both dwell on the same theme – Rosenberg's reputation as a Lothario. Bellow's character, Wulpy, an art critic with a gammy leg, was a "bohemian long before bohemianism was absorbed into everyday life". And he is described as still taking Marx as his gospel and giving talks about the "application of *The Eighteenth Brumaire* to American politics and society – the farce of the Second Empire. Very timely".

Balken, summing up his life, offers this account: "Rosenberg knew that his ideas could not be spun into lasting theory. Unlike formalism, *action* was evanescent. He also knew that his signature term had run its course with the demise of the avant-garde in the late-1960s. With this demise, intense debate had ceased to matter". He was out of place in the new art world and looked on Andy Warhol, and other Pop and Colour Field painters as "virtuosos of boredom".

Debra Bricker Balken has written a fascinating, well-documented biography of Rosenberg which brings to life a long-lost world of radical politics, bohemian writers and artists, and serious debates. It was a world of little magazines, disputes, and near-poverty in its early days. It would be wrong to romanticise the social situation which helped create it, but likewise it would be wrong to dismiss what came out of it as lacking interest. With so much art and politics now focusing on novelty and triviality, Rosenberg and Greenberg could claim they've been proved right about the threat from mass culture. Rosenberg's "Herd of Independent Minds" has particular relevance in terms of how large numbers of people, including intellectuals, can be persuaded to admire and desire the same things, though some might want to question his role in advertising in relation to this. But it's useful to look back to a time when it appeared that "ideas were worth fighting for" and being serious mattered.

HAROLD ROSENBERG : A CRITIC'S LIFE
By Debra Bricker Balken
University of Chicago Press. 640 pages. $40. ISBN 978-0-226-03619-9

SUZANNE VALADON : MODEL, PAINTER, REBEL

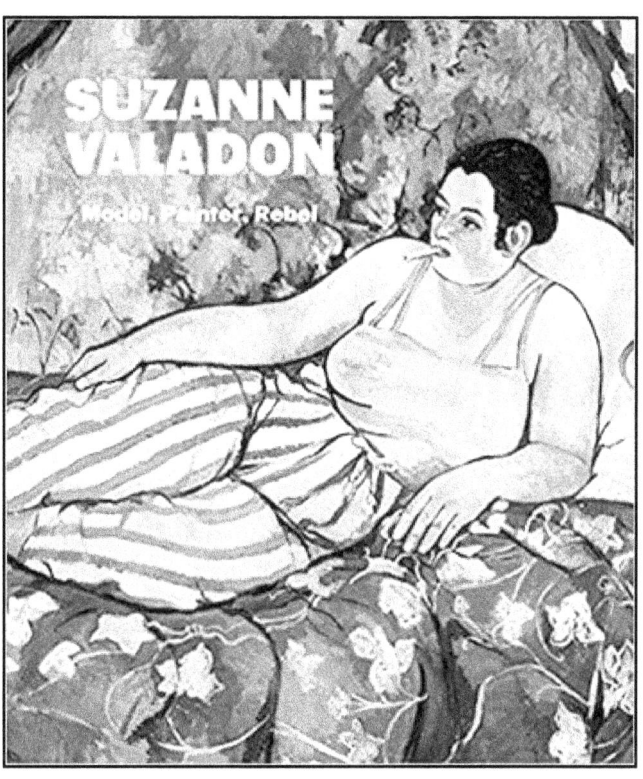

Establishing a reputation in the art world has never been an easy process, especially for women artists. And it must have been particularly difficult for a woman aspiring to be a painter to succeed in the competitive and male-dominated art world of late-nineteenth and early-twentieth century Paris. That Suzanne Valadon, despite coming from a poverty-stricken background and having had no formal art training, became a talented and critically-acknowledged painter is a remarkable story of natural skill allied with perseverance.

Valadon was born in 1865 and christened Marie-Clémentine Valadon. She was brought up in Paris by her mother, and by the age of fourteen was employed at a series of low-paid jobs, such as a waitress and a seamstress. She was rumoured to have worked as an acrobat in a circus at one point, though this has never been proven, and Valadon was not averse to embroidering the facts of her life when interviewed in later years. One of her occupations involved delivering laundry around Montmartre, including to the artist, Toulouse-Lautrec. It's said that he nicknamed her "Susanna" after the Biblical story of Susanna and the Elders. Did this happen after Valadon began to model for Lautrec, and possibly became his lover? It may have been his oblique comment on older artists viewing a naked young girl.

One of the Lautrec paintings reproduced in this book is a splendid portrait of a twenty-year old Valadon. But it's relevant to point to Lautrec's "The Hangover" which shows a somewhat bedraggled woman seated at a table with a glass and a bottle of wine in front of her. In other words, she was a model and Lautrec could make use of her as he wanted to obtain an effect on canvas. But, in contrast, there is "Young Woman at a Table", with a tidier and fresher-faced female (modelled by Valadon) gazing into space.

Lautrec wasn't the only Parisian painter Valadon posed for. She modelled for Puvis de Chavannes and Pierre-August Renoir, and it's more than likely had sexual relations with both. Whatever else she talked about she didn't ever divulge who she had slept with. It's perhaps true to say that it is the paintings by Renoir that are best-known in terms of the presence of Valadon. Catherine Hewitt's biography of Valadon, *Renoir's Dancer: The Secret Life of Suzanne Valadon* (Icon Books, 2017) has his "Dance at Bougival" on its front cover. And it has been reproduced widely on calendars and posters.

Lesser-known but striking in their way are the Spanish painter Santiago Rusinol's "Laughing Girl" (1894) and Jean Eugene Clary's "Portrait of Suzanne Valadon Age 20" (1885). Both are in the book, and I have to say that I was immediately taken with the charm of the Rusinol. It must have been painted towards the end of her career as a model. She gave it up when she married a businessman, Paul Mousis, in 1896. The laughing girl is leaning forward and looking directly at the viewer, as she must have looked directly at Rusinol, and the look on her face is infectious. The Clary catches her only in near-profile, but is an attractive fashionable painting.

How did Valadon get started on her own career as an artist? She had been drawing since the age of nine, though without any sort of encouragement. It was only when she encountered Lautrec, watched him working, and then showed him some of her drawings, that matters began to improve. Lautrec is said to have commented to a friend, "She arrived at this result without taking a lesson from anybody, ever, eh? It's marvellous". And another friend told him to show the drawings to Degas. He had a reputation as a harsh critic, but became a supporter of Valadon's work. It needs to be recorded, too, that she took note of Renoir's use of colour when she posed for him.

In 1893, when Valadon was eighteen, she gave birth to a son who was to become the painter, Maurice Utrillo, famous for his evocative pictures of the streets of Montmartre. He was also to become notorious for his drinking. Valadon never acknowledged who was the father. All that is known is that, in 1891, the Spanish painter, Miguel Utrillo, gave Maurice his surname, though it's unlikely that he was his actual father. Nancy Ireson says: " Nineteenth century men often viewed female models as easy conquests. Valadon did not speak about her intimate relationships with those for whom she posed, but it is likely that the boundaries between will and obligation were blurred".

Valadon's marriage to Paul Mousis was over by 1910, and she had, in fact, started an affair with André Utter, a much younger man who was a friend of her son. And it was around this time that, because she was making only a little money from the sale of drawings and prints, Valadon began to paint seriously in oils. Her 1912 "Family Portrait" focuses on herself, her elderly mother, a confident-looking Utter, and a somewhat morose-looking Utrillo. The painter is central to the picture and her firm presence suggests that she is the one who holds the family together in more ways than one. To which Ireson wryly comments: "Consequently, while Valadon's early canvases are in many ways progressive, they also perpetuate pre-existing notions of how women should appear in paintings. A woman cares for her partner, son, and mother, she is at the heart of the home".

In an interesting essay by Lisa Brice the question of nude representations of women is discussed. Valadon painted various self-portraits, including three (1917, 1924, 1931), all of which show her bare-breasted. Following Brice's analysis of each painting, we see Valadon in 1917, when "there is a toughness that can be felt through the treatment of the subject and the handling of the paint". Despite the death of her friend Degas, problems with Utrillo's alcoholism, and Utter being wounded during the Great War, the painting, in

Brice's words, emphasises her "femininity". By contrast, the 1924 portrait "shows a masculine body with shrunken breasts and pronounced neck muscles". Valadon is "ready to confront the outrage she knew a depiction of a naked, aged woman would provoke – after all, the raison d'etre for the nude in French art was sexuality".

It's easy to understand what Brice is protesting against when one considers what a hostile critic in 1929 said of Valadon's work: "If Suzanne Valadon has painted hideous shrews in tones of great vulgarity, it is because she wants to. That is the most disturbing thing. Apart from two or three works, the most recent, like the large bathers which are normal and healthy if not graceful, her female nude studies are treated as caricatures…..As for her flower paintings, the charm of their colour, their fragility, is always spoilt by a detail, a basket or ladder, placed there to look unpleasant. Does it spring from her poverty or her spite?" (as quoted by June Rose in *Mistress of Montmartre: A Life of Suzanne Valadon* (Richard Cohen Books, 1998).

A 1927 self-portrait has bright colours, and Valadon's expression might indicate a sadness, or discontent that only a painting can suggest. Contrast it to a photograph of her with Utrillo and Utter, taken in 1926, where she appears happy enough. And, a few years later, she has "calmed herself" and "looks ahead with dignified resignation" in the 1931 self-portrait. All of which brings me to Martha Lucy's assertion that Valadon "defied long-held conventions for presenting the female body as flawless, sensual, and passive". Elderly women had been portrayed on canvas in the past, but rarely, if ever, in a manner that openly pictured the way in which age affects the body.

It is the female nude that is heavily featured, though some of Valadon's early drawings do involve the young Maurice Utrillo. But she additionally painted landscapes, still-life canvases, and portraits. I recall exhibitions in 2001 at the Musée Utrillo-Valadon in Sannois, and in 2009 at the Pinacothèqhe in Paris, which featured both Valadon and Utrillo, and finding her work, which seemed to have a greater variety than his, much more appealing. It's difficult now to remember in detail exactly what was in those exhibitions. Utrillo's pictures of the streets of Montmartre admittedly had an attractive quality in terms of postcards and calendars, and the myth of

Montmartre, but Valadon, in my memory, came across as more-assertive, original, and colourful.

From a personal point of view I find Valadon's paintings of more interest than her drawings, though I accept that it's necessary to see both in context. Artists develop over time and operate in different areas as their ideas formulate. There is, also, the practical question of earning a living with one's work, and there's no doubt that it was necessary for Valadon to make money. Her impoverished upbringing had hardened her view of the world. She was not an idealist with a private income which enabled her to choose what to do: "in practical terms, her family depended on her income. She began to exhibit in the Salon d'Automne and the Salon des Indépendants, and she promoted her work to art dealers".

She started to achieve some recognition for her work, though this mostly seems to have occurred post-1918, and it can only be assumed that the 1914-18 War had interfered with both her activities as an artist and responses to them. The chronology of exhibitions featuring Valadon lists nothing between 1914 and 1924, though there is a critical evaluation of her "Black Venus" which was shown in the 1919 Salon d'Automne.

The 1920s and 1930s saw Valadon earning both critical and financial success. She could afford to buy property, live comfortably, and travel, but by 1933 she "suffered from mood swings" and eventually gave up painting, though her 1936 "Still Life with Herring" and the 1937 "Portrait of Madame Maurice Utrillo (Lucie Valore)" indicate that it must have been a gradual process. Utrillo had married Valore in 1935, and it is suggested that Valadon did not get along too well with her daughter-in-law. The relationship with Utter had broken down, and in June Rose's words : "Utter had become a semi-detached member of the family, coming in and out as he pleased". He had a string of mistresses and was not averse to gossiping about Valadon and her problems to members of the Parisian art community.

Suzanne Valadon died in 1938. She had been successful in her lifetime, though she was entering into her fifties when critics began to notice her and her work sold. To quote June Rose again: "When she was a beautiful young woman, the art critics had applauded, somewhat reluctantly, the willpower and independence that had enabled her to become an artist. But the middle-aged aesthetes who ruled the Paris art scene in the 1920s found Valadon's lack of education and defiance of etiquette distasteful, and the emotional whirlpool in which she floundered an embarrassment".

Suzanne Valadon: Model, Painter, Rebel accompanies an exhibition which was held at the Barnes Foundation in Philadelphia from September 26, 2021, to January, 9, 2022, and will transfer to Ny Carlsberg Glyptotek, Copenhagen on February 24, 2022 to August 1, 2022. It is effectively a catalogue of the exhibition, and is well-illustrated. There is a useful bibliography, and a selection of "Texts on Suzanne Valadon", one of which is an entertaining interview with her from 1921, in which she talks informatively about her years working as a model for various artists.

SUZANNE VALADON : MODEL, PAINTER, REBEL

Edited by Nancy Ireson

Paul Holberton Publishing. 159 pages. £35. ISBN 978-1-913645-13-7

SICKERT : A LIFE IN ART
An exhibition at the Walker Art Gallery, Liverpool, 18th September, 2021 to 27th February, 2022
SICKERT : A LIFE IN ART
By Charlotte Keenan McDonald

Walter Sickert was born in Munich in 1860. His father, a painter and illustrator for a weekly satirical paper, was Danish, and his mother was the daughter of an Irish dancer who worked on the London stage. The family moved to England in 1868, "partly owing to the increasing political and social tensions in Prussia". He had no conventional art training, but received "an informal arts education" through his father and "the family's artistic social network", which included Oscar Wilde, William Morris, and Edward Burne-Jones.

It's relevant, also, to point to Sickert's early activities as an actor. He had some success on the stage, but suddenly decided to turn to painting. There is a suggestion that this may have been brought about by his friendship with the American artist, James Abbott McNeill Whistler. He enrolled at the Slade School of Fine Art in 1881, but didn't stay long, disillusioned by the "formal teaching and rigid hierarchies", and then became an apprentice in Whistler's studio. Learning on the job suited him better. Years later, in 1907, Sickert painted a self-portrait with the title, "The Juvenile Lead", which was a somewhat satirical look at his early days as an actor.

Sickert met Edgar Degas in 1883 and through him began to pick up ideas from the Impressionists, though it would be wrong to suggest that he can be easily slotted into that category. His work, almost from the beginning, was far too original, and with its own colour interests, to place him alongside the French painters, or even those English artists who more-closely followed the Impressionist leanings in relation to light and colour. "The Laundry Shop, Dieppe", painted in 1885, is darker in tone than most Impressionist works.

I think Sickert really began to come into his own when, in the mid-1880s, he painted pictures set in the music halls. Some of the resultant canvases are possibly among his best-known paintings. "The Gallery of the Old Bedford", with its working-class audience almost hanging over the balcony, had me humming one of the most charming of music-hall songs, "The Boy I Love is up in the Gallery", as I stood in front of it. In his own way Sickert was recording the music-hall before it began to bring in more middle-class customers and toned down the bawdiness and working-class participation that often marked performances.

The music-hall section of the exhibition particularly delighted me, but there is much to be gained from Sickert's work as he painted in Dieppe and Venice. Some people, expecting a lightness of touch about the views of both places, might be disappointed with what they see. Colour is there, but Sickert did not overplay it in the way that a more-conventional painter might have done in order to create an attractive picture. His darker colours refuted some Impressionist ideas, and in fact Sickert was critical of Monet's attempts to record shifting arrangements of light and shade in, for example, his Haystack series.

I have to admit that I was a little disappointed that the exhibition didn't devote much attention to Sickert's involvements with the artists of the Fitzroy Street, Camden Town, and London Groups. Sickert's presence was important to all of them. There are passing references to some of the painters and, considering that he can be seen as a key influence in their activities, more might have been made of what they did. There are some examples of a number of women painters who worked alongside Sickert – Sylvia Gosse, Ethel Sands, Anna Hope Hudson, and most of all Thérèse Lessore – and, to be fair, the catalogue for the exhibition does mention Spencer Gore, Harold Gilman, and one or two others. Some examples of their work could have been useful. Sickert was a firm believer in getting art out of the drawing-room and into the kitchen. In other words, in portraying what might be dismissed as the "ordinary" and not considered as suitable for painting.

Leaving that aside, it was good to see that quite a few of Lessore's works are on display. It's noted that her "Brighter palette and delicate brushwork were more in keeping with the style associated with the Bloomsbury Group". She had links to it through her marriage to her first husband, Bernard Adeney. Sickert is reputed to have commented that Lessore, who married Sickert after his second wife died, "was the first women who took no notice of what he said and did exactly as she wanted". But they appeared to have had a good, working relationship, with Lessore's contributions to his later work (particularly the photo-based paintings) being considerable. It may also have been a fact that she "completed works bearing Sickert's signature when, towards the end of his life, he was too infirm to finish them".

Sickert's so-called Camden Town Nudes are often seen as among his best-known works and have gained a degree of notoriety because of stories about his supposed involvement in the Jack the Ripper saga. He did create a canvas called, "Jack the Ripper's Bedroom", and a painting with the title, "The Camden Town Murder or What Shall We do for the Rent?" but that was in 1908. The Ripper murders had had taken place many years before in Whitechapel and not Camden Town. Sickert's painting had been based on newspaper reports of the 1908 murder of a prostitute.

There are a great many of Sickert's drawings in the exhibition, the Walker having a major collection, and the catalogue has a useful guide to them by Keith Oliver: "The drawings range from quick on-the-spot sketches made to capture a particular pose or detail, to squared-up final studies for paintings, as well as drawings made as art works in their own right". Taken together they support the paintings in the exhibition and indicate how Sickert arrived at his final version of a scene or portrait.

Both the exhibition and the catalogue follow Sickert's life in art from his early days as a student to his final years when ill-health sometimes prevented him from working, but at other times he often used photographs as a basis for paintings. And he collaborated with Lessore on some works. He did have a degree of popular success in his late-years, though it's noted that critics have occasionally tended to overlook the paintings based on photography, primarily because they're not seen as original compositions. But they seem to me to work in their way. And their inclusion in what is, in effect, a study of Sickert's career, completes a splendid exhibition. He had a long, productive life, and died in 1942.

It should be noted that the catalogue is well-produced, has informative texts, and is liberally illustrated.

SICKERT : A LIFE IN ART

By Charlotte Keenan McDonald

National Museums Liverpool. 104 pages. £14.95. ISBN 978-1-9027-00632

BEYOND BLOOMSBURY : LIFE, LOVE AND LEGACY

An exhibition at the Millenium Gallery, Sheffield, 25th November 2021 to 12th February 2022

Interest in Bloomsbury never seems to wane. Books, newspaper and magazine articles, films, radio and TV programmes, all crop up regularly. And visitors flock to Charleston, the country home of Vanessa Bell and Duncan Grant. There are also exhibitions, including the current one in Sheffield. I have to admit that my first impulse on hearing about it was to wonder if there is anything new to say or see about the "Bloomsberries", a name applied to Virginia Woolf, Vanessa Bell, and the rest, by Molly McCarthy, wife of the writer Desmond McCarthy. She was captured on canvas by Bell.

It was the word "beyond" which attracted my attention and persuaded me that the exhibition might offer more than a round-up of the usual suspects. They are all there, of course. Woolf and her husband Leonard, Bell, Duncan Grant, Roger Fry, Dora Carrington......the list goes on. And they are amply represented in paintings and photographs. The National Portrait Gallery provided a number of items from their extensive collection of material, and devotees of Bloomsbury won't be disappointed with what they find on display.

Of more interest, at least to me, were works by artists who, in one way or another, might be said to have been on the fringes of Bloomsbury. Matthew Smith, Edward Wadsworth, Nina Hamnett, William Roberts, Wyndham Lewis, David Bomberg, and Mark

Gertler. Paintings and drawings by them can be seen in the exhibition, and to my mind often overshadow the visual work by "insider" Bloomsbury artists like Bell. Fry, and Grant. I don't dislike Vanessa Bell's paintings, for example, but they seem to lack individuality. You couldn't say the same about Matthew Smith's colourful portrait of Angelica Garnett.

The presence of the artists I've referred to does indicate that those in the close Bloomsbury group were meeting a variety of painters. When the London Group was formed in 1913 it included members of the Camden Town Group, Wyndham Lewis's Vorticists, and people like Bell, Grant, and Fry. There is a delightful illustration by William Roberts which satirises the Bloomsbury contingent as they appear to be debating something that Cezanne did or said. Roberts himself had been influenced by Cubism, and would have been aware of Roger Fry's important work in introducing French Post-Impressionist art into Britain. But a little gentle mockery doesn't go amiss.

There are examples of publications from the Hogarth Press and products from the Omega Workshop. The display cases have interesting items with accompanying details. There were some minor errors (two different dates given for Vanessa Bell's date-of-birth, for example) and a curious mistake in relation to Molly McCarthy. A note about her is accompanied by a copy of the American writer Mary McCarthy's *Memories of a Catholic Girlhood.* Surely someone should have spotted this? There appears to be no connection between the two McCarthys.

Beyond Bloomsbury is a generally worthwhile and informative exhibition. It will obviously appeal to those fascinated by the legends of Bloomsbury – the affairs, intrigues, and arguments – and the work, whether written or visual, created by the likes of Virginia Woolf and Vanessa Bell. But it also has the added value of widening the usual picture to incorporate other artists, writers, and personalities.

Sadly there isn't a catalogue for the exhibition, nor were there postcards on sale. But there isn't an entrance fee, just a request to make a donation. Its next stop will be York from 4th March to 5th June.

LIGHT ON FIRE : THE ART AND LIFE OF SAM FRANCIS

I don't know if Sam Francis's name will mean a great deal to people in the U.K. who take an interest in twentieth-century art. This despite the fact that his work attracted world-wide attention at one time. He had established a reputation in France, and was admired in Japan, as well as being widely acclaimed on the West Coast of the United States, though perhaps less so in New York. But there appears to be few examples of his work in public galleries in Britain, and I can't recall any major exhibitions of his paintings in this country.

Francis was born in 1923 in San Mateo, south of San Francisco. His father, Canadian by birth, was a Professor of Mathematics at the University of California and his mother an accomplished pianist and a French teacher. Francis grew up in relatively comfortable surroundings, and doesn't seem to have been greatly affected by the widespread social and economic impact of the Depression. He preferred the outdoors to more-academic pursuits, and didn't show any signs of an aptitude towards taking up art as a profession. He did have some skills at sketching. But his early inclinations about a career were in the direction of medicine.

When America entered the Second World War in 1941 he enlisted in the Army Air Corps and was selected for pilot training, something which affected him in terms of making him aware of space and its possibilities. An accident cut short his flying ambitions and while in hospital he was diagnosed as suffering from spinal tuberculosis. It would take several years for him to recover enough for the armed forces to discharge him. It was during his lengthy stay in hospital, where he was encased in a plaster cast from his chest to his hips, that he was given paints as a form of therapy. He was encouraged to express himself through art by David Park, an established West Coast artist and teacher, who, Francis once said, "pulled me out of myself". Another California painter, Hassel Smith, also encouraged Francis.

He was initially interested in surrealism, though he also looked back to the work of El Greco. However, figuration soon began to disappear from his work as he moved towards abstraction. There was an active West Coast movement of painters who were not copying, but paralleling what was being established in New York as Abstract Expressionism. Hassel Smith, Richard Diebenkorn, Clyfford Still, Edward Corbett, and others were producing work which was too often overlooked as attention was focused on New York and the activities of Pollock, de Kooning, Rothko, and Kline.

Susan Landauer's authoritative *The San Francisco School of Abstract Expressionism* (University of California Press, 1996) demonstrates just how vital and inventive the West Coast artists were. Sam Francis was, for a time, probably influenced by Corbett's "serene simplicity" which critics suggested related to "Zen Buddhism and Chinese landscape painting". There is some irony in the fact that Corbett wasn't particularly interested in either Chinese art or philosophy. Francis was, as his later involvements would indicate.

Francis was never one to settle for very long in a single place, and in 1950 he travelled to Paris with Muriel Goodwin. He had earlier married his childhood sweetheart, Vera Miller, but it had become obvious that his increasing involvement in the world of art and artists was not to her taste. The marriage soon broke down. There was, too, the possible problem of Francis being caught up in the anti-communist purges sweeping across America. He had once belonged to a group called American Youth for Democracy, an offshoot of the Young Communist League. There doesn't appear to be any evidence to show that he ever took a deep interest in politics, but it was, perhaps, an opportune moment to move to Paris.

It was there that, as the painter Al Held put it, "Sam found his truth". Paris in the early-1950s was artistically and intellectually alive. Francis, thanks to the G.I. Bill which gave veterans an opportunity to choose where to study, enrolled at the Atelier Fernand Léger, though Gabrielle Selz is of the opinion that his real education "took place around café tables, among his contemporaries". Besides Al Held, others like Joan Mitchell, Norman Bluhm, Shirley Jaffe, and the Canadian Jean-Paul Riopelle were in Paris. But it wasn't only fellow-painters that Francis encountered. He met Sartre and various French writers, artists and intellectuals, such as "the dynamic art historian and man of letters Georges Duthuit", described by Francis as "a Baudelairean dandy, very emotional, always on stage". He was also able to see Monet's "Water-lilies", a large work which had an influence on him.

By 1952 Francis, despite having to operate in a "cramped room at the Hotel de Seine" had enough paintings ready for an exhibition at the Galerie Nina Dausset. Critics received his work enthusiastically. Duthuit thought that the images were "shrouds of mist" and "fine-nets" that were "between the painter and the beholder's eye". Another critic said that the paintings "appear to be a window into another, more vast world of which we are only seeing a detail", while the Swiss art collector Franz Meyer was "stupefied by the constant swirls of movement on each canvas". Meyer was to become one of Francis's key patrons and a keen collector of his work.

Francis remained in France for five years, during which time the campaign to replace Paris with New York as the centre of Western art had built up. From his point of view it resulted in some problems when he returned to America. There was a certain amount of envy involved because of his success in Paris, and this, linked in with his absence from his home country, meant that he was overlooked when critics took stock of the achievements of the abstract expressionist artists. He was even thought of as primarily a French artist in some ways: "His scale was large, on par with Pollock's, but his surfaces had a European delicacy".

I recall an exhibition in Paris some years ago of what was called "Lyrical Abstraction" and it occurs to me to suggest that it might be a term usefully applied to some of Francis's paintings, and to ask whether certain of the French artists involved might have seen his work? He did have contacts with the Tachisme movement in Paris, and it was from this group that the idea of lyrical abstraction was formed. It was less "raw" than American Abstract Expressionism.

Another factor which may have had something to do with Francis not receiving his due was his tendency to move around. He had a need to be in different places, which may have been a way of escaping from certain realities that he wasn't prepared to face up to. He did spend some time in New York, but he was not "tied to the Cedar Tavern", the meeting place where the Abstract Expressionist painters drank, fell out, and sometimes fought. It could have been that, to the older generation, shaped as they were by the Depression and not achieving fame until they were middle-aged, someone like Francis had it too easy. As Selz puts it: "Now his growing wealth cast another shadow over him. How had Sam succeeded so quickly? Was he too market-driven? Was he a sellout?".

There was possibly some truth in the idea that he had landed lucky by being in at the start of an art-boom: "The sale of art had become its own form of theatrical spectacle. Guests attended auctions in dress jackets and dinner gowns and drank champagne. *Fortune* magazine compared investments in the art market to investments in the stock market, calling old masters 'gilt-edged securities' ". There's no doubt that Francis made a lot of money from his paintings, and it enabled him to purchase properties in California, Japan, Paris, and other locations, so that he was constantly moving from one to another, as well as attending exhibitions of his work in Tokyo, Paris, Dusseldorf, Rome, and Vienna. His trips to California were expressions of his "describing and apprehending light and in capturing light's material thingness". It was akin to his taste for white as a colour, and he described it as "like the space between things".

But was there, perhaps, a degree of self-doubt expressed about the quality of some of his later work as his wealth accrued? He told a friend, "Great art comes from poverty". Was he thinking of his early days living the bohemian life in Paris and breaking new ground with his paintings?

One of his favourite places was Japan where his paintings were seen as having something in common with traditions of Japanese art. He was interested in Eastern philosophies, and claimed an awareness of Zen Buddhism, though some might wonder how his often-chaotic lifestyle could fit in with the order and discipline that Zen demanded? The intensity he gave to his work may have certain connections to his ventures into Zen. But equally it could have been just the self-absorbed condition of the creative artist. Other people found it difficult to deal with. His second wife, Muriel, was of the opinion that "Sam had a fecund intensity that could be hard to live with".

There was something in the art that gave it a relationship to Japanese and Chinese painting, a kind of touch of the "floating world" we associate with art from those countries. It is not surprising that he became interested in sky-painting and the visual effect of vapour trails. And financed light show acts supporting rock performers in the Sixties.

Francis lived out his later years in California and was involved in establishing a Museum of Contemporary Art in Los Angeles, along with other projects. His health, never good, declined and in 1991 he was diagnosed with prostate cancer. He died in 1994. His estate, valued at around 79 million dollars, included several properties, businesses, a library, many art works (his own and those by other artists), cars, and more. Inevitably, his will became a matter of dispute. Selz provides a summary of what eventually happened, but it may be of interest to note that his fifth wife, Margaret, an artist, was born on a farm near St Helens, England. She was twenty-five years younger than him when they met in Japan. The substantial amount she received under the terms of the will enabled her to buy Gledstone Hall, near Skipton, where she lived with her son, Augustus, also an artist.

It's impossible to know how Francis's reputation will stand in the future. Will those large canvases, with their invitations to reach beyond the painted surfaces, still continue to fascinate? And will we ever get an opportunity to see them? There could be difficulties with "Berlin Red" which Selz refers to as "the largest single canvas in the world". Was it an expression of Francis's desire to outdistance Jackson Pollock's larger works? He was a complex man, and needed to be recognised and treated as an important artist. He could be generous and encouraging to younger artists. But his relationships with the opposite sex were less than perfect, as his five marriages (two of them to Japanese women), and many affairs, indicated. Nor was he always the most reliable father.

Gabrielle Selz has written a tightly-packed book which combines the facts of Sam Francis's life with astute comments on his paintings. It's not always easy to define abstract works in words. Francis's canvases need to be seen if their intentions of taking the viewer beyond the obvious are likely to be achieved. And even then it may all depend on whether or not the viewer has the potential to enter into the artist's frame of mind and understand what William Blake (admired by Francis) said: "If the doors of perception were cleansed then everything would appear to man as it is, infinite".

LIGHT ON FIRE : THE ART AND LIFE OF SAM FRANCIS

By Gabrielle Selz

University of California Press. 367 pages. £27. ISBN 978-0-520-31071-1 (UK distributor: John Wiley & Sons)

LONDON YIDDISHTOWN : EAST END JEWISH LIFE IN YIDDISH SKETCH AND STORY, 1930-1950: SELECTED WORKS OF KATIE BROWN, A.M. KAIZER, AND L.A. LISKY

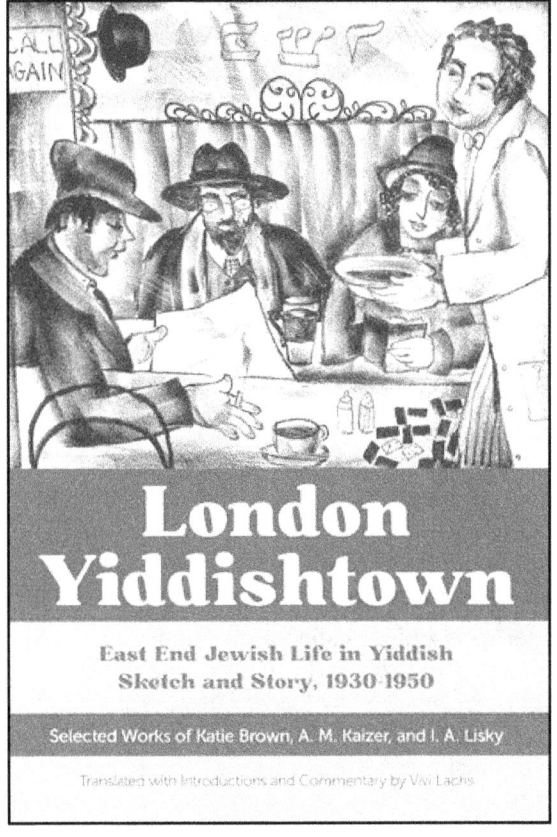

Whitechapel was once the home of a thriving and lively Jewish community. The largest in the United Kingdom, it had started to grow as thousands of Jews arrived from Russia and Eastern Europe from around 1880. There were already Jews in Britain, especially London and also in other big cities such as Manchester, but they were often members of the middle-class, keen to assimilate as much as possible, and mostly not in favour of using Yiddish as their favoured method of verbal and written communication. For the majority of the Jews arriving from Russia, Poland, and elsewhere, Yiddish was the language they used in the home, at work, and on the streets. They came from the shtetls and were predominantly working-class. It was a flexible language, taking in expressions from whichever country people were living in, while at the same time having a broad enough base so that it could be understood wherever Jews came together.

Although it's clearly angled towards one aspect of the Jewish immigrant experience it could be useful to refer to William J. Fishman's *East End Jewish Radicals 1875-1914* (Duckworth, 1975) for information about the early days of Jewish life in Whitechapel. Fishman quotes the poet, Morris Winchevsky, on the subject of the Anglo-Jewry's attitudes towards the newcomers: "They are ashamed of us; not as one is ashamed of poor relations, but as one is shamed by a leper, a black sheep……and their charity always has a flavour of riddance payment". Fishman also refers approvingly to Emanuel Litvinoff's novel, *A Death Out of Season* (Michael Joseph, 1973), set at the time of the Siege of Sydney Street, and "which presents a rare insight into Jewish immigrant life".

It shouldn't be assumed that all the Jews in London lived in Whitechapel. But they were noticeably concentrated there for several decades. And even those choosing to live in other areas (North London, for example) often worked in Whitechapel, or chose to visit it regularly because the Yiddish theatres were there, along with friends, clubs, restaurants, shops, and other facilities.

There is an entertaining piece called "The Whitechapel Express" by A.M. Kaizer in *London Yiddishtown* which follows the route of the number 47 tram (later replaced by the 647 trolleybus) which ran from Stamford Hill to Whitechapel. Kaizer's descriptions of the variety of passengers and their activities, ranging from reading Yiddish newspapers to knitting, talking, and sometimes even singing, has a humorous angle but deftly establishes a record of a specific time and location. His sketch, originally published in 1934, was designed to be read by Yiddish speakers, but has lasting qualities because of its social values.

It's probably true to say that, by 1934, there were signs of a lessening of activity in Whitechapel. Vivi Lachs suggests that the writing was on the wall even before that : "By the 1920s, however, the Jewish East End was in decline". And she goes on to point out that those still living there "were mostly an older generation of working-class immigrant tailors, cabinetmakers, and market-stall holders who still spoke Yiddish. Many of these Yiddish speakers did not want to pass on the language to their children, worried that it would hold them back or cause them to suffer anti-Semitism. The children, who were in or had been through Anglo-Jewish and local authority schooling, were, in any case, firmly anglicised". The tensions that arose between the generations were often referred to by the writers Lachs has translated.

In Katie Brown's "Breadwinner" the assertive Rachel, who is going hiking, upsets her mother, who says "I haven't brought up a girl to dress in men's trousers and go off wandering around forests and fields with a strange boy. I didn't behave like that at all". And she wants to know if the boy is "at least Jewish". Rachel simply laughs at her, points out that she is the breadwinner in the house, and tells her mother not to speak Yiddish when the boy arrives. In Brown's "Too Jewish" a son-in-law explains to his wife's mother that they can't name their child "Yisroel" because it sounds "too Jewish" and "in the neighbourhood where he lived it wasn't the done thing to give a child a Jewish name. It wouldn't fit in with the neighbours, or in the school he would attend, and even he would find it hard, because then people would know that they were Jewish, and these days you had to be careful with this sort of thing".

The question of being identifiably Jewish occurs in the more-overtly political writings of L.A. Lisky. He had direct experience of Fascist anti-semitism in Vienna, and left that city to move to London in 1938. His story, "Fascist Recruits" explores how and why someone joins Oswald Mosley's British Union of Fascists, and "On the March with the Hungry" is centred around one such march and the difference in attitudes between a father, who is reluctant to join in demonstrations despite being unemployed, and his son, a more militant-minded person, who does go to Trafalgar Square and is clubbed by a policeman.

Lisky's "Nationalist Feelings and Class Interests" concerns Mr Klepman, a factory owner, who instructs his manager to fire the female workers when they laugh at him and quickly hire new ones: "Don't you know what to do with slackers like that?" said Klepman. "Let them work till the end of the week and then throw them out". He then returns to his comfortable home and is glad that he's living in London and not in Germany where Jews are being persecuted.

It's a fact that many of the sketches and stories in *London Yiddishtown* are didactic in intention. They're making points about life and its problems, though they frequently do it with humour. It's easy to see how they fitted into the context they were designed for, i.e. publication in the Yiddish newspapers and magazines that flourished in Whitechapel. Kaizer's "When You Go to a Yiddish Theatre" makes easy-going fun of people who eat peanuts and scatter the shells, not only the on floor, but on those nearby, or who take out slices of watermelon to gorge on.

And Kaizer's "Moses in London" is the story of how, when Moses led the Jews out of Egypt and into Israel, he discovered that he had forgotten to provide himself with an immigration certificate so had to remain outside the Holy Land. He somehow gets to London and approaches various Zionist organisations for the appropriate documentation. He's turned away by them all for one reason or another, and eventually ends up in the London Jewish Hospital, where he dies. Upon which the different Zionist bodies compete to claim him as their own.

Katie Brown could also use humour to good advantage, as in "Jewish Readers" which anyone reading it would recognise from their own experiences of being asked to lend someone else on the bus their newspaper, or being conscious of the person behind them peering over their shoulder to read the news. And "I Need a Flat" tells of the difficulties encountered when living alongside neighbours who complain, while "My Prince, the Socialist" is a light satire on having a son who suddenly takes to speaking on soapboxes about the iniquities of the capitalist system. Brown was herself active in the Workers' Circle, a left-wing mutual-aid society. There is satirical intention, too, in "When a Woman Becomes a Person" where she is taken to task by her husband because she makes fun of him in her column in a Yiddish newspaper. She then offers some tongue-in-cheek advice on how wives should treat their husbands.

It's essential to see the three writers picked out by Lachs as operating in the context of a wider circle of Yiddish authors. Her "The Literary Landscape of London's Yiddishtown and the Fight for the Survival of Yiddish, 1930-50" does just that, and provides an informative and provocative survey of what was taking place in the period referred to. She points to the fact that, by the 1930s, younger Jewish writers often preferred to write in English, even if they knew Yiddish. Books like

Simon Blumenfeld's *Jew Boy,* and Willy Goldman's *East End My Cradle* aimed to reach readers outside the Jewish community, as did Louis Golding's *Magnolia Street*, though that was based among Jews in Manchester and not Whitechapel. A little later there were Roland Camberton's *Scamp* and Bernard Kops' *The World is a Wedding*, both entertaining and not restricted to the world of Yiddish readers.

It has sometimes occurred to me to wonder if Julius Lipton knew Yiddish? I'm sure he must have done, though his book, *Poems of Strife,* published in 1936 in an edition of 95 copies by Lawrence & Wishart, is written in English. He's quoted in the introduction by C. Day Lewis as saying that when he does find employment he works "fifteen hours each day, in a 'sweat shop' wielding a heavy press iron". The copy of his book that I have is signed by Lipton and dedicated to someone called "Joy". From references in the poems I would guess that Lipton was a member of the Communist Party.

Lachs is mainly concerned to look at the fate of Yiddish after 1930 and, in particular, in the post-war years of the late-1940s and early-1950s. Yiddish didn't disappear, but it was largely used by older people. Many of the anglicised young had moved away in search of jobs, wider educational opportunities, and what they saw as less-restricted social activities. There was also the situation with regard to housing, the East End having suffered badly during the Blitz. The docks were a key target for German bombers.

The Yiddish writers carried on, despite the audience for their work having diminished. Yiddish publications continued to appear, though sales of newspapers, magazines and books were never enough to ensure that the writers contributing to them would be paid reasonable fees for their work. Life had never been a bed of roses for Yiddish authors, and, as Lachs says, "it was almost impossible to make a living from writing for the Yiddish press in Britain, and few were full-time professional writers".

The poet Avron Nokhem Stencl perhaps put it in more personal terms when he wrote in 1938: "It has not been easy to plough the arid cultural earth in London. The field of Yiddish culture is hard and stony. Hard, as is every place that has not felt the warm kiss of human work for a long time". Stencl, who founded a new Yiddish literary magazine during the early days of the Blitz, is remembered as "standing at the door of every literary or Yiddish-language event, selling his *Heftlekh* and, later, *Loshn un Lebn*". There are photographs of both publications in *London Yiddishtown*.

When the older generation died, so to a great degree did Yiddish. Lachs, who did not initially speak Yiddish herself, relates how around 2000 she began to attend meetings of the Friends of Yiddish : "A small group of very elderly Yiddish speakers, augmented by a couple of Yiddish learners like me, read poems and stories, sang songs, and told jokes in Yiddish. I couldn't understand most of it, but I particularly loved Phyllis, who with a broad London accent would read a different sketch by Katie Brown each week. I managed to understand whole sentences here and there in the story, but never seemed to be able to catch the punchlines at the end, at which everyone laughed".

London Yiddishtown is a book that packs in a great amount of information about what is now a lost world that we can only recreate from the literature (novels, stories, poems, journalism) of the period and old photographs. From these we can, if we're lucky, imagine what the people were like and how they dealt with everyday problems as well as larger social and political issues. Vivi Lachs has done a wonderful job in translating a selection of Yiddish writing, and providing a commentary on it and its creators. As she suggests, it is "literature that can be enjoyed today on its own merits, and within its historical context". Her book can stand alongside the earlier *Whitechapel Noise: Jewish Immigrant Life in Yiddish Song and Verse, London 1884-1914.* (See my review, *Northern Review of Books,* March, 2019, and in *Militants, Artists, Poets,* Penniless Press, 2020).

LONDON YIDDISHTOWN : EAST END JEWISH LIFE IN YIDDISH SKETCH AND STORY, 1930-1950: SELECTED WORKS OF KATIE BROWN, A.M. KAIZER, AND L.A. LISKY

Translated with Introduction and Commentary by Vivi Lachs

Published by Wayne State University Press. 240 pages. £23.50. ISBN 978-0-8143-4847-5 (Distributed in the UK by Eurospan)

ALIAS AKBAR DEL PIOMBO ; ANNOTATIONS ON THE LIFE AND WORK OF NORMAN RUBINGTON

There was, for a time, a belief that the novels published under Akbar del Piombo's name by the notorious Olympia Press in Paris were really the work of William Burroughs. Olympia had published his *Naked Lunch* and other books, and Maurice Girodias claimed that the mistaken attribution came about because of a printer's error. It was a claim that Norman Rubington, the man actually behind the Akbar del Piombo pseudonym, rubbished. He was convinced that Girodias deliberately fostered the supposed link with the better-known Burroughs in order to further sales of the del Piombo titles.

Who was Norman Rubington? Born in 1921 in the United States he served as a map maker in the American army in China during the Second World War. He returned to New York, but soon decided to take advantage of the G.I. Bill which provided ex-servicemen with funds to study at locations of their choice. Rubington went to Paris and enrolled at the École des Beaux Arts, and later at the Académie de la Grande Chaumière. He took to the city immediately, and in fact stayed on even when his entitlement to US government funding ended. It was 1969 before he returned to America.

Gregory Stephenson, working from letters exchanged with Rubington in the 1980s, and books by Joseph Barry and Maurice Girodias, describes how he survived. Barry tells how he visited the artist in 1951/52 and found him living in a room above a fish shop in a street off the Boulevard San Michel; "There were no toilet facilities and he had to get all his water from the fish shop". Girodias, writing after he had fallen out with Rubington, was inclined to offer what Stephenson refers to as a "defamatory characterisation", and asserted that he had married "a pleasant pharmacist…..in order to secure for himself a cosy nook by the fire while winter winds were blowing". Girodias even suggested that Rubington wasn't averse to seducing "bourgeois women of luxurious habits and opulent bodies, to whom he was pleased to offer himself". Rubington's response when he was told what Girodias had said was, needless to say, less than happy. He described it as "genteel calumny".

While in Paris Rubington exhibited at the Salon d'Automne and had a solo exhibition at Galerie Huit. In 1951 he won the prestigious Prix de Rome. But, in need of money, he turned to writing pornography for Olympia Press. His first book, *Who Pushed Sylvia?* by Akbar del Piombo, appeared in 1956 and was followed by several others with titles like *Cosimo's Wife* and *Skirts*. There was also, in a somewhat different vein, *Fuzz Against Junk*, published in 1959, and perhaps capitalising on the rise of the Beats and the growing interest in the so-called "underground" and similar subjects. I recall picking up a copy during a visit to Paris in 1962, though I later disposed of it somewhere along the way.

I don't think Rubington had any great commercial or critical success as an artist when he returned to America, though he did contribute collages and humorous pieces to *Rolling Stone, International Times*, and other publications. He also published poetry in little magazines.

And he wrote novels, not necessarily of a pornographic kind, under various aliases. Stephenson looks at a western called *The Comancheros* by Jack Slade, and at least two, and possibly four, "Gothic Romance novels" by Leslie Paige from Tower Publications in the 1970s. An idea of the contents might be gained from a line Stephenson quotes from one of them: "Ellen longed for a tranquil life, but the fates seemed to be working against her".

It seems that Rubington described his status in the art world as one of "ever-abiding amateurship", by which he meant "a sense of non-status, as opposed to professional as meant by what Wall Street means by it......it is a state of mind, akin to a child's, a state too easily sacrificed for the schemes and cunning required for merely coping in this vale of commerce". Stephenson adds that the "particular sense in which Norman understands the word 'amateur' is related to that of its Latin root in the word *amare*, meaning to love, to be in love with, to take pleasure in"

Norman Rubington died in 1991. His archive is held at Yale University, and there is information about him and his activities available on YouTube. Gregory Stephenson gives a good picture of the man in this illustrated chapbook. As for the novels, pornographic or not, you may be very lucky and come across one or two of them in a second-hand bookshop, but on-line they're expensive to buy.

ALIAS AKBAR DEL PIOMBO ; ANNOTATIONS ON THE LIFE AND WORK OF NORMAN RUBINGTON

By Gregory Stephenson

Ober-Limbo Verlag, Heidelberg. 48 pages. ISBN 978-87-971569-9-5

THE WORST MILITARY LEADERS IN HISTORY

On the 25th June, 1876, General George Armstrong Custer led the 7th Cavalry towards the Little Big Horn River where, his scouts had informed him, there was a large Indian village. Custer's unit comprised almost 650 soldiers, scouts, and civilians, and was part of a larger force which, in turn, was made up of three columns working to a plan to surround the Indians and force them onto reservations. They had been deemed to be hostiles for not adhering to an order to go to the appointed locales on a voluntary basis. For the Indians, basically Sioux along with some Cheyenne and Arapaho, such an order conflicted with their natural nomadic instincts. And the twenty or so years since the end of the Civil War had seen them harried by the intrusion of settlers and soldiers into what the Indians saw as their traditional hunting grounds. It's difficult to know what, as a group, they thought of their situation, but it's possibly true that they realised their traditional way of life was under threat, and were consequently in no mood for compromise.

Custer had been given orders to find the Indian encampment and observe it, but to wait for the main column, commanded by General Crook, to arrive before taking further action. What he didn't know was that Crook had been stopped at the Rosebud River by a clash with the hostiles and his advance brought to a halt. From the available evidence it seems probable that, even if Custer had been aware of Crook's setback, he wouldn't have delayed his attack on the village. He was impulsive, and anxious to re-establish the reputation as a cavalry commander he'd gained in the Civil War. And later he had cultivated the image of a practised Indian fighter after action against a Cheyenne village in the winter of 1868. He wanted to be seen as the man who effectively brought the Indians to heel, and was confident that his regiment alone could defeat whatever forces they came up against.

The problem was that Custer was inclined to ignore warnings from both white and Indian scouts that the village was the largest they had ever seen. He underestimated the number of warriors he was likely to encounter. He then divided his force, using the tactic of launching an attack from each end of the encampment. This might have succeeded on a smaller scale, but it soon became obvious that things weren't going to plan. The troops attempting to enter one end of the village were quickly in retreat and forced into a defensive position. Custer's command of over two hundred soldiers and scouts was likewise overwhelmed, but in their case they all died. When the casualties were added together they totalled 268 killed, not to mention numerous wounded. Custer's ambitions and arrogance had caused the deaths of almost half of his regiment.

I suppose the Custer debacle is the best known of the various stories of blunders and bungling that are included in this book. There have been novels, films both factual and fictional, academic studies, paintings, and articles too numerous to count looking at what was, in contrast to some other examples, a fairly minor incident in terms of the numbers involved. But you didn't have to be American to know about the Little Big Horn when I was growing up in industrial Lancashire in the 1940s. The cinema saw to that and Errol Flynn died gallantly, if not accurately, in They Died With Their Boots On.

This isn't the place for anyone in the United Kingdom to claim superiority in military affairs. Bonnie Prince Charlie hadn't a clue what to do at Culloden (not included in the volume under review) and his incompetence resulted in hundreds of deaths among his followers. And Chelmsford's actions during the Zulu War might be questioned. His decision to divide his army made it easier for the Zulus to kill around one thousand troops at Isandlwana. But I'm moving away from what is in the book, and Lord Wolseley is there and taken to task for the failure to relieve General Gordon in Khartoum in 1884. His push up the Nile and on land just didn't move fast enough and the Mahdi and his followers soon had Gordon's head on the end of a lance. Joseph Moretz, writing about Wolseley, does try to be fair, and points out that not all the blame can be attached to him. There were shortcomings in the general organisation of the British Army. It could have been that not having to fight what Moretz refers to as a "first class enemy" for many years had brought about a degree of complacency with regard to training, equipment, and related matters.

Wolseley's reputation as a commander largely rested on campaigns fought in China, India, Canada, the Gold Coast, and Egypt. It could be argued that his experiences in colonial warfare ought to have equipped him to deal with the Mahdi, but he badly underestimated the strength of the Mahdi's forces. And he also seemed to have lacked the organisational skills necessary to put together an efficient relief column. It's suggested that Wolseley attempted to shift the blame for failing to reach Khartoum in time onto others. I suspect it was, and no doubt still is, a not uncommon practice among military men.

Incompetence is bad enough, but when tied in with what might have been a form of madness, it can become terrifying. Roman Fedorovich von Ungern-Sternberg is not likely to be a household name, even among many historians. He was a relatively minor figure during the Civil War that swept across Russia in the years following the Bolshevik Revolution of 1917. He was a junior officer in the Russian army during the First World War. When Civil War started he fought for the Whites, the anti-Bolshevik forces that sprang up under different leaders and were eventually defeated by the Red Army. The Civil War was a particularly brutal episode, with both sides indulging in atrocities, but Ungern appears to have gone further than most in his application of terror as a means of obtaining compliance with his orders.

Ungern formed his own army which was never very large, but operating as it did along parts of the Trans-Siberian Railway, and in small towns and villages in Mongolia, achieved some minor successes. Unger had a dream of creating a form of Mongolian Empire which would in time have an army strong enough to sweep into Russia, defeat the Bolsheviks, and re-institute the monarchy. He was anti-semitic so pogroms against Jews were part of his strategy. And he was a strict disciplinarian when it came to his own men. It's said that he had one officer who disobeyed him burnt at the stake. Ungern was never the most-capable of commanders, and as the Red Army became more powerful his grip on his soldiers began to slacken while his cruelty increased. Some of his officers plotted to overthrow him, but he escaped and tried to enlist help from nearby Mongolian auxiliaries. They, however, handed him over to the Reds who, after a brief interrogation, shot him.

Most of the chapters concern military leaders on land, so the diversion into naval warfare with an essay on Vice-Admiral Sir David Beatty is useful. I think I might be forgiven for declaring a personal interest. My father joined the Royal Navy as a boy-sailor when he was sixteen in 1911. He served until 1925, and I grew up knowing the names of Beatty and Jellicoe. He was present at the Battle of Jutland in 1916, though he was below decks most, if not all of the time. And he was lucky enough to have been on board a battleship and not a battle cruiser, three of which were lost to enemy gunfire.

That was, according to Chuck Steele, Beatty's fault. He was in charge of the battle cruiser fleet at Jutland, but though the ships represented the "largest concentration of cutting-edge naval technology", Beatty appears to have lacked an awareness of what they were capable of. Steele says, "Beattie had not done well in preparing or controlling his forces". There were poor communications between various ships, and "British gunnery was abysmal". It would seem that there was a campaign by Beatty and his supporters to blame Jellicoe for what happened at Jutland.

Steele's opinion is that, "Beatty proved himself to be not only a poor fleet commander but a thoroughly ignoble man for his efforts to escape accountability for his actions".

What are we to make of some of the other examples of poor leadership and worse? Gideon J. Pillow was a lawyer with political ambitions, and, despite a lack of military qualifications, was appointed Adjutant General of the Tennessee state militia in 1833. He returned to his law practice in 1836. He appears to have been someone who knew how to cultivate the right people, including the future President, James K. Polk. When the United States invaded Mexico in 1846, Pillow was with the army and had the rank of Brigadier General, thanks to Polk's influence. His incompetence was noted by other officers, one of whom remarked that Pillow's command capability was "one of the smallest capacity that has ever been elevated to so high a command". During one battle Pillow was found to be "more than a mile and a half away from his troops", and it was suggested he rejoin his regiment. Later the same day he reported to headquarters and said that he'd been unable to find it.

Pillow's activities with the Confederate army during the Civil War didn't improve his standing among officers on either side. He was shunted to recruiting duties, the authorities having realised that it was best not to have him around when there was any fighting to be done. Robert P.Wettemann sums him up in these words : "Gideon Pillow was the nadir of a martial system that valued personal ambition, party loyalty and the supposed innate martial abilities of the American citizen over military professionalism, general knowledge of military art and science, and the ability to inspire and lead men into battle".

Or there was the leader, of whom it is said: "In a conflict notorious for failed generalship, Austro-Hungarian Field Marshall Franz Conrad von Hotzendorf repeatedly demonstrated that he was the worst of a bad lot during the First World War". Admired for his theoretical views as an "innovative tactical thinker", he often advocated war against just about every other nation in Europe. When war did arrive in 1914 he showed little real talent for it and "habitually disregarded such crucial factors as proper force ratios, sufficient firepower, terrain, weather, logistics, intelligence, unit training and troop morale".

I've only managed to pick out a few from the fifteen selected to represent the worst military leaders in history, and there are others I could have held up for examination. General Nogi Maresuke was a "semi-forgotten pensioner living in quiet retirement" who was brought back when the Russo-Japanese War started in 1904. His problem was that he tended to look down on technology and "engaged in full frontal assaults because he saw no other way". In one engagement his losses amounted to eighteen thousand, around one-third of his total force. Japan did win the war, but at a cost. And General Antonio Lopez de Santa Anna, victor at the famed siege of the Alamo, managed to lose what later became Texas when his confidence in his military skills, and his contempt for the rag-tag-and-bobtail Texan army, led to his defeat at the Battle of San Jacinto. It lasted just eighteen minutes. It was siesta time and he and his troops had been caught napping.

The Worst Military Leaders in History is not definitive, and I'm sure a different group of failed leaders could easily be assembled to illustrate how wrong they were. It's difficult to decide if any one characteristic was common to them all, but arrogance, a refusal to accept that they might not be right, could stand out. "You do the scouting, I'll do the fighting" was what Custer is alleged to have said in response to one of his scouts attempting to alert him to the dangers of dividing his command when he had no information about the number of Indians he would be facing. His men died because he was certain that he knew best.

THE WORST MILITARY LEADERS IN HISTORY
Edited by John M. Jennings and Chuck Steele
Reaktion Books. 337 pages. £16.99. ISBN 978-1-78914-583-0

BRITISH ARMY OF THE RHINE : THE BAOR 1945-1993

I'll declare an interest before I start to write about this book. In September 1954, as a young, short-term regular soldier – I'd volunteered for three years instead of waiting to be called up for the standard two years National Service – I was sent to Germany, where I served until March 1957. I can't claim to have done anything of importance and was just one of many who spent time in Germany in the 1950s.

Paul Chrystal's short, but informative survey of BAOR and its role in the Cold War doesn't attempt to do more than provide a sketchy account of what life was like for the average soldier (and his wife and family, where relevant) and is angled more to showing how the army was designed to be a part of NATO strategy to confront the forces the Soviet Union could assemble if war broke out In Europe.

The British Army was one of several which, at the end of the Second World War, occupied Germany. The country was then split into four zones under the control of the French, American, Russian, and British occupying forces. The British Zone was in the North and spread roughly from just below Bonn to beyond Hamburg, back to Holland and Belgium, and had the longest border facing the Soviet Zone. It was obvious that the number of British troops needing to be stationed long-term in Germany would require conscription to continue, not to mention the huge expense involved in supporting thousands of troops, the establishments and equipment they required, and in some cases their families.

I've often wondered how many young men like myself spent time in Germany in the 1950s? It was a fairly commonplace experience, and if I was in uniform when home on leave I'd sometimes be approached by strangers who'd recognised the divisional flashes on my sleeves, told me where they had been, and wanted to know where I was stationed. Chrystal says there were 129 different locations where British soldiers were based. I spent time in three of them – Mönchengladbach (Rhine Workshops), Bielefeld (REME light aid detachment with 106 Company RASC) and Lippstadt (2nd Armoured Workshop) – working mostly as a clerk and occasional storeman. At one location I was the unit postman which meant going into the town each day with a German driver to collect and distribute the mail. I liked that job. It gave me opportunities to look in the local record shops while I waited for the mail to be sorted.

But I'm lapsing into personal reminiscences, and Chrystal's survey has a much more serious purpose. He provides a great deal of information about armaments and equipment which will surely fascinate those with an interest in such matters. I had the impression from his comments that, faced with a large Russian presence in East Germany, backed by a strong East German Army and others from Iron Curtain countries, BAOR's role in the event of a war actually breaking out would be to fight a kind of holding action "to buy time for NATO'S political leaders to negotiate a peaceful end to the crisis without resort to the use of nuclear weapons". I can't say I had any awareness of overall tactics at the time. What does an eighteen year-old know? And Crystal makes the point that "it is unlikely that many troops or their dependents spend that much time agonising over their potentially precarious location". One just got on with the daily routines and looked forward to going to the NAAFI or the local pubs later.

Chrystal looks into the question of the army's relations with the local public. Obviously, in the early days, soldiers were seen as foreigners occupying a defeated nation and a degree of resentment was only to be expected. Likewise, soldiers were naturally suspicious of civilians who had supported a regime of such terrifying proportions as the Nazis. Initially, any kind of fraternisation was frowned on, and intense efforts were made to investigate the past activities of many officials. But it soon became impractical to get things like local government functioning again without the co-operation of people who had been involved with such matters under the Nazis. It seems that ninety percent of all lawyers, for example, had been members of the Nazi Party.

Chrystal also points out that, in a race to grab the best brains, "ex-Nazi scientists and engineers from major (ex-Nazi) industrial firms….found their way to the US and Russia…….the slave labour of tens of thousands, the toxic gases they had employed in concentration camps, the tanks they churned out for use against the allies were all quietly forgotten in the name of scientific progress".

Once the army had settled in, and certainly by the time I arrived in 1954, military installations employed numerous local people in a variety of occupations. There were drivers, mechanics, administrative staff, and many others. And the presence of British soldiers in towns and cities was generally accepted by most people. There were moments of friction, often caused by the activities of soldiers. Putting young men together and giving them easy access to alcohol inevitably leads to noisy, disruptive and sometimes violent behaviour.

But on an individual level it was often possible to have conversations with individuals without problems arising. I was reminded of one encounter in a bar with a man who had served with the Wehrmacht and told me that Britain should have fought alongside Germany and against Russia. Chrystal refers to SS General Karl Wolff "who was guaranteed immunity at the Nuremberg Trials by the Office of Strategic Services (OSS) and later CIA Director Allen Dulles when they met In March 1945. The US was considering enlisting Wolff and his forces to help implement "Operation Unthinkable", basically a secret plan for victorious US and defeated Germany to invade the

Soviet Union, a plan which Winston Churchill advocated". Chrystal says that information about the plan only came to light in 1998 when documents were declassified. The Russians possibly knew about it thanks to the activities of the spy, Guy Burgess.

I suppose a basic anti-German feeling may have levelled off somewhat after 1970 or so. Conscription had ended in 1960, and an eighteen year-old joining the army in, say, 1978 would have been born in 1960, and entered a whole different social world than someone born in 1938. Memories of the war, and the experiences of their fathers and other relatives would have changed a great deal. But Chrystal makes reference to "the innate British xenophobia and insistence on monolingualism, the stereotypical German portrayed as a goosestepping thug in British media and culture" as difficulties that could affect relations between soldiers (bored, and "animated by alcohol") and civilians. It sometimes occurs to me that, in many ways, the British even now seem obsessed with the Second World War. A friend of mine said that he always knows when it's Christmas because of the number of war films being shown on British TV.

On the subject of "boredom" affecting soldiers' behaviour, it always struck me that, outside of a few main centres, little was done to provide cultural and social activities. Even sports facilities seemed fairly sparse on the ground in many places. And, in fact, the overall impulse of officers was to try to force conventional taste and habits on other ranks. Books I had in my locker were looked at askance during inspections. And I recall being stopped from going to a jazz concert in Düsseldorf. "I'd have let you go if it had been classical music", the officer told me with a smirk on his face. Perhaps I was just unlucky? On the other hand, I always had a feeling that I was sometimes isolated for stepping out of line at any level. Most of the time I practised blending in. It made life easier.

Chrystal includes a chapter on Berlin, though strictly speaking it wasn't part of BAOR. I only ever got to the city twenty or so years after my army service ended, but the Wall was still there and seeing how it divided the streets made me realise what a shocking thing it was. A friend served in Berlin in the 1950s and married a German girl. I'm also reminded of another friend who had been in an armoured car patrolling along the then mostly unmarked country border between the British and Russian Zones. The driver made a mistake and they found themselves surrounded by Russian troops.

They were held for a few days while the appropriate protocols were followed and they were handed over to the British authorities. He said they weren't badly treated, though the Russians relieved them of all their cigarettes.

I have never regretted my time in the British Army, and the two-and-a-half years I spent in Germany, though I couldn't see myself making a career as a soldier. When I've been asked which university I went to, now that so many people assume that if you enjoy reading books you must have been to university, I like to say BAOR. And it's true, it was my university. I was in a different country, I met different people, I heard a different language. And there were practical reasons for enjoying being in Germany. The German music shops stocked American jazz records I couldn't obtain in Britain, and the bookshops, even in relatively small towns, often had a section of American paperbacks. The selections were much more adventurous than those in the NAAFI or other military-related retail outlets which never seemed to carry much of interest. And I always turned my small radio to the American Forces Network (AFN) and mostly ignored the British Forces Network (BFN) where the programmes seemed dull and the music pretty dire. On AFN I could catch a range of sounds, from jazz to country-and-western. So, yes, BAOR was very much my university.

I realise that, despite not intending to, I have made this into a subjective review by bringing In my own experiences and interests. It was difficult not to. So many of the names Chrystal mentions brought back memories. He highlights Soest a couple of times, and my thoughts returned to 1956 or so and sitting on a bench with my German girlfriend, waiting for a rail connection. Some years later, in 1962, the first poem I ever had published ended with the lines: "At Soest,/ The Dutch/ Were loading a train/ With tanks/ In the rain".

Leaving aside my own personal response to this book, I have to say that it is packed with information about the Cold War and the BAOR. Anyone wanting to know about either subject could learn a great deal from It. There are relevant illustrations, including maps, and a useful bibliography.

BRITISH ARMY OF THE RHINE : THE BAOR 1945-1993
By Paul Chrystal
Pen & Sword Books. 128 pages. £14.99. ISBN 978-1-526728-53-1

CLEM BECKETT : MOTORCYCLE LEGEND AND WAR HERO

In 2016 I went to Oldham to see a play called *Dare Devil Rides to Jarama*. A small theatre production with minimum props and two actors, it told the story of Clem Beckett, a one-time star of the speedway circuit of the 1920s and early-1930s who died fighting with the International Brigades in Spain. It was a lively evening with something of the spirit of an old-style agit-prop performance.

So who was Clem Beckett? He was born in 1906 in Saddleworth, "an anomalous amalgam of Yorkshire villages left on the doorstep of the Lancashire town of Oldham". Like many young people in those days he quit school early, "starting work as a 'half-timer' with Platt Brothers, Oldham's leading textile engineers". Rob Hargreaves says that Oldham at the end of the nineteenth century was "the most productive cotton-spinning centre in the world". But Beckett soon moved on from Platt Brothers and became an apprentice blacksmith. It's suggested that he was keen to work with horses, hence his decision to opt for employment as a blacksmith.

Horses may have been important to him, but it's perhaps an indication of their declining relevance as various forms of road transport developed that Beckett, at the age of fourteen, was already interested in motor-cycles. A self-taught mechanic he was known as "Daredevil Beckett" and had a reputation as a "tough guy". When he was eighteen he joined the Young Communist League (YCL) after being politicised by a socialist farrier he worked with. He also joined the Territorial Army (TA) and so gained an awareness of weapons that became useful years later. It's difficult to know how long he remained in the TA, or how active he was with the YCL, but both involvements no doubt widened his field of experience beyond that of many working-class males of his age.

The 1920s saw the rise of "speedway riding" or "dirt track racing" as a spectator sport that could appeal to big audiences. And it provided opportunities for young men, most of them from backgrounds similar to Beckett's, to live a little dangerously, earn some money, and possibly attract attention as star performers. Beckett's own initial appearance took place at Audenshaw Race Course in May, 1928, riding a home-made machine. The event attracted ten thousand spectators.

Hargreaves does a good job in showing how quickly race tracks opened up around the country. There were fifty stadiums by the end of 1928, twenty of them in the Manchester area. One of the main ones was, of course, Belle Vue. With the rise of interest in dirt track racing and the opening of new venues came the advent of the Auto-Cycle Union (ACU), an organisation that functioned rather like the Royal Automobile Club (RAC) and primarily represented the concerns of conservative-minded members and officials. They regulated the activities of motor-cycling enthusiasts who took part in competitions of an amateur nature, and were consequently disturbed by the fact that speedway racing brought in professional (or semiprofessional) riders who were keen to be paid for putting on performances that included lots of thrills and spills.

There was also an organisation called International Speedways (ISL) which had a power-base in three London stadiums and aimed to extend it beyond them. Hargreaves says that "the growing commercialisation of speedway by ISL would soon mean that it controlled riders' remuneration and other matters such as transfers between stadiums, just as automatically as the Football Association was able to control the pay and conditions of professional footballers". The fact that Clem Beckett and others were responsible for organising the Dirt Track Riders Association (DTRA), a quasi-trade union which would fight for better pay and conditions for riders, soon put him at odds with the ISL and the ACU.

In the meantime Beckett's fame was spreading. He visited Denmark and Sweden in 1929, and also made trips to Turkey, Romania and Bulgaria. He had direct experiences of the rise of Fascism when he took speedway to Germany. And he spent time in Marseilles. At home he mixed with the "Cheshire Set, taking flying lessons and enjoying speedboat racing on the Cheshire lakes (or meres)". He also attracted a number of young ladies, though doesn't appear to have taken any one of them too seriously. What Communist Party officials thought of his activities, if they knew about them, isn't documented.

By the early 1930s the effects of the Depression were being felt around the country, but especially in the North. Attendances at speedway events declined and tracks began to close. If people had money to spare they preferred to spend it on football matches, which had always been speedway's main competition in terms of holding the loyalty of working-class spectators. In an effort to continue attracting the attention of audiences some riders, including Beckett, turned to the Wall of Death.

"Motorcycle riders defying gravity by hurtling horizontally round a wooden bowl" had no sporting angle to it. Hargreaves describes it as "sheer entertainment, more of a fairground attraction". He might have added that, from the spectators' point of view, there was probably a voyeuristic aspect involved as they waited for a rider to come a cropper. The dangers inherent in such an activity were obvious, especially as riders attempted to distinguish their performances by "a variety of stunts and gimmicks". A photograph in the book shows Beckett with his arms outstretched as his machine nears the top of the bowl and spectators look down impassively. More than one rider, including Beckett, sustained injuries when things went wrong and they fell.

The decline in interest in dirt-track racing, together with the numerous injuries he had suffered, were not the only reasons for Beckett having to look for other sources of income. He wrote articles for *The Daily Worker*, the Communist Party newspaper, about the state of speedway racing and the exploitation of the riders by "promoters" and the "sport's administrators". The main focus of his attack was the ACU, and it represented, in Griffith's words, "a professional suicide note". Beckett found himself blacklisted from appearing at ACU-registered tracks.

The Depression had hit the North badly, but there were areas of the country which were booming. Beckett and a friend headed south and obtained jobs in the Ford factory at Dagenham. His employment there didn't last too long. Not accustomed to working to the timed conditions of a production line, nor to the controls asserted over workers' behaviour, Beckett soon tangled with a foreman and was dismissed. Drifting back North he opened a motor-cycle sales and repair shop. I'm compressing his activities and the early Thirties saw him visiting Russia and taking part in the famous Kinder Scout mass trespass. It was largely a Communist Party-organised event, though involving many non-communists, and the policed targeted and arrested known local communists like Benny Rothman. But Beckett wasn't among them.

In 1934 he was in Denmark and it's hinted that he may have been acting as a Party courier, carrying messages and cash through intermediaries either to or from Russia. He also developed a relationship with a Danish woman called Lida who is described as "mysterious" and was a Communist and most likely a courier for the Party. Beckett married her and she came to live with him "over the shop" in Miles Platting. Hargreaves, noting that "From the accession of Hitler to the German Chancellorship after 1933, it would have been too dangerous for messages between King Street (Communist Party HQ in Britain) and Russia to go through Northern Germany. The route through Denmark would be all the more vital", Beckett and Lida made several visits there in 1935 and 1936.

When the Spanish Civil War started in July, 1936, and the call went out for Communist Parties in various countries to raise volunteers to fight for the Republic, Beckett was one of the first to enlist in the International Brigades. The general situation was that Franco and his Nationalist fellow-conspirators had the advantage of leading an army which included the Spanish Foreign Legion and regiments of Moorish troops. And although a Non-Intervention policy had supposedly been agreed to by most countries, Hitler and Mussolini supplied men and equipment to the Nationalists. The only countries willing to provide the Republican government with arms were Mexico and Russia. Little of quantity or quality came from Mexico, and the Republicans paid heavily, in more ways than one, for what they received from Russia.

Beckett headed to Spain in late-October, 1936, ostensibly as part of a British Medical Aid convoy. It was while this was being prepared in London that he met and became friends with Christopher Caudwell (Christopher St John Sprigg), a Marxist writer, literary critic, and intellectual. Hargreaves suggests that their friendship was perhaps not as incongruous as it seems. Beckett's range of experiences travelling throughout Britain and Europe may have set him apart from many of the British working-class volunteers in Spain.

His time with the British battalion of the Fifteenth International Brigade was not without incident, and at one point he was arrested and accused of "disaffection". Hargreaves says that it was probably because of his "general irreverence towards the political commissars and Party propaganda…..It was as natural for straight-talking Clem to criticise battalion command as it was to ridicule the 'old-fogeys' of the Auto-Cycle Union". And, as his encounter with an overbearing foreman at Dagenham had demonstrated, he wasn't likely to take kindly to petty rules and regulations. The charges against him were soon dropped and he returned to his unit.

When the British battalion moved towards Jarama in February, 1937, Beckett and Caudwell were in charge of a French Chauchat machine-gun, a left-over from the First World War. At some stage during the battle they were providing covering fire for troops who had been ordered to withdraw, and found themselves isolated. They both died when their position was over-run by Moorish infantry. Hargreaves provides a more-detailed account of what happened and also notes that their bodies were never recovered.

The Party promptly hailed them as heroes, and claimed that Beckett had written to his wife to say, "I am sure you'll realise that I should never have been satisfied had I not assisted". Her account was that his last words to her were "So long, kid, don't worry", which sounds more like what "Daredevil Beckett" might have said in the circumstances.

Writers and academics still argue about what happened in Spain during the Civil War, and no-one who has read about it in histories and memoirs would want to deny that many mistakes were made, and that the motives of some of those supporting the Republic were not always pure and simple. But I've always thought that the majority of the volunteers in the International Brigades deserved the high praise given to them.

Rob Hargreaves has written a detailed and lively account of Clem Beckett's life and activities. His participation in the Spanish Civil War was only one relatively small, but significant part of it. Hargreaves supplies a great deal of information about his involvement in dirt-track racing, along with informative portraits of some of his co-riders, their backgrounds in the social conditions of the 1930s, and much more. His book has a great deal to offer in terms of its broad range.

CLEM BECKETT : MOTORCYCLE LEGEND AND WAR HERO
By Rob Hargreaves
Pen & Sword Books. 239 pages. £25. ISBN 978-1-39909-842-7

WRITING IN THE DARK : BLOOMSBURY, THE BLITZ, AND HORIZON MAGAZINE

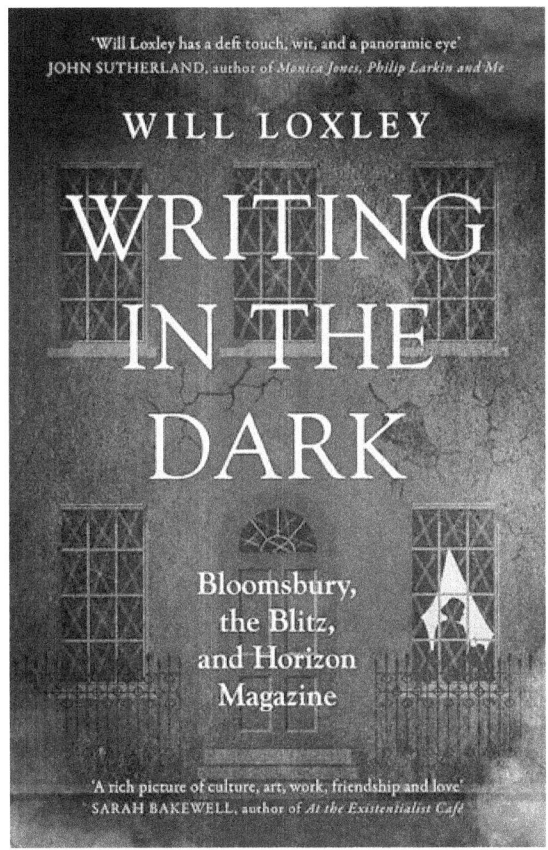

There is something about the period covered by this book – roughly 1939-45, give or take a little bit on either side – that continues to intrigue. Is it because it was a time when the threat of death or serious injuries seemed possible, so living was more intense? Or is it because the people who were then active in the literary world appear to have been, in some ways, more talented and courageous than we are? It's difficult to imagine that going to work in an office or factory in the morning might mean returning home in the evening to find the place where we lived no longer in existence. And, of course, there was always the threat of conscription hanging over the heads of those eligible to serve in the armed forces. Some people didn't wait to be called up and volunteered, others went when summoned, perhaps not always willingly but with a broad feeling that wearing a uniform was an unfortunate necessity.

Certain people managed to find ways to serve without having to don khaki or whatever. They worked for government departments, such as the Ministry of Information, producing material to boost national morale. A few found ways around conscription by faking illnesses. Will Loxley tells the tale of Dylan Thomas deliberately drinking himself into a state where his appearance before the draft board would show him as unfit for service. It can be seen as a not very noble act, but I doubt that he would have made a useful soldier in any case. Julian Maclaren-Ross did have a brief army stint, but was soon discharged on medical grounds. Some of his short stories record the experience of life in a barrack-room in his usual laid-back manner.

And then there were Auden and Isherwood who decided before hostilities got under way that life in the United States would suit them better. Oxley discusses their roles in the literature of the 1930s and the impact their leaving Britain had on the literary left-wing of the time. From Loxley's account, both were experiencing a feeling of dissatisfaction with the "Popular Front, the party line, the anti-Fascist struggle". Or were they just bored and had never truly been all that committed? For many people, not necessarily always from the left, it was an act of betrayal, especially so where Auden was concerned. Loxley seems to come down harder on him than on Isherwood, and his account of the poet passing through London in an American Army officer's uniform at the end of the war, and extolling the virtues of life in the United States, has a slightly disapproving, if understandable ring to it.

Writing in the Dark isn't concerned to tell us what life was like in uniform. As its title indicates it mostly revolves round the denizens of Bloomsbury, their literary activities, and their experiences of the Blitz. Virginia and Leonard Woolf, and their Hogarth Press, clearly have a part to play in the narrative, and so does John Lehman. Although at one time deeply involved with the running of the Hogarth Press, Lehman eventually fell out with Leonard Woolf. He was soon to become editor of *Penguin New Writing* which proved popular and easily outsold *Horizon*. To be fair, the aims of the two magazines differed. In simple terms, *Penguin New Writing* considered itself very much of its time in that it printed a wide range of material from a wide range of contributors and reflected life in the forces and the factories. It would be wrong to suggest that it only used such material, however, and its contents were varied.

Horizon, on the other hand, was designed more to sustain an air of cultural independence. It looked back to past periods to summon up a tone of intellectual seriousness that, it seemed, needed to be cultivated in the dark days of the War. It would have been hard to imagine *Penguin New Writing* publishing Enid Starkie's two-part essay about "Eccentrics of Eighteen-Thirty", which *Horizon* did in May and June, 1944. But would John Hampson's "Movements in the Underground" have appeared in Cyril Connolly's magazine? It was published by Lehman in the Spring and Summer 1946 issues of *Penguin New Writing*. It's doubtful if many of the writers referred to by Hampson would have been of great interest to Connolly. To add a personal note, I was delighted when, visiting second-hand bookshops, I picked up somewhat worn but readable copies of the issues of *Horizon* with the Starkie essay. It is entertaining and informative.

Stephen Spender appeared in both magazines and receives much more than a passing mention in *Writing in the Dark*. Described by Loxley as "the poster boy of the movement of British intellectuals against fascism", he seemed to be everywhere in literary London. He had something of a colourful personal life, too, with "sexual adventures" with both men and women. I can recall a conversation with an old poet and communist who had been around in the 1930s when one of Spender's male companions ran off to join the International Brigades in Spain. He was quite scathing about Spender's own reasons for going to Spain – "in pursuit of his boyfriend" – but Loxley says that he felt guilty for having persuaded the man in question that communism was beneficial and Franco had to be defeated. He is, in fact, largely sympathetic to Spender during the wartime years, and acknowledges that, as opposed to Auden and Isherwood, he'd stayed in England, and served in the Auxiliary Fire Service during the Blitz.

It's fascinating to read about Cyril Connolly and what might on the surface seem his haphazard way of editing *Horizon*. As was made clear in D.J. Taylor's *Lost Girls: Love, War and Literature 1939-59*

(Constable, 2019), much of the work essential to keep the magazine appearing regularly in difficult circumstances was done by various women who, for one reason or another, found Connolly attractive and interesting. It might be difficult now to understand why that was so, though it could be that he overwhelmed them with his intellectual capabilities. He was better-educated than they were, and presumably had some sort of charisma to persuade them that he was worthy of their admiration. But reading about his general behaviour during the war years doesn't make him out to be an endearing character.

The impression is that he was selfish and almost viewed the war as a personal affront to his needs and interests. Loxley has a pointed comment to make about how Connolly probably saw the general situation with regard to what he looked to for inspiration: "Literature was in fact becoming more democratic but less important". The success of *Penguin New Writing*, and of another similar pocket-paperback magazine, Reginald Moore's *Modern Reading*, indicates how a democratic spirit prevailed both in the contents and distribution. And was literature "less important" because of that fact? Connolly's elitist (some would say) opinion may not have been the right one.

Having said that, I have to admit to thinking that he made a major contribution to asserting the need to maintain a belief in a civilised way of living and appreciating art and literature. I have a copy of *The Golden Horizon* (Weidenfeld & Nicolson, 1953), an anthology edited by Connolly from the magazine, and it shows how much excellent writing appeared in *Horizon.* And that, whatever Connolly's own feelings about the war may have been, he didn't overlook the way in which writers were responding to it. A line like "Sweet the grey morning, and the raiders gone", from a short poem by E.J. Scovell, captures the sense of relief at having survived one more night that must have been a common experience at the time.

The atmosphere during the Blitz Is well-evoked by Loxley, as is the later phase when "flying bombs" began to hit London in 1944. That it was possible to hear them approaching, and then the motors cutting out so they could fall, meant that apprehension became a part of daily life: "The fact that the doodlebugs were coming over at all hours of the day meant that not only sleep but also work, meetings and parties were now constantly being interrupted". Loxley quotes an anecdote about a poetry reading involving Edith Sitwell and her brothers,

Osbert and Sacheverell. She was reading as the sound of an approaching doodlebug became obvious: "Only once, between a line or stanza break, did her eyes lift to the ceiling, before continuing to read at greater volume". John Lehman recalled that it was a "magnificent performance", and Loxley adds that "The implication, as everyone in the audience felt at the time, was that poetry was more important than all the terrors that Hitler could launch against them". I can't help wondering if Cyril Connolly was present at the reading?

Anecdotes often illustrate a time and place better than detailed descriptions, and more than one of the personalities who appear in *Writing in the Dark* can provide material for them. Dylan Thomas is an obvious example, and his behaviour was usually guaranteed to upset many people. But the story that made me smile is the one about Thomas's reaction when Julian Maclaren-Ross suggested keeping a bottle in the office where they both worked so they could have a pick-me-up for the inevitable mornings-after both often suffered from. Thomas, it seems, was shocked at the idea of drinking in the office.

Loxley, incidentally, has a short, but interesting discussion about whether or not Thomas can accurately described as a "war poet". He comes to the conclusion that, although he may not have been in uniform, and perhaps gave the impression that he wasn't much involved in the "war effort", he did produce poems about what was happening. Looking back, Connolly included "Deaths and Entrances" and "A Refusal to Mourn the Death, by Fire, of a Child in London" in *The Golden Horizon* anthology.

When Paris was liberated Philip Toynbee wrote an article for the November 1944 issue of *Horizon* in which he said: "I know that praise of France at the expense of England is a greatly hated activity, but after sixteen days in this astonishing Paris of September 1944 it is an activity which cannot honestly be avoided……..the galleries are opening. The bookshops are anything but bare, the people are a thousand times more alive than London people". He doesn't seem to have offered an explanation of why Parisians were "more alive". Was it simply the joy they felt at being liberated, whereas in September 1944 Londoners were still being bombed and it would be several more months before the war ended? There probably isn't a single reason for the difference.

Loxley doesn't take his account much beyond the end of the war. *Horizon* continued for a few more years, and it was significant that its large October 1947 issue featured American writers and critics. It was a sign of the increasing importance and influence of American literature. But 1950 saw the magazine calling it a day, as did *Penguin New Writing* with its 50th number. The boom years for little magazines were over as the realities of peace-time brought worries about work, housing, families, and other concerns. The late-1940s and into the early-1950s were years of austerity and there was little spare money to spend on producing or buying literary publications. And many of the writers who had written a few poems or a story or two in response to their experiences no longer felt the need, or had the time, to write when they returned to civilian life.

It may seem that Will Loxley has covered some familiar ground in *Writing in the Dark* as he works his way through the lives and wartime writings of Cyril Connolly, Stephen Spender, George Orwell, Virginia Woolf, Dylan Thomas and other well-known names, with asides about the lesser-known, like William Sansom, whose stories of firefighting in London are worth reading, and George Garrett, a now-forgotten working-class writer from Liverpool. But he's managed to bring it all together in a very assured and readable manner. He quite successfully evokes the atmosphere of wartime London with its ever-present threat of death or injury and its effects on the literary scene. There are ample notes and recommendations for further reading.

WRITING IN THE DARK : BLOOMSBURY, THE BLITZ, AND HORIZON MAGAZINE
By Will Loxley
Weidenfeld & Nicolson. 388 pages. £25. ISBN 978-1-4746-1570-9

NOTHING TO LOSE BUT OUR CHAINS : WORK & RESISTANCE IN TWENTY-FIRST-CENTURY BRITAIN

These are not good times for trade unions, nor for the majority of workers by hand or brain. Union membership is low when compared to earlier years, and is mostly concentrated in mass terms in areas such as the National Health Service, local government, and similar bodies. But even there the practice of contracting out services has meant that agency workers and the like are often not organised in unions. And changes in what Jane Hardy refers to as "the economic structure of Britain" have resulted in a decline in industries requiring large numbers of people and which were once central to the role of unions in representing the interests of at least a substantial part of those in employment. And they often also set the pace for improvements in the working conditions of many of those who didn't belong to a union.

Hardy points out that "traditional areas of the economy have been replaced by innovative forms of production and changing ways of consuming". This may have been beneficial in some ways for certain employees, but it has also brought about the creation of what is referred to as the "precariat" who "experience unstable work and Zero Hours Contracts (ZHCs)". These are people often employed in what is known as "the hospitality sector" (pubs, clubs, restaurants, etc.) but also cleaning, deliveries, home care, and any situation, in fact, where there are few, if any, guarantees of regular hours and long-term conditions of employment such as sickness and holiday pay, and pensions. There is evidence that even in a middle-class occupation such as university education there is a growing body of part-time lecturers with few assurances of any forms of permanent work and a steady income.

It's true to say that there is little or nothing new about the "casualization" and "on-call" arrangements in the labour market. My father had served twelve years in the Royal Navy and when he returned to civilian life in 1925 he worked at a variety of jobs, including as a steeplejack, docker, labourer, and more. He could tell tales of lining up outside the dock gates, hoping to be chosen for a day's work, and of working all night on a railway bridge in the pouring rain with nothing in the form of protective clothing and no health and safety precautions. To question the conditions was to invite the response that "There are a hundred others waiting to take the job if you don't want it". During the dark days of the Depression he would walk miles in search of any kind of work. It was thanks to the onset of war in 1939 that he obtained a regular job when, too old for military service, he was directed to work in a factory.

The difficulties of organising workers in the "gig" economy will be obvious. And it's open to question whether or not the established unions have been, and perhaps still are, unwilling to take on the role of persuading people that it could be in their own best interests to join a union. If there is a large concentration of workers in a factory or similar location then organising might be relatively easy, even in the face of management intransigence. People may feel that they have skills they ought to be properly paid for. And they may see themselves as having interests (security, pensions, etc.) in common with their work colleagues. So, they will be more susceptible to the notion of joint action through a union. But with groups of workers who often don't have a fixed location (home carers, for example moving from one address to another and rarely encountering fellow-workers for any length of time) it needs imagination and perseverance to persuade them to unite to improve their pay and conditions. Would-be organisers will also be faced with the fact that part-time employees, which many are in the gig economy, may be reluctant to pay union dues. And there is often a high turnover among those employed on part-time or ZHC terms. Someone working in a low-paid agency job in the home care sector may find it more advantageous to stack shelves in a supermarket. A floating work force is difficult to organise from a union point of view.

There is an interesting historical reference when Hardy mentions the IWW (Industrial Workers of the World), formed in 1905 in the United States with the intention of organising workers who were ignored by the established craft unions. The IWW burned brightly for a few years, primarily in America and Australia, and it's relevant to take note of the difficulties the organisation encountered with regard to recruiting and retaining members among transient workers who followed the harvests or moved from job to job for one reason or another.

To be fair, Hardy does indicate that the established unions are slowly waking up to the fact that, if they want to build up a healthy membership, and exert any kind of influence in the workplace, wherever it is, or on the economy, they will need to broaden their tactics and their appeal. She also points to the appearance of certain new unions such as the Independent Workers Union of Great Britain (IWGB) and United Voices of the World (UVW), and that they have had some success in organising among what have sometimes been seen as the unorganisable.

The IWGB union was formed by cleaners breaking away from Unison and Unite who felt "frustrated that their action was being undermined and their participation in union structures sabotaged in their fight for better working conditions at the University of London". There was a feeling that, with Unison in particular, a too-cosy relationship existed between the union leaders and management. My own experiences as a one-time Unison member would incline me to believe that this was probably true. UVW members are "mainly migrant cleaners and workers in other outsourced or low-waged industries and have strong associations with the Latin American community".

The successful campaigns by the IWGB and UVF are not often reported in the press, with the exception of the *Morning Star*. They are admittedly mostly small-scale and don't have the impact that industrial action by railwaymen or local government employees can have when their strikes affect day-to-day life for a large proportion of the general public. But they do demonstrate that workers can fight back against low wages and poor working conditions. I've recently read of inroads made into supposed anti-union establishments like Starbucks and Amazon in the USA. I'm not sure what the situation is in the UK with regard to those employers, but one hopes that if they don't currently recognise and negotiate with unions then they soon will. Hardy refers to the notorious example of Sports Direct and the struggle to organise there. Those trying to recruit members were faced with a hostile management, and a less-than enthusiastic response from the well-established Unite union. It was reported that some officials had been overheard saying that recruiting at Sports Direct "was more trouble than it was worth".

The impact of the current conditions in the labour market ought to arouse a sympathetic response from those, like myself, who spent most of our working lives in relatively benign employment circumstances. When I came out of the army in 1957 there seemed sufficient jobs to choose from. I lost the first one after a few months when I was sacked for "industrial misconduct". I was young and after three years hearing officers and sergeants barking orders I wasn't much inclined to listen to more from a bullying section-head. But I easily walked into another job in a couple of weeks and at a higher rate of pay and with less-travelling involved. Later, when I was made redundant from an oil company, I took time off to re-think my life and got along for a few months on the redundancy pay and the dole. Benefits were better then and easier to come by.

And when I quite easily found employment again I opted to work part-time in a low-grade administrative job in local government and do some part-time teaching in adult education (though it wasn't regular or guaranteed in any way) which, along with earnings from free-lance writing, provided enough to live on. The point I'm making is that, even if my income was somewhat up-and-down at times, personal circumstances, and a more-flexible economic situation, enabled me to choose to get by in this way. The precariats now don't have many choices. They take low-paid, insecure and sometimes temporary jobs because they have to. And to "get by" doesn't mean to live cheerfully and satisfactorily in a modest, but intellectually fulfilling way, but to worry from week-to-week about paying the bills and eating or heating.

Speaking from a personal perspective I'm convinced that more than a few members of the current government, along with many employers, are happy to have this situation continue. It's a handy way of ensuring that a workforce worried about sliding into the abyss of the precarious will inevitably be afraid to venture too near the edge. There will always be doubts about what an employer can do (fire and re-hire, for example) when faced with any demands for improvements in pay and conditions. And those doubts will inhibit action.

Jane Hardy has written a thoroughly informative and in many ways inspiring book. She gives numerous examples of the ways in which groups of workers have come together to fight back. Sometimes their actions have been spontaneous, sometimes they've been organised through a union. It always made sense to me to join a union, even if I never called on its support, no matter whether I was working full or part-time. She also has a great deal to offer in terms of outlining general economic conditions and the prospects for unions. The UK has some of the most-restrictive legal barriers to industrial action in Europe. These, combined with the precarious nature of many sources of employment, might explain both the poor level of union membership and the relatively low activity in terms of industrial action taken to obtain better pay and conditions. But that struggle does go on, as Jane Hardy clearly indicates in her very readable and well-researched book.

NOTHING TO LOSE BUT OUR CHAINS : WORK & RESISTANCE IN TWENTY-FIRST-CENTURY BRITAIN

By Jane Hardy

Pluto Press. 248 pages. £19.99. ISBN 978-0-7453-4104-0

1922 : SCENES FROM A TURBULENT YEAR

Nick Rennison describes the 1920s as having a "distinctive character". It is said to have been the "Jazz Age", the "Roaring Twenties", a time when the stock market boomed, lots of people thought they could make money quickly, and there was a determination to party and have a good time. I'm not sure it was that way for everyone. To point to just three contrasting factors - there was plenty of poverty around, in Britain there was a General Strike which bitterly divided the nation, and civil unrest, of one sort or another, occurred in various countries. But I suppose it's like the so-called "Swinging Sixties" and we choose to pick out certain happenings and events and suggest that they represent the decade when, in fact, there was much more going on that didn't involve pop music, flower power, and summers of love.

But Rennison's brisk survey of 1922, a "turbulent year" in his view, helps to dispel the notion of the Twenties as being all fun and games. He doesn't get far into January when a major snowstorm has hit Washington D.C. in the United States and the weight of the snow on the roof of the Knickerbocker Theatre has caused it to collapse. Almost a hundred people died and many more were injured.

January, 1922 was also when "the second trial of the comedian and film star Roscoe "Fatty" Arbuckle began". It may be significant that the account of how and why he came to be in court takes precedence in terms of space over the death of the explorer Ernest Shackleton, the first performance of Edith Sitwell's *Façade* accompanied by William Walton's music, a successful treatment of diabetes with Insulin, and the Washington tragedy. I'm not criticising Rennison, but it's a fact that we all like a good scandal. And the details of the Arbuckle case certainly provided enough material for the public to gloat over and feel morally outraged by. It involved a wild weekend with hints of an orgy in a hotel room, and the possibility of some odd sexual practices. A young woman died and Arbuckle's glamorous Hollywood career was destroyed, as much by inference than proven hard evidence.

Arbuckle's wasn't the only scandal in 1922, and in Britain in December of that year newspaper readers picked up copies each day to learn how Edith Thompson and her lover Freddy Bywaters had killed her husband. Rennison again devotes ample space to the case. But it's justified because of the way in which the trial brought out "the extraordinary frenzy of righteousness into which elements of the media had whipped themselves". There were doubts about how far Edith Thompson was involved – Bywater always insisted she knew nothing about his intention to kill her husband – and Rennison probably has a point when he suggests that, given the moral climate (or hypocrisy) of the time, she was really hanged for her sin of committing adultery with a younger man.

There may have been sexual scandals at both the start and the end of 1922, but plenty occurred between those dates. What Rennison says is "One of the most significant works of twentieth-century literature" was published in Paris in February. He's referring, of course, to James Joyce's *Ulysses*, a book beloved by professors, at least, who can analyse it in every which way and find allusions on every page. Academic careers have been constructed around it. The story of its creation and publication has been told many times, with the bookseller Sylvia Beach playing a central role, and a key little magazine of the period, *The Little Review*, bringing it to the attention of a limited American readership. There were few readers of the actual book itself at first for the simple reason that it was banned in Britain and the United States. And reactions even among informed readers who somehow got hold of a copy varied wildly. Virginia Woolf wrote disparagingly about it. But other writers and critics were more positive.

Rennison also writes approvingly of "The most influential poem in twentieth-century English literature", meaning T.S. Eliot's *The Waste Land*. It was published in another little magazine, *The Criterion*, in October. Like Joyce's *Ulysses* it immediately attracted extremes of attention. One critic called it "a pompous parade of erudition", and John Squire, editor of the *London Mercury,* said that he was "unable to make head or tail of it". But there was nothing in it that caused it to be banned, and it went into circulation and provided more material for those who like to ponder and even puzzle over what they are reading. I have come across comments to the effect that its influence was not necessarily widely beneficial. Too many other poets wanted to imitate its "parade of erudition" and instead simply left comprehension behind.

If there were battles in the literary world they didn't result in deaths. That wasn't true of the world of industrial relations in America. In June major strikes broke out in the mining and railroad sectors. American labour disputes were often violent affairs and 1922 was no exception to that rule. In Herrin, Illinois, a small mining town, a strike in June led to management bringing in strike breakers and armed guards to protect them. The miners were also armed and, after an exchange of gunfire, which resulted in deaths on both sides, the strike breakers agreed to leave the mine if they were given safe passage out of the district. Once out in the open, however, they were rounded up, marched away, and many of them gunned down or otherwise killed. Rennison says that 23 people died. Around the same time more deaths occurred as railwaymen fought with guards hired by the rail companies to break a strike.

It wasn't only in the United States that violent situations occurred. In Ireland in June a vicious Civil War started as pro and anti-Anglo-Irish Treaty forces battled in Dublin and around the country. If we jump ahead to August Michael Collins, who had been blamed for signing the Treaty, was killed in an ambush by IRA dissidents. And in November the newly-established Irish government tried and executed Erskine Childers, author of the spy novel, *The Riddle of the Sands*, for being in possession of an unlicensed firearm. He had supported the anti-Treaty forces when the Civil War got underway.

It's a relief to turn from the killing for a time and look at sport, and I was delighted to see my old home-town of Preston mentioned on a couple of occasions. In April the last FA Cup Final before they were held at Wembley Stadium took place at Stamford Bridge. The teams involved were Huddersfield Town and Preston North End, and Huddersfield achieved a one-nil victory when the Preston goalkeeper, Jim Mitchell, failed to save a penalty kick by Billy Smith. Mitchell, we're told, "may well have been the only person to appear in both a Cup Final and an international match wearing glasses".

The other Preston reference relates to the Dick, Kerr Ladies Football Club which toured around the United States in September. The team had been formed during the First World War from workers at the Dick, Kerr and Co., munitions factory and achieved some success. Rennison notes that a match they played at Goodison Park on Boxing Day, 1920, attracted 53,000 spectators. But "It was all too much for the men of the Football Association. In December, 1921, they banned women's football matches at their members' grounds". Which is why the Dick, Kerr Ladies played the initial game of an American tour in September. The name was changed to Preston Ladies FC later in the 1920s. Dick, Kerr and Co. was taken over by English Electric after the First World War, but the factory was still sometimes referred to locally by its old name when I worked for English Electric in the early-1960s.

Scott Fitzgerald's collection of short-stories, *Tales of the Jazz Age,* was published in August 1922, and may have been partly responsible for establishing the term as descriptive of the 1920s generally. There's no doubt that jazz firmly established itself then, much to the dismay of social critics who saw it as leading to a widespread moral collapse. Doctors, journalists, and religious leaders lined up to point to its dangers, with the *Ladies Home Journal* launching an anti-jazz crusade and calling for its "legal prohibition". But, as Rennison makes clear, "Jazz was not intended for middle-class matrons and septuagenarians. It was the music of the post-war younger generation and they lapped it up".

Some of the future stars of the music – Louis Armstrong, Kid Ory, Sidney Bechet, Fats Waller –were already performing, and the availability of cheap radios and phonograph records meant that they could be heard across America and in other countries. There were, too, efforts to make jazz more respectable by incorporating it into semi-classical settings. White bandleader Paul Whiteman came up with a large orchestra including strings and "A watered-down version of African-American jazz", and, in August, George Gershwin's "jazz opera" *Blue Monday* was staged as part of *George White's Scandals of 1922*. For anyone really interested in jazz they were poor imitations of the genuine stuff.

I've moved around Rennison's book, and by doing so I've tried to give an impression of what it has to offer. Which is, largely, something that is, in his own words, "entertaining and enlightening". But I hope that I've not suggested that it is in any way designed to avoid the disturbing. Racial violence reared its ugly head in May in Kirven, Texas, when a white mob burned alive three blacks who had been accused of murdering a white girl. When they tried to crawl out of the fire onlookers pushed them back in. The mob then went on the rampage and "somewhere between 11 and 23 blacks died", while many others moved away from the area. Across the world in September Turkish troops embarked on an orgy of murdering, raping, and looting in Smyrna, a town in Turkey but with a largely Greek population. The ambitions of politicians in both Greece and Turkey had brought about a war between the two countries. Not much has changed in that line in the past one hundred years.

1922: Scenes From a Turbulent Year is a good book for armchair browsing, and reading about Mussolini's march on Rome in October, and the staging of Bertolt Brecht's first play, *Drums in the Night* in September. It's sad to read about events like those in Texas and Smyrna, but it's amusing to follow the account of the decline of the Dada movement. In May members of the group staged a mock-funeral "at the Bauhaus school in Weimar". There was an inevitability about the death of Dada. It wasn't designed to last for very long and had been a hotbed of rival egos almost from its inception in Zurich in 1916. By 1922 two of the leading egotists, Tristan Tzara and André Breton, were competing in Paris (where else could something like it happen?) for leadership of the so-called avant-garde. Breton came out on top and took his followers into the longer-lasting Surrealism.

1922 : SCENES FROM A TURBULENT YEAR
By Nick Rennison
Oldcastle Books. 255 pages. £12.99. ISBN 978-0-85730-467-4

EILEEN AGAR : ANGEL OF ANARCHY

Leeds Art Gallery, 29th January, 2022 to 7th May, 2022

The role of women in the Surrealist movement has often been underplayed, at least until relatively recently. And there's no getting past the fact that there was a great deal of misogyny among the Surrealists. Women were wives, mistresses, sex objects, but rarely given credit as creators of Surrealist art. And yet major exhibitions, such as *Angels of Anarchy: Women Artists and*

Surrealism at Manchester Art Gallery in late-2009 and early-2010, and *Women Artists and Surrealism* at the Picasso Museum, Málaga, in 2017, have demonstrated how much imaginative work was produced by women functioning within a framework of Surrealism.

Eileen Agar was represented in the exhibitions I've referred to, and the earlier neglect of her work might be explained not only by the fact of her female status, but also perhaps because she was usually identified as a British Surrealist. And for a long time British Surrealism was looked on by critics as mostly being a weak imitation of the real thing that came from the Continent. The British artists were said to be too whimsical and less convincing and unlikely to portray a deeper, darker and more disturbing aspect of Surrealism. An exhibition, *British Surrealism in Context: A Collector's Eye,* at the Abbott Hall Gallery, Kendal, in 2014 certainly demonstrated that whimsy could play a part in some British Surrealist paintings, but it wasn't the whole story.

Eileen Agar was born in Buenos Aires in 1899 to a Scottish businessman father and an American mother. From an early age she was sent to private schools in England, and was encouraged by sympathetic teachers to develop an interest in art. Later, she studied for a time at the Slade, though she expressed dissatisfaction at the teaching and general atmosphere there. By the early-1920s she had experienced a brief, unsuccessful marriage, toured in France and Spain, and met the Hungarian writer Joseph Bard with whom she had a fifty-year relationship. This didn't prevent her from having an intense affair with Paul Nash, and another with the French poet, Paul Éluard. I'm compressing details of Agar's life, and she studied Cubism in Paris and mixed in circles which included Picasso, Ezra Pound, Brancusi, André Breton, and other talented poets and painters.

She also encountered people in what might be called the British avant-garde when Herbert Read and Roland Penrose visited her studio and selected some of her work for the now–famous New Burlington Gallery, *International Surrealist Exhibition* in London in 1936. Agar used to say that she hadn't known she was a Surrealist until Read and Penrose told her she was. And it seems she didn't like the label. Artists and writers often do deny a group identification, preferring to have their work judged on its own merits rather than those of a supposed movement. It's usually critics and art historians who want to place people in neat and tidy categories. But things are much more complicated than that and individuals don't observe boundaries and take what they want from various sources.

Was she a Surrealist? Walking around the Leeds exhibition it's easy to see that elements of what is usually referred to as Surrealism can be located in the paintings, photographs, and other items on display. But she was interested in "found objects" and took pictures of rock formations shaped by accidents of nature, and trees broken and gnarled by the effects of extreme weather conditions. It was the physical appearance of these objects that seemed to intrigue her rather than any deep meaning that may have been attached to them.

Her paintings incorporated elements of Cubism and Surrealism, without falling into any kind of slavish imitation or pattern of prescribed Cubist or Surrealist intentions. And, yes, the whimsical is there and why not? It's noted that Agar had a liking for Lewis Carroll, and I recall the American poet Robert Bly (I think It was) expressing his objection to a British assertion that we didn't really need Surrealism because we have, among other things such as Edward Lear and a long tradition of Gothic novels and ghost stories, the Lewis Carrol books. There may be a case for the whimsical and the idea that the gloomy is not necessarily profound, nor the cheerful shallow.

It's a pleasure to see an exhibition that features a wide range of work produced across a lifetime (she died in 1991) of activity. And to have it backed up by a selection of documents – among them exhibition catalogues and old magazines such as the four issues of *Island,* a publication part-edited by Joseph Bard and to which Agar contributed. A true little magazine it lasted only a short time, but played its part in the artistic ferment of the period. The role of magazines like it should never be under-estimated because they seem slim and fragile and few people saw them at the moment of their appearance. The audience they reached was an informed and important one.

Back to the question – was Aileen Agar a Surrealist? She's in the books and the exhibitions, and that's useful in terms of drawing attention to what she did. But it doesn't really matter. The work, with its vibrant use of colour and subtle suggestions of humour, has its own values and is worth looking at on those grounds.

AMERICANS ABROAD

I'm looking at an anthology, *Americans Abroad*, edited by Peter Neagoe, and published by the Servire Press, The Hague, in 1932. There are fifty-two contributors and all the names one might expect from a book dealing with American writers who spent time in Europe in what Neagoe refers to as the "after-war period" are there: Henry Miller, Ernest Hemingway, Malcolm Cowley, William Carlos Williams, John Dos Passos, E.E. Cummings, Robert McAlmon and others. The histories and memoirs of the expatriate experience provide information about them, and their writings have often been reprinted.

But what intrigues me are the names of those who are no longer remembered, and who haven't had books and scholarly articles written about them. What do we know about Virginia Hersch, Allan Dowling, Muriel Draper, Ruth Jameson, Robert Sage, and Cary Ross? There are notes in the book which indicate what and where they had published prior to its publication. They were young then, so hadn't appeared in print a great deal. And recourse to browsing the Internet, or finding their names on Abe Books, does sometimes indicate that they went on to write novels, short stories, poetry, and other material after their time in Europe. Hersch, for example, wrote several novels, one of which, *To Seize a Dream,* was based on the life of the French artist, Delacroix.

One person who I have been able to track down in some detail is Sherry Mangan, a poet, novelist, journalist, and follower of Leon Trotsky, the exiled Russian revolutionary. Mangan's contribution to *Americans Abroad* is called "Spot Dance" and consists of a series of short sketches which focus on some of the inconsistencies and contradictions of personal relationships. Earlier Mangan had edited a little magazine, *larus: the celestial visitor*, been involved with another publication, *Pagany,* and appeared in various magazines, such as *This Quarter* and *Poetry*.

He had also published a novel. *Cinderella Married or How They Lived Happily Ever After: A Divertissement*, which, according to Professor Alan Wald, reflected his experiences when he was hired as a tutor by a wealthy Boston family. Wald also described it as emulating the work of Ronald Firbank "too closely" in concentrating on "some of the same precious, contrived, bored, and lethargic characters". A short story, "The Coat", published in the *London Mercury* in 1933 can be seen as dealing with people who, while not being wealthy, want to be and are affected by their yearning for money and material goods to the extent that the husband influences his wife into committing adultery with a wealthy admirer who will buy her a fur coat.

Mangan had published poetry, and his 1934 collection, *No Apology for Poetrie*, was described by one critic as "the latest book the intelligentsia like". As a Harvard graduate, and a poet, he associated with R.P. Blackmur, Ezra Pound, William Carlos Williams, Robert Fitzgerald, and others. He was a friend of John Wheelwright, a Boston poet from a wealthy family who had turned radical in politics, and was responsible for introducing Mangan to the ideas of Trotsky. Mangan became a firmly-committed and active Trotskyist, something which may have seemed incompatible with his career between 1938 and 1948 as a journalist for firmly-capitalist publications such as *Time, Life,* and *Fortune*. But travelling in Europe and South America as part of his journalistic duties no doubt gave him an opportunity to maintain contacts with a variety of Trotsky's supporters. It's appropriate to note that when there was a factional fight, and a split in the American Trotskyist group, Mangan followed James P. Cannon rather than Max Shachtman, and helped form the Socialist Workers Party.

In the early-1950s he turned away from direct political activity, though without losing his commitment to the Trotskyist movement, and tried to reconstruct his career as a creative writer. Some of the poems and stories from this period can be found in a small book, *Blackness of a White Night*, published in 1987. What is significant is that, bearing in mind Mangan's involvements, there are few direct political references in the poetry and fiction. A poem, "Activist Miliciano" relates to the Spanish Civil War, and the long story, "Snow", clearly has links to Mangan's own activities as a kind of courier for the international Trotskyist movement. It's set in the post-1945 period when it seemed necessary to reconstitute an organisation, the Fourth International, shattered by the events of the Second World War. Another story, "Blackness of a White Night", is based on an "affair with an intellectual ……in the circle of Hannah Arendt".

A third story, "Reminiscences from a Hilltop", was published in 1957 in the final issue of *Black Mountain Review*, edited by Robert Creeley, and mostly devoted to Black Mountain and Beat writers. It would be interesting to know how Mangan's story came to be alongside them. It is worth noting that "Reminiscences from a Hilltop", and another story from the early Fifties, "A Night in Scranton", are inclined towards fantasy or science-fiction in the way they extend reality into the surreal. And in this connection Mangan had contacts with Surrealists in Paris in the 1930s. It might also be relevant to mention that when the Surrealists broke away from the Communist Party they moved politically towards the Trotskyists.

The 1950s were, on the whole, not a good time for Mangan. They were years when anti-Communism meant that prejudice was rampant against anyone with even the slightest leanings in that direction. . As an active Trotskyist Mangan experienced great difficulty in obtaining work in the field of journalism. What little he published in the way of stories and poems wasn't likely to attract fees of any consequence. And he devoted a lot of time to editing the Trotskyist magazine, *The Fourth International*, which was more a matter of commitment to a cause than a way of earning a living. In addition his health was bad. He moved to Spain and lived in a small village, hoping to be able to live frugally, and then to Rome, where he died in 1961, "alone, destitute, forgotten, not quite fifty-seven years old", to quote Alan Wald.

Sherry Mangan was a minor writer, and a political activist with a small group which perhaps had little or no influence on wider events. But he has always fascinated me because of his dedication to both writing and politics. His family background and education could have enabled him to live differently, but he chose to involve himself with matters that meant he would, out of necessity, exist on the sidelines.

As I said earlier, it's the lesser-known figures in the *Americans Abroad* anthology that intrigue me. I doubt that very few people, apart from a handful of scholars, know or care about Ernest Walsh. He was described by Edward Dahlberg as having "all the fever of a tubercular who knew his days were few", and, although he was a poet, is probably remembered mostly for his brief editorial role with *This Quarter*, a magazine he started with financial assistance from Ethel Moorhead. *This Quarter* is now seen as one of the key publications of the Paris expatriate scene and printed work by Hemingway, James Joyce, William Carlos Williams, Ezra Pound, and Djuna Barnes. Walsh was portrayed in Kay Boyle's novel, *Year Before Last*, a fictionalised account of their affair. He died in 1926. The third issue of *This Quarter*, edited by Ethel Moorhead, was dedicated to Walsh and had a substantial amount of prose and poetry by him.

And there is Wambly Bald. He had a story, "Dreary", in *Americans Abroad* which had previously appeared in *The New Review*, a magazine edited by Samuel Putnam, and was about a couple of lesbians in Paris. Bald had led a colourful life before arriving in the French capital, having wandered around the United States and been a merchant seaman. He obtained a job as a proof reader for the European edition of the *Chicago Tribune*, where he worked alongside Henry Miller and Alfred Perles. He is in Miller's *Tropic of Cancer* under the name, Van Norden. But his main claim to fame is as the man who wrote the lively and informative "La Vie de Bohème" column for the paper between 1929 and 1933. Bald didn't achieve much when he returned to America later in the 1930s. He worked for the Office of War Information during the Second World War, and then seems to have been a freelance writer, living in Greenwich Village and occasionally contributing pieces about his time in Paris to magazines.

Mangan, Walsh, and Bald are just three of the forgotten writers from *American Abroad,* and there are others I could have written about. Emily Holmes Coleman wrote a single novel, *The Shutter of Snow*, and had work in little magazines like *transition* and *Seed*, but published little else due to her fragile mental state, though the novel has been reprinted in recent years. Or there is Emanuel Carnevali, who was published in *This Quarter*. He suffered from a form of sleeping sickness, and was partially supported financially by William Carlos Williams and Robert McAlmon. An Italian-American, he returned to Italy in 1922, needed constant medical attention, and died there in 1942. And Peter Neagoe, a now-forgotten novelist as well as editor of *Americans Abroad.* His final book, *The Saint of Montparnasse*, was a fictionalised account of the life of the sculptor, Constantin Brancusi, who Neagoe had known in Paris.

I make no claims for the writers I've mentioned being major talents, though Sherry Mangan deserves to be written about because of the way in which he combined journalism, creative writing, and political commitment in his life. But they all produced work of interest and were a part of the overall literary scene of their time. And for that they ought to be remembered.

NOTES

1. *Americans Abroad* edited by Peter Neagoe. The Servire Press, The Hague, 1932

2. Alan Wald, *The Revolutionary Imagination: The Poetry and Politics of John Wheelwright and Sherry Mangan.* The University of North Carolina Press, Chapel Hill, 1983

3. Sherry Mangan, *Blackness of a White Night: Stories & Poems,* Arts End Books, Newton, 1987

4. Sherry Mangan, "Reminiscences From a Hilltop" in *The Black Mountain Review 7 ,* Black Mountain, Autumn, 1957

5. Sherry Mangan, "A Night in Scranton" in *New Directions 14,* New York, 1953

6. Sherry Mangan, "Coat" in *The London Mercury,* London, April, 1933

7. Ernest Walsh, "Some of His Latest Poems and Writings" in *This Quarter 3,* Monte Carlo, 1927

8. Wambly Bald, *On the Left Bank, 1929-1933*, edited by Benjamin Franklin V, Ohio University Press, Athens, 1987

9. Emily Holmes Coleman, *The Shutter of Snow,* Virago Press, London, 1981

10. Emanuel Carnevali, *The Autobiography of Emanuel Carnevali*, edited by Kay Boyle, Horizon Press, New York, 1967. Some of Carnevali's poems can be found in *This Quarter 2,* Milan, 1925

11. Kay Boyle, *Year Before Last,* Faber and Faber, London, 1932

12. Henry Miller, *Tropic of Cancer,* John Calder, London, 1963

POLPERRO : CORNWALL'S FORGOTTEN ARTS CENTRE

Most people heading to Cornwall with art on their minds will naturally be conscious of St Ives as the main centre of activity for painters and those who cluster around them. Newlyn might also come into the picture. But how many hands would be raised if Polperro was named and a question posed about its place in Cornish art history? Not too many, I suspect, and I put myself among them. I knew next to nothing about Polperro prior to visiting the small, but excellent exhibition at Falmouth Art Gallery, and looking at David Tovey's two-part history of the village and the artists who spent time there.

It is worth noting that both Tovey and the gallery are careful to refer to an Arts Centre and not an Art Colony. Unlike St Ives and Newlyn it seems fewer artists actually resided in Polperro on a permanent basis, especially in the early period that Tovey looks at. They were often mostly summer visitors. David Tovey names Herbert Butler, who married a local girl, as one of the few long-term residents, and rightly devotes space to his paintings and the art school that he opened in Polperro. And he says that "the contrast between the busy summer months, when the village was full of visiting artists, and the deserted winter period will have been stark". With regard to summer visitors, Tovey notes that the French painter, Auguste Joseph Delécluse, brought a party of thirty female art students to the village in 1894. Tovey suggests that Chrissie Ash may have been among them. One of her paintings is in his book on Polperro's early days.

As happened so often in Britain and on the Continent it was the development of the railway system that enabled more artists to visit Polperro from around 1901 when a branch line from Liskeard to Looe was opened. Polperro is situated on the south Cornwall coast between Looe and Fowey. Its main commercial activity was fishing and two pilchard factories were located in the village. It was obvious that the port and its fishing boats, the local people, and the tangle of cottages and other buildings, would provide material for artists concerned to produce attractive scenes which would have some commercial appeal. From this point of view it becomes obvious that few, if any, of the painters either in the exhibition, or in Tovey's informative books, were innovators. Saying this doesn't lessen their achievements. There are never more than a handful of artists who bring about major changes. The rest then absorb them into the mainstream.

Like most of their contemporaries in St Ives and Newlyn the Polperro painters worked within what might be termed traditional representational frameworks. Many of them had studied in Paris and elsewhere, and as Tovey makes clear, more than a few foreign artists – from America, Germany, Holland, France – spent time in Polperro and painted what they saw. Impressionism had clearly had an influence, though not to any extreme extent. Paintings by the Dutch artist, Hendrik Jan Wolter, do indicate that his days in Paris had opened his eyes to the work of Signac and Seurat.

Tovey notes that though "Polperro was undoubtedly thriving as an arts centre in the years leading up to 1914……there is very little art activity recorded during the War years". Things began to pick up in the 1920s when tourists began to return to the village and Frederick Thomas Nettleinghame became what Tovey describes as a "tourist operator" and set up a business dealing in artefacts for the tourist market. He was assisted by a couple of young would-be artists, Arthur Wragg and Frederick Roberts Johnson, both of who would later bring some radical political intentions to their own work.They each contributed drawings to *Tribune* and *Peace News* in the 1930s.

Wragg is of particular interest and his anti-war statements still retain their powerful visual impact. He was a friend of Walter Greenwood (the author of *Love on the Dole* lived in Polperro in the 1930s) and illustrated his book of short-stories, *The Cleft Stick*. Wragg's 1934 book, *Jesus Wept*, was described as "a commentary in black and white on ourselves and the world today", and its sharp pictorial representations of poverty, unemployment, and other social problems were, and still are, striking. The exhibition has a short video with the title "The Polperro Polemicists", which provides information about the friendship between Greenwood and Wragg. Greenwood shared Wragg's left-leaning political ideas.

Wragg's friend, Frederick Roberts Johnson was also a prolific illustrator in the inter-war years, "producing cartoons, caricatures, comic adverts and other funnies for a range of periodicals". Using the pseudonym "Essex" he did a series of caricature portraits for *Punch* of well-known people such as Lord Halifax and Montagu Norman. And he came up with a wonderful sequence of caricatures of Polperro fishermen which Tovey uses in his book on the post-1920 village.

I think it's important to look at what Wragg and Johnson did to earn a living. They both spotlighted Polperro in some of their paintings and drawings, but clearly had other concerns in terms of either making a little money or using their art to make socio-political comments. But it's interesting to refer to Tovey's comments on Johnson who, he says, "as a painter….never sold or exhibited his work". What he earned from his commercial work, together with a marriage to someone with money, enabled him to paint purely for pleasure. The still-life paintings reproduced in Tovey's book show him to have been a skilled artist.

The 1939-1945 War had an impact on Polperro. The noted artist. Oscar Kokoschka, was there for almost a year, and inevitably tended to be remembered whereas many others were overlooked. There are Kokoschka canvases from his Polperro sojourn in Tovey. And in the exhibition a Johnson painting that is based on one by Kokoschka. He seems to have struck up a friendship with the Austrian painter.

There were talented artists in Polperro in the 1950s, among them Stuart Armfield, whose work displayed some surrealist influences, and Jack Merriott, "painter, poster-designer, author, illustrator and teacher". He was less-adventurous than Armfield in that he painted in a "direct method" and didn't seem to deviate from the established details of what he was portraying. According to Tovey, "Merriott was one of the most successful Polperro artists. Furthermore, he managed to be successful in an age where representational art was totally out of fashion. – a not insignificant achievement".

There perhaps isn't any one single reason why interest in Polperro as an artistic community faded over the years. The 1950s saw attention focused mainly on St Ives where an influential group of abstract artists – Bryan Wynter, Peter Lanyon, and others – held sway. And St Ives became a key place for would-be artists, writers, and others to drift to when there was a surge of what might be called commercialised bohemianism in the late-1950s. The St Ives poet Arthur Caddick satirised the beatniks who cluttered up the streets and slept on the sands in his humorous verses.

It's refreshing to see attention being brought to bear on Polperro. The Falmouth exhibition offers a selection of some of the artists who, at one time or another, lived and worked there. David Tovey's books go into much greater details about their activities, and provide a far greater range of illustrations to show how much good work came out of a small place. In addition, he looks at various writers – Walter Greenwood, Hugh Walpole, and some others – who spent time in Polperro. Greenwood, in fact, wrote a trilogy of novels set in an "imaginary Cornish fishing port" called Treelooe. Some of the characters were allegedly based on real-life residents of Polperro, and it was suggested that Greenwood's decision to leave the area and move to Looe was determined by their reactions to how he had portrayed them. Tovey's research in relation to both artists and writers is to be admired.

POLPERRO : CORNWALL'S FORGOTTEN ARTS CENTRE

Falmouth Art Gallery, 2nd April, 2022 to 18th June, 2022

POLPERRO : CORNWALL'S FORGOTTEN ARTS CENTRE : VOLUME ONE – PRE-1920

By David Tovey

Wilson Books, 256 pages. ISBN 978-0-9955710-1-3

POLPERRO : CORNWALL'S FORGOTTEN ARTS CENTRE : VOLUME TWO - POST-1920

By David Tovey

Wilson Books, 346 pages. ISBN 978-0-9955710-2-0

VICTOR GRAYSON : IN SEARCH OF BRITAIN'S LOST REVOLUTIONARY

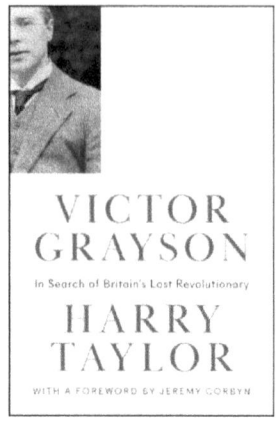

Back in the 1980s I had a conversation with an elderly lady who told me that she remembered being taken as a child by her father, a socialist, to hear Ben Tillett speak. He stood on a brewer's dray, she said, and he didn't speak to the people, he spoke for them. I guessed from her age that she was talking about the period before the First World War, when radicalism, in all its variations, was in the air and hopes of revolutionary change ran high.

Victor Grayson came out of the same working-class background as Tillett, but unlike him he didn't live to reach a ripe old age. Or did he? There is a mystery about Grayson. He disappeared in 1920, and though several theories have been advanced as to what happened to him, no-one has managed to come up with a definitive solution.

Who was Victor Grayson? He was born in Liverpool in 1881 and was one of six (or it could be seven) children. The family was poverty-stricken, with the father liking to work only when necessary and to drink whenever he could. Grayson's mother was probably illiterate. Grayson was said to have been a sickly child and stammered badly as he learned to talk. He was also afflicted with epilepsy. Neither condition appears to have been a factor in his later activities. It would seem that his family had somehow scraped enough money together for him to have elocution lessons to help cure the stammer. And there are no references to epilepsy affecting him as he got older.

Grayson would have seen at close hand how low wages, casual employment, poor housing, a lack of educational opportunities, and similar factors, affected the lives of the dockers and other workers. He started work when he was fourteen as an apprentice engine turner at the Bank Hall Engine Works of J.H. Wilson & Sons. Grayson enjoyed reading Penny Dreadfuls at first, but soon took to more-serious literature, usually with a religious and sometimes political base. He listened to street-corner speakers standing on soapboxes and preaching either the message of the Bible or the promises of socialism. And he began to develop a flair for public speaking.

His skills as a speaker were noted by the people he associated with and he passed through different religious groups in Liverpool and Manchester. But he was developing a keen interest in socialism and more and more of his activities as a speaker were soon focused on politics. His reading, too, had moved from scriptures to Darwin, Max Nordau, and Edward Carpenter. There was also a book that had a specific influence. Popular in its day, *The Roadmender* by Michael Fairless told the story of "a few days in the life of a roadmender in East Sussex as he reflected on living a simple and charitable existence". Harry Taylor says that it was not a political work, but "some of its passages could be construed as vaguely anti-capitalist and socialist". The author was actually the Christian writer, Margaret Barber.

In Liverpool Grayson had met the future Irish trade union leader Jim Larkin, and in Manchester he had been introduced to the Suffragette Emmeline Pankhurst and her daughters. He supported the Suffragette calls for votes for women and the general case for greater autonomy. This didn't go down well with some on the Left, especially trade unionists who were suspicious of any changes which might encourage women to enter the workplace. Grayson identified with the more-radical elements in the Independent Labour Party (ILP) than with the members of the Labour Representation Committee (LRC, soon to become the

Labour Party) which had negotiated pacts with the Liberal Party and believed in a gradual development of socialist ambitions via the ballot box.

It came as a surprise to many people when a by-election in the Colne Valley constituency saw Grayson chosen as the Labour and Socialist candidate despite opposition from the official Labour leaders. There are interesting parallels with more-recent situations where the central Labour administration has refused to accept a locally-nominated candidate. But it was more complicated in the Colne Valley district due to previous Labour and trade union agreements with the Liberals regarding not contesting too closely what were seen as safe Liberal seats. Grayson, who had built up a large amount of popular support through his speeches advocating socialism, was clearly going against the wishes of Labour notables like Keir Hardie and Ramsay MacDonald when he stood identifiably under the socialist banner.

Grayson won, though not by a substantial majority. His victory gave a boost to socialists throughout Britain and he was in demand as a speaker. It was probably the constant pressure to keep travelling to various destinations, coupled with the need to forever be on top form when addressing an audience, that started his problems with alcohol. A whisky or two seemed a good way to overcome the tiredness and mental strain associated with always having to respond to demands to appear in public. But it quickly developed into more than a pick-me-up and reports of Grayson's drinking began to circulate in socialist circles.

His tenure in Parliament was short-lived, though marked by some disruptive acts and a period when he was suspended from the House of Commons because of his behaviour. It's worth considering at this stage whether or not Grayson fulfilled any duties as a constituency MP. Provocative speeches both in and out of the House, and a capacity to arouse a crowd into action, brought him publicity, but did he achieve anything on a local level that might have benefited those who voted for him? I can't imagine that he would have been content to sit through dull meetings dealing with routine matters. Edward Carpenter, who knew him, said that "for detailed or constructive arguments he was no good".

Grayson was becoming increasingly unreliable in terms of turning up at meetings. He failed to appear at a major Labour Party conference in Portsmouth in 1909, where his supporters had been expecting him to present the case for "an alternative, more definitively socialist policy". In addition, when he did arrive on time at meetings "some of his performances were erratic and blundering, where they had once been spellbinding". His drinking was getting out of hand. And rumours about his sexuality were circulating and alienating some of his supporters. He was bi-sexual and had, for a time, been in a homosexual relationship with someone he knew in Liverpool. This was something that would come back to possibly shape his actions a few years later. When there was a General Election in 1910 Grayson again stood as a candidate for Colne Valley, but came in third behind the Liberal and Conservative contestants.

The formation of the British Socialist Party (BSP), with Grayson at its head, offered "a fresh beginning for the whole socialist movement in Britain", as various groups on the Left seemed prepared to join together in unity. But it soon became apparent that the members of the Social Democrat Federation (SDF), a Marxist-oriented party inclined to be doctrinaire, were intent on taking control of the BSP. And when Grayson failed to turn up for the first annual conference of the BSP the SDF were soon firmly in the saddle. As Taylor notes, the failure to give the BSP a genuinely revolutionary programme was "a wasted opportunity for the British left". 1911 "had seen a wave of industrial unrest, the like of which Britain had never before witnessed". Railway workers, seamen, dockers, and others, went on strike, and there were signs of a growing commitment to a socialist programme across the country, but there wasn't a truly efficient radical party that could provide a leadership and a system of co-ordination to direct activities towards a common goal. The BSP never made any great impact on British politics, and is probably only remembered now as one of the groups which formed the British Communist Party in 1920.

Grayson married the actress Ruth Nightingale in 1912, but his health was poor and he was said to have been drinking a bottle of whisky each day. He had a breakdown in 1913, travelled to Italy, and then to New York where he gave an interview in which he sympathised with the syndicalist aims and actions of the Industrial Workers of the World (IWW). He and his wife returned to Britain and when war broke out in 1914 he reported on events in France. Grayson was not a pacifist and supported the government's war programme. In 1916 he went to Australia and New Zealand to encourage people to volunteer, and in 1916 he enlisted himself. He was wounded at Passchendaele and suffered from shell shock. He toured Britain speaking in factories against strikes and also wrote articles in favour of greater efforts to defeat Germany.

It was during this period that Grayson's wife died in childbirth in February, 1918, along with the child. He was working for the National War Aims Committee (NWAC), a "shadowy propaganda unit", visiting factories and shipyards to make speeches in favour of the war and denigrating "growing industrial militancy", He was making money with his speeches and writing articles and pamphlets and living well, but still drinking heavily. Taylor refers to a visit to Hull in November, 1918, when Grayson arrived late and apologised for his "battered" appearance which, he claimed, was caused by falling down some stairs.

What happened to Grayson when the war ended? Taylor says that his life "is shrouded in mystery". As a result several suggestions have been made regarding his disappearance. He may have been associated with J. Maundy Gregory, "the flamboyant fraudster and Lloyd George fixer", perhaps knew too much about "the illegal sale of honours", and was threatening to go public with the information. Maundy Gregory was said to have had him murdered. Taylor easily demolishes this theory, and says that a likelier reason for Grayson suddenly going quiet was that he was more or less blackmailed into silence by leading lights in the Labour Party. They threatened to release some letters that he had written to his male lover in Liverpool many years previously. Taylor says that the letters had been in the possession of J.H. Thomas, one-time head of the railwaymen's union and then a

Labour MP, Cabinet Minister, and a prominent supporter of Grayson's old antagonist Ramsay MacDonald.

Whatever the reason, Grayson never surfaced in public again, though there were alleged sightings of him here and there over the years. There was the curious fact of a Scotland Yard investigation into his disappearance as late as 1942. Reg Groves, who wrote an earlier book on Grayson, was called in by the police and asked what he knew. He gave them some documentation, which was never returned, but heard nothing further. Groves, years later, tracked down the retired police officer he'd dealt with in 1942 and was told that Grayson was "married – settled in Kent". When Taylor, researching for his book, contacted Scotland Yard he was informed that there was no record of the 1942 investigation. I've abbreviated the search for Grayson, and Taylor's more-detailed account certainly makes for intriguing reading.

I suppose that, at this late date, it is the mystery surrounding Grayson's sudden silence that will interest most readers. But Taylor has written an account of his rise and fall that also throws light on the early days of socialism in Britain, and in particular the years between 1900 and 1914 when many people believed that radical change could be achieved either by direct action of the kind that Grayson so often espoused, or by following the path to parliamentary power through the ballot box. It's worth asking the question if Grayson's methods could ever have succeeded, and if he himself, even without the intervention of the First World War or his alcohol problem, could have stayed the course. Taylor seems to have doubts about Grayson's activities. To him it is obvious "That a dizzying array of parties on the left will never further the cause of socialism in Britain, that the Labour Party was formed to represent working people in Parliament, not to be an instrument of protest, and strong party structures and organisation are the basis of electoral victory".

VICTOR GRAYSON : IN SEARCH OF BRITAIN'S LOST REVOLUTIONARY
By Harry Taylor
Pluto Press. 268 pages. £16.99. ISBN 978-0-7453-4398-3

WRITING RED : AN ANTHOLOGY OF AMERICAN WOMEN WRITERS , 1930-1940

"*Writing Red* corrects the failure of most collections from the 1930s to include a substantial amount of writing by women". So says Paula Rabinowitz in her introductory essay to this useful and stimulating anthology of the kind of material she considers ought to have been represented in the books she lists. I don't intend to mention them all here, but will acknowledge that she has a point when asking why so few women appear in them. And it's very often noticeable that the same names – Josephine Herbst, Meridel LeSueur, Muriel Rukeyser, Ruth McKenney, one or two others – tend to crop up. It's as if the compilers of these selections had only a limited range of women writers to choose from. *Writing Red* sets the record straight by delving a little deeper in the archives to discover some of the overlooked and forgotten.

I think it needs to be pointed out that a kind of pattern of male dominance had been set earlier. The 1930s anthology, *Proletarian Literature in the United States*, edited by an all-male team of six including Granville Hicks and Michael Gold, had only seven women in a contents table that listed a total of over sixty contributors.

It can, of course, be argued that numerous male writers of the 1930s have been forgotten, and that the anthologies on the whole focus on many of the well-known names – Steinbeck, Farrell, Nelson Algren, Richard Wright – to the exclusion of others who didn't produce a great deal and never became famous. The literary world has always been littered with casualties, both male and female, and it requires a lot of effort to provide most of them with suitable memorials.

Another factor that perhaps needs to be taken into account when considering American left-wing writing in the 1930s is how a shift in policy in the Communist Party influenced who was given attention by critics and appeared in print. The early 1930s had seen the foundation of the John Reed Clubs in major cities like New York and Chicago. Magazines were started to publish work by Club members, with an emphasis on proletarian literature. There was always some confusion about what that meant. Did it refer to writing about proletarians, or writing by proletarians? It seems true that many working class writers did find it an advantage to be connected to a John Reed Club and its magazine, and there were other little magazines and small presses which seemed to be open to work by them.

However, in 1935 Communist Party policy changed to one of a Popular Front and the Clubs, which were Party institutions, were closed. The proletarians were out and middle-class writers who would ally themselves with the aims of the Popular Front against Fascism were welcomed. I'm generalising out of necessity, the politics of the 1930s often being complex, especially where Communist motives were concerned. The League of American Writers, which was started when the John Reed Clubs were dissolved, made no claims to represent writers of proletarian fiction. Its membership included numerous well-known novelists and poets and, on the surface, didn't emphasise its communist connections. It was meant to enlist a wide range of established novelists, poets, journalists and others who could be described as fellow-travellers and would give the League a veneer of moderation and respectability. The FBI considered it a "Communist front" organisation. A glance at the list of members of the League in Frederick Folsom's *Days of Anger, Days of Hope*

(Colorado University Press, 1994) shows that male writers predominated, and I'd hazard a guess that the majority of them were white middle-class in their social backgrounds.

It's obvious that, one way or another, most women writers faced a hard time getting into print and having their work evaluated by critics. In addition to which their domestic demands, if they were married and had children, worked against them being able to produce anything sustained. Novels and long narrative poems were not compatible with family life, other than in exceptional circumstances. It could also be true that, during the days when proletarian writing was looked on favourably, "By linking the proletariat, and its culture, with masculinity, the metaphors of gender permeated the aesthetics debates of male literary radicals throughout the 1930s". Those are Paula Rabinowitz's words, and she quotes from a striking passage by Mike Gold, one of the Communist Party's key commentators on cultural matters, which extols the virtues of young, working-class males who write "in jets of exasperated feeling" do not "polish their work" and are "violent and sentimental by turns".

The value of an anthology like *Writing Red* is that it can demonstrate how women were just as likely as many men to be directly involved in problems relating to political protest, union work, and other practical matters. Josephine Herbst was a novelist, short-story writer, and journalist whose literary reputation faded after the 1930s, but revived to a degree when some of her novels were re-issued in the 1980s. And her fine memoir, *The Starched Blue Sky of Spain and Other Memoirs* which initially came out in the 1960s in Saul Bellow's magazine, *The Noble Savage*, and Theodore Solotaroff's *New American Review*, did help to focus some attention on her earlier books. Her contributions to *Writing Red*, one a short-story, the other reportage, are both set in Cuba, and point to her awareness of the political situation on the island.

Herbst was not the only woman to travel and write fiction or journalism relating to what she saw and experienced. Ruth McKenney is probably remembered now for *My Sister Eileen*, which was the basis for a popular film, but her *Industrial Valley,* from which a section is used, was a novel combining fiction and snatches of newspaper items to look at the unemployment and general economic situation around Akron, Ohio, in 1932.

And there was Mary Heaton Vorse, a veteran labour journalist and novelist (see, for example, *Strike!*, based on the 1929 textile dispute in Gastonia, North Carolina) with radical roots going back to the early part of the twentieth century. She was writing about militant labour activity in 1916. Her "School for Bums" looks at the kind of facilities available to the homeless and unemployed during the dark days of 1931. With regard to Vorse's Gastonia novel it's worth reading Ella Ford's "We are Mill People". She's described as a "Striking mill worker in Gastonia, North Carolina", and her account is a bleak narrative of violence and intimidation by local officials, the police, and vigilante groups.

Agnes Smedley and Anna Louise Strong both moved outside America and reported extensively on events in China, though Strong also covered revolutions in Mexico, Russia, and Spain, as her "Front Trenches – North West" indicates when she talks to Spaniards and foreign volunteers in the International Brigades about the fight against fascism. Smedley wrote fiction alongside her factual work. Her "Shan-fei – Communist" tells the story of a young woman from a wealthy family who becomes a communist and infiltrates a Kuomintang headquarters by pretending to be anti-communist and then secretly passes information to communist forces outside the city. She is captured and badly treated but still retains her faith in communism. I suppose it could be argued that a story like this is essentially a form of propaganda, but it is tidily written and retains some of its vitality, as well as being a record of a time and place.

I've taken just a few examples of the prose works in *Writing Red* to give an indication of what it has to offer, and I could just as easily have chosen others. Tess Slesinger's story, "The Mouse-Trap", isn't obviously political but does show how a young, ambitious woman refuses to go on strike with her office colleagues and tries to ingratiate herself with the boss. By doing so she leaves herself open to his sexual advances. Leane Zugsmith's "Room in the World" is about unemployment and its effects on family life. Vivian Dahl's "Them Women Sure Are Scrappers" looks at women members of the Agricultural and Cannery Workers Industrial Union battling on the picket lines against scabs, police, and deputies.

There are also several stories by black women writers. They clearly had the additional problem of racism to deal with, along with poverty, harsh living conditions, and unemployment. The writers among them also had limited access to publishing outlets. There were publications such as *Crisis* and *Opportunity* which did focus on black writers, and *Writing Red* has Edith Manuel Durham's powerful "Deepening Dusk" which deals with "the theme of the tragic mulatto". As Rabinowitz stresses, for many black women during the Depression "their imperative desire was to maintain their families". But Elaine Ellis's "Women of the Cotton Fields" refers to the organisation of the Sharecroppers Union in Alabama and its newspaper, *The Southern Worker*, which aimed to bring together both black and white cotton field workers.

Of the poets in *Writing Red* possibly only the names of Muriel Rukeyser, Genevieve Taggard, and Margaret Walker may ring some bells. And even then, only among academics and a few individuals who care to look beyond the immediate and to the past for some inspiration. Rukeyser's "Ann Burlak" and "Fifth Elegy – A Turning Wind" still speak powerfully and directly and their political inclinations are evident. Rukeyser's novel, *The Savage Coast,* dealt with her experiences in Spain during the early days of the Civil War. It remained unknown until 2013 when the Feminist Press published it.

Charlotte Nekola, in her introduction to the poetry section, says: "Poetry by women in the 1930s matched leftist arguments against ironic despair, aestheticism, and meaningless or elitist erudition in the works of such modernist poets as T.S. Eliot and Ezra Pound". She mentions Lucia Trent's biting "Parade the Narrow Turrets" with its final couplet: "Go live in your Ivory Tower. Build it as high as you can,/And parade the narrow turrets as a cultivated man".

Genevieve Taggard's "Silence in Mallorca" brings in the Spanish Civil War and "Ode in Time of Crisis" looks at a world in turmoil but raises hope for a brighter future. I have a copy of an anthology, *May Days*, that Taggard edited in 1925 and which is compiled from poems published in *The Masses* and *The Liberator*, so it's easy to see where her socio-political ideas were located. Margaret Walker's "For My People" and "Dark Blood" have long-lined stanzas in the Whitmanesque mode, and are perhaps also reminiscent of Arturo Giovannitti's verse, which she would possibly have been familiar with. Walker was one of the few black writers to achieve some success in the 1930s and her collection, *For My People* won the Yale Younger Poets award in 1942.

There are other poets worth reading, including, I'm glad to say, Florence Reece and Aunt Molly Jackson, two working-class women writing out of their direct experiences in strikes. Reece's "Which Side Are You On?" stems from a miners' strike in Kentucky ("If you go to Harlan County,/There is no neutral there/You'll either be a union man/Or a thug for J.H. Blair"), while Jackson's "I am a Union Woman" likewise relates to the mine wars: "If you want to join a union/As strong as one can be,/Join the dear old NMU/And come along with me". The NMU was the National Miners Union, a short-lived Communist Party creation.

Both Reece and Jackson wrote poetry that was meant to have an immediate practical use, and kept their use of words simple and straightforward. There is an interesting collection, *You Work Tomorrow: An Anthology of American Labour Poetry, 1929-1941* (University of Michigan Press, 2007), with poems from union newspapers. What is obvious is that the majority of them focus on bread-and-butter issues, such as shorter hours, higher pay, working conditions, unemployment. There is little, if any, political posturing or theory. I doubt that the names of the poets, female and male, will mean anything to most readers of poetry. I recognised a couple, Ralph Chaplin and Arturo Giovannitti, from their links to the Industrial Workers of the World. A collection of Giovannitti's poems was published by El Corno Emplumado in Mexico in 1966.

One final poem I want to mention is Tillie Olsen's "I Want you Women up North to Know" which is about how the clothes that are on sale in big stores in New York, Boston, and other cities are made by exploited Mexican labour – "those dainty children's dresses you buy/are dyed in blood, are stitched in wasting flesh". It has relevance today if we think of poorly-paid workers in India and elsewhere producing clothes for the UK market and facing violent opposition from managers and police when they protest about low wages and bad employment situations or try to unionise.

Writing Red was first published in 1987 by the Feminist Press in New York, and it's good to see it back in print. It has a great deal to offer in terms of the mostly-neglected writing it features, but also for the information it contains about obscure publications and the detailed commentary by Charlotte Nekola and Paula Rabinowitz. And it can take its place alongside the other anthologies of left-wing American writing that Rabinowitz challenges for their lack of female representation. It helps to round out the picture of what was being written by novelists, poets, and others with a radical perspective about the state of things in the turbulent 1930s.

WRITING RED : AN ANTHOLOGY OF AMERICAN WOMEN WRITERS , 1930-1940
Edited by Charlotte Nekola and Paula Rabinowitz
Haymarket Book. 349 pages. £19.99. ISBN 978-1-64259-583-3

MAGRITTE : A LIFE

A train seeming to appear from a fireplace, a pipe with words beneath it telling the viewer that it isn't a pipe, a torso, tuba, and chair hanging over a calm sea. These are all images now instantly recognisable as the work of René Magritte, the Belgian surrealist artist. They've been seen a thousand times and adapted, in various ways, for commercial purposes. But the man who created them consistently denied that he was an artist. He was a "man of thought", he said, and communicated his thoughts through paintings, as "others do through music, words, etc.". He admired philosophers and "always preferred the company of writers and poets to that of painters". Alex Danchev says that "Magritte's art is a cross between Wittgenstein's thought and *Alice in Wonderland*, with a seasoning of surrealism, a pinch of eroticism, and a sizzle of dread".

Magritte was born in 1898 in Lessines, though he grew up in Gilly. His father is described by Danchev as a "chancer", a man who made money and lost it, liked pornography, and was a womaniser. Magritte's mother was "prayerful, dutiful, heedful" and suffered from depression. Magritte and his two brothers lived in an atmosphere of "domestic upheaval", further exacerbated by their mother's suicide when Magritte was thirteen. They ran wild in the streets, playing practical jokes on their neighbours and in shops and the local café. He wasn't a good student at school and was often a truant. Magritte rarely, if ever, talked about his mother and, when questioned in later life, said: "No-one can say whether the death of my mother had an influence or not".

He had some early painting lessons from a local teacher. And he developed what became lifelong passions for popular literature and the cinema (he liked Westerns and especially John Wayne). He read Edgar Allan Poe and *Treasure Island*, along with detective stories (he particularly enjoyed Rex Stout, the American novelist) and Fantômas, a fictional character who "slipped the bounds of bourgeois morality" and "mocked the canons of good taste". Magritte wasn't alone in his admiration for his escapades, and Franz Kafka, Guillaume Apollinaire, Max Jacob, and Pablo Picasso were all Fantômas fans. Many years later, in 1943, Magritte painted his portrait of Fantômas based on the poster advertising the original stories. It may be of relevance to note that the knife carried by Fantômas had been replaced by a rose in Magritte's version.

In 1915 Magritte moved to Brussels to study at the Académie des Beaux-Arts, though his attendance was irregular. The Académie closed for several months in 1918 due to fuel shortages, and Magritte re-registered in 1919, though his studies were interrupted by military service in 1920-21. He did not take the final exams, and appears to have spent a lot of time in the bohemian cafés of Brussels, associating with fellow art-students but also with writers and philosophers. Magritte read widely and was familiar with the work of Comte de Lautrémont, whose famous phrase about "the chance meeting on a dissecting table of a sewing machine and an umbrella" was of significance in "the thought crimes of the surrealists", according to Danchev. It was during this period that he met up again with Georgette, who he had first encountered in 1913. They were married in 1922.

It's difficult to know exactly what Magritte was painting in those early days, though there are references to canvases in the style of the Hague School, the group of painters largely specialising in coastal landscapes and seascapes. It's also suggested that he produced some Cubist-influenced works. As an art student he would have been informed of what was happening in Paris, and what people like Picasso and Braque were doing. I would guess that he was facile enough in technical matters to be able to turn his hand to different approaches to painting while developing his own method of expression.

In order to earn enough to provide for himself and his wife Magritte worked as a wallpaper designer, though he had, by the early-1920s, become aware of what the surrealists were up to in Paris. He could identify with them in some ways, though his basic concern was for what Danchev quotes the poet Elizabeth Bishop referring to as "glimpses of the always more-successful surrealism of everyday life". It might be useful to mention at this point Magritte's objection to references to "symbols" in his paintings. They are not symbols, he said, they are objects. His visual inspiration was drawn from the real world. And, as Danchev points out, "he had no truck with *le fantastique"*, and when asked to paint something in that vein he bluntly replied, "I am not a painter of the fantastic".

Magritte's first exhibition of surrealist paintings took place in Brussels in 1927. It didn't arouse a great deal of positive critical reaction, and few, if any, sales. But it was around this time that he met the colourful E.L.T. Mesens, a precocious and talented youngster who had launched himself into the world of the avant-garde by contacting the Futurist F.T. Marinetti and the Dadaist Tristan Tzara. As a budding composer he had got to know Erik

Satie. He no doubt intrigued Magritte when he talked about these people and their ideas, and they were to remain in contact for many years. Mesens became a collector of Magritte's work and helped to promote it in more ways than one. He moved to London in 1938 and opened a gallery which spotlighted the surrealists.

It was obvious that Magritte would have to spend some time in Paris, then the key centre of avant-garde activity. The surrealists were entrenched there and André Breton dominated their gatherings and decided who was suitable for acceptance into their ranks. Magritte and his wife arrived in the French capital in 1927, and were at first welcomed by writers such as Louis Aragon and Paul Eluard. But it was significant that the Magrittes chose not to live in the artistic areas of the city, Montparnasse or Montmartre, but instead several miles outside them. And Magritte didn't look for a studio. He always preferred to work where he resided, preferably painting in the living room.

Magritte spent three years in Paris, but I doubt that he was ever truly accepted into Breton's inner circle. The Parisians looked on him as a provincial and mocked his French, which he spoke with a heavy Walloon accent. And he deliberately exaggerated it when he thought he was being patronised. Insofar as fitting in with the surrealists' collective thinking was concerned, he was too much of an individual to submit his ideas to group inspection. He was, Danchev says, "a maverick, a case apart".

Breton and his associates may have found his work of interest, but not all of them were happy with his sense of humour, nor his refusal to take all their posturings too seriously. Breton spoke scathingly about the idea of having to go to work – "There is no use being alive if one must work" – but, according to Danchev, "the Belgians by contrast operated under bourgeois cover", and Magritte's Brussels surrealist friends had jobs as teachers, civil servants, journalists, and in the case of the influential Paul Nougé, as a bio-chemist. Nougé was to be a key factor in Magritte's intellectual endeavours. Magritte often relied on friends to provide titles for his paintings and Nougé was particularly good at finding something appropriate.

A break with Breton was almost inevitable, and happened in a somewhat bizarre way. The surrealists were noted for being anti-religion and Breton one day in 1929 noticed that Georgette was wearing a cross. He ordered her to remove it, she refused and left the room, and Magritte himself followed her. The poet Paul Éluard ran after them in an effort to persuade them to return, but the Magrittes were adamant. Breton had insulted Georgette and they weren't about to apologise. It was several years before what might be called "normal" relations between Breton and Magritte were resumed, though they never again became totally relaxed and informal.

Magritte and his wife returned to Brussels in 1930 and a house in a "dull street in a drab neighbourhood", with him attempting to earn a living through commercial work, a situation that more or less shaped his life for several years and probably into the early-1950s. Danchev sums up how it was: "Painters have always been part of the 'precariat'. Magritte was practically a life member". There were some improvements in the 1930s, partly thanks to Claude Spaack, a novelist and playwright from a wealthy family, who purchased some of Magritte's paintings and persuaded his brother to do likewise.

And Magritte also benefited from the patronage of another wealthy person, the eccentric Edward James. He bought several Magritte canvases, but also commissioned him to construct three panels behind two-way mirrors in the ballroom of his house in Wimpole Street. It would mean Magritte having to spend several weeks in London. He was "like a fish out of water in Wimpole Street", didn't care for English cooking, and depended on Georgette to keep him supplied with crime novels by Dashiell Hammett, Agatha Christie, Ellery Queen, and similar writers. He did socialise to a degree and met Henry Moore and Humphrey Jennings.

There is a suggestion that Magritte, while in London, may have had an affair with Sheila Legge. He would have most likely first met her in 1936 when several of his paintings were included in the London International Surrealist Exhibition. She was photographed as the "Surrealist Phantom of Sex Appeal" in Trafalgar Square with her head obscured by red roses. It could almost have been a study for a Magritte painting, but it was, in fact, created by Salvador Dali. Artists sometimes work along the same lines.

When Belgian resistance to the Germans collapsed in 1940 Magritte initially made his way to France, afraid that some of his political affiliations might lead to his arrest. He had never been a political activist, but he had lent his support to various left-wing causes, and he knew people who were communists. His friend, Paul Nougé, for example, had been a founder member of the Belgian Communist Party and the Belgian Surrealist Group. Magritte did eventually return to Belgium but lived quietly outside Brussels. Interestingly, when the war ended, he joined the Communist Party, but didn't remain a member for very long. The restrictions the Party attempted to impose weren't to his liking, and he pointed out that "Conformism was as blatant in this milieu as in the most narrow-minded sections of the bourgeoisie"

Things were changing by the late-1940s and early-1950s. Surrealism's day as a movement had passed, the Belgian group had splintered and broken up, old friends and acquaintances had died or moved on, Nougé was drinking himself to death. There had previously been some dubious involvements in Magritte's life. During the war he had happily forged paintings by, among others, Picasso, Braque, and de Chirico. And when hostilities ceased he was, for a short time, working with one of his brothers in the production of counterfeit bank notes. Both activities were undertaken to boost his income from painting which was still miserably low. Danchev mentions that, in 1998, when Magritte had become respectably established as a Belgian icon, his portrait was used by the National Bank on a 500 franc note. He would have been amused at the idea of a one-time counterfeiter being celebrated in that way.

But the situation began to alter when a 1951 exhibition of his work in New York attracted attention. The city was beginning to take over from Paris as the main centre for art. Marcel Duchamp took on the role of promoting Magritte's paintings to American collectors. Young American artists like Jasper Johns, Robert Rauschenberg Andy Warhol, and Roy Lichtenstein who, a few years later, would become the stars of Pop Art, enthused about Magritte's work. In 1954 he was given a solo exhibition at the Palais des Beaux-Arts in Brussels, and his work was shown at the Venice Biennale. With all this attention, and the income from sales in America, Magritte was finally financially secure. His lifestyle began to change in line with his new-found affluence.

But it may not have brought him contentment. An old friend, Louis Scutenaire, described as "poet, anarchist, surrealist, and civil servant", who often gave titles for the paintings, thought that Magritte was uncomfortable with success: "It bothered him. He was much less agreeable than when he was poor, less warm, less happy with himself". However, he was still producing intriguing pictures in 1963, as can be seen from the reproduction of *La Lunette d'approche* where what seems to be a window through which one can observe clouds actually opens onto a blank wall. He died in August, 1967.

Magritte: A Life is a splendid well-illustrated book, packed with information about Magritte's life and insights into his paintings. Alex Danchev sadly died before he finished it, but Sarah Whitfield has done a first-rate job of putting the finishing touches to the story. It should be invaluable reading for anyone interested in knowing more about the always-provocative and entertaining René Magritte.

MAGRITTE : A LIFE

By Alex Danchev with Sarah Whitfield

Profile Books. 439 pages. £30. ISBN 978-1-78125-077-8

I USED TO LIVE HERE ONCE: THE HAUNTED LIFE OF JEAN RHYS

I am looking at a copy of *The Transatlantic Review*, a magazine edited by Ford Madox Ford from Paris. It's dated December, 1924, and the list of contributors includes Ernest Hemingway, Gertrude Stein, Robert McAlmon, Tristan Tzara, and Jean Rhys. Her story is entitled "Vienne", and a note says that it's an excerpt from a novel called *Triple Sec* which remained unpublished in its complete form. But the presence of the story in a publication which had status in the world of the literary avant-garde of the Twenties brought its author to the attention of people who knew and cared about new writing.

Jean Rhys was born on Dominica, a "small and sternly beautiful Caribbean island", in 1890. Rhys wasn't her real name which was Ella Gwendoline Williams. Her father was Welsh and had been a ship's doctor but had set up a practice on shore. Her mother was Irish and had been born on the island so was classified as a "white creole" in the same way that her daughter would be, a fact that had relevance in terms of jean Rhys's later experiences. Gwen, as she was called at home, was discouraged from associating with darker skinned relatives. Miranda Seymour has some useful things to say about distinctions between the minority white population of Dominica and the coloured people who constituted the majority. Power and wealth were largely in the hands of the whites when Rhys was growing up. But she had a nursemaid who told her tales of witchcraft, Obeah and Zombies. Rhys later said, "Meta had shown me a world of fear and distrust. I am still in that world".

She was brought up in the Anglican faith but was sent to a Catholic Convent school. Seymour offers a vivid account of Rhys's adventures as a young girl, including probing into the "forbidden world of the islanders", and her love of reading. It's of some importance to know about her background in order to understand why Rhys always felt like an outsider and often looked back wistfully to some aspects of her earlier life in Dominica. At the school she was introduced to French poetry. At home her unsympathetic mother punished her for any infraction of the set rules of behaviour and told her, "You'll never be like other people".

In 1907 she was sent to school in England where, as a colonial with an accent (she had what was described as a sing-song voice), she was ridiculed by other girls. She had ambitions to go on the stage, and in 1909 gained a place at Sir Herbert Tree's Acting School. Her accent worked against her taking on leading roles and she eventually joined the chorus of a touring musical comedy group which visited places like Oldham and Southport. The life of a chorus girl with its sequences of dingy lodgings, cheap meals, and different men with the same idea in mind, is evoked in *Voyage in the Dark*, Rhys's third novel published in 1934.

She worked in pantomime and in the chorus for a 1911 production of Franz Lehar's *The Count of Luxembourg*, but it was evident that she was going nowhere as an actress, and was struggling to keep afloat financially. When a wealthy admirer, Hugh Lancelot Smith, offered to support her she took to the arrangement quite willingly. She soon had to have an abortion and her liaison with Lancelot Smith came to an end, though he continued to keep in touch with her and bail her out when she had money problems. She worked as a film extra and as a model for the artists Sir Edward Poynter and William Orpen. And she frequented Augustus John's club, The Crabtree, where she mixed with Nina Hamnett, Jacob Epstein, Mark Gertler, Paul Nash, and Wyndham Lewis. There are references to the club in *After Leaving Mr Mackenzie*, which appeared in 1930.

Rhys helped out in a canteen catering for soldiers during the First World War, and in 1919 met Jean Lenglet, a Dutchman with a somewhat shady background. She was warned against involvement with him but their relationship developed and they married, despite Lenglet already having a wife. A job for Lenglet with the Inter-Allied Commission took them to Vienna (see the story I mentioned earlier) and Budapest. Rhys gave birth to a son, William, who died. But Lenglet had been embezzling money from the Commission and was arrested and imprisoned. An idea of how Rhys survived can be gleaned from her story, "Hunger". She had another child, a girl named Maryvonne, who was "cared for at a series of baby shelters or orphanages". When she grew up Maryvonne opted to live with her father in Holland just before the Nazis invaded. Both became involved with the Dutch Resistance.

I'm moving quickly through the facts of what was frankly a somewhat rackety life. Rhys ended up in Paris where she met Ford Madox Ford, and had an affair with him which later provided the basis for her novel, *After Leaving Mr Mackenzie*, published in 1930. It was during her time in Paris that her first book, *The Left Bank*, a collection of stories, was published in 1927. Seymour gives a full account of Rhys's involvement with Ford and his wife, Stella Bowen. Whatever the facts, there's no doubt that, from a literary point of view, Ford was of great use to her, both in terms of advising on her writing and widening her choice of reading. Like virtually all of Rhys's work the stories in *The Left Bank* were autobiographical, so it is possible to identify many of the real people behind their fictional counterparts. For example, Seymour says that a staid English couple in "La Grosse Fifi" were probably based on the artist Paul Nash and his wife.

The marriage with Lenglet having foundered Rhys took up with Leslie Tilden Smith, who soon became her second husband. A heavy drinker, like her, he acted as her agent, and regularly argued and even physically fought with her. The marriage survived, despite the couple's financial and other problems. Rhys's novels, *Voyage in the Dark* and *Good Morning, Midnight* were published in 1934 and 1939 respectively, but after that there was what became a long silence insofar as publishing was concerned. And Rhys's behaviour tended to work against her widening her reputation in the London literary world, not to mention any kind of respectability among neighbours. When intoxicated she could quickly turn both orally and physically aggressive. She was arrested in Soho for drunkenness and fighting with her husband. When she moved to live in a village in Norfolk in 1940 while her husband was in the RAF she quickly fell out with the locals and was again arrested for being drunk and disorderly. "I Spy a Stranger", one of Rhys's excellent wartime stories ("rich in black humour", in Seymour's words), is illustrative of how she saw her situation with regard to other people. She was always the outsider.

Tilden Smith died in 1945, and in 1946 a collection of Rhys's stories was rejected as being "too dark". She continued to drink, and in 1947 married Max Hamer, a man described as "unreliable". There were more disputes with neighbours, one of which involved her throwing a brick through a window, and another a confrontation with a policeman. Hamer was arrested and charged with attempted fraud when he stole several cheques from his employer. Again, I'm compressing details of Rhys's life and activities. Seymour covers them fully and they can occasionally make for fairly depressing reading. Perhaps the one positive aspect of this period is that Rhys did continue to write and was working on what was to become her most well-known work, *The Wide Sargasso Sea*, though it wouldn't be published until 1966.

In the meantime a few people tried to keep track of her. She had admirers, among them Alan Ross, Lucian Freud, Julian Maclaren-Ross, Francis Wyndham, Sonia Orwell, Diana Athill, and Selma Vaz Dias. There were occasional glimpses of her when the BBC broadcast a radio adaptation of *Good Morning, Midnight*, and short-stories appeared in *Art & Literature* and the *London Magazine*. But the usual problems of poverty and excessive drinking continued. Rhys's brother bought her a cottage in the Devonshire village of Cheriton Fitzpaine, though she complained about the local people and feeling isolated. Seymour is of the opinion that, in fact, Rhys's loneliness "was always more of a state of mind than a fact of her existence". People helped her in various ways, and the well-educated local vicar often visited to talk about books and other matters. He encouraged her to continue writing when she was depressed and about to give up. But she shocked other people with her drunkenness and her rages. An attack on a neighbour in 1964 led to her brother having her sent to a mental health clinic for observation and possible treatment.

When *Wide Sargasso Sea* was published in 1966 her fortunes began to improve. Thanks to her supporters the book received advance publicity and was guaranteed reviews in the right places. Not all of them were positive. Kay Dick dismissed it as an "awkward annotation" of Charlotte Bronte's *Jane Eyre*, and Alan Ross said it was just "romantic evocation". But Rhys's creation of the story of the mad woman locked in Mr Rochester's attic proved popular. I have to admit to preferring Rhys's other writings to this book. Stories of chorus girls in pre-1914 London, and bohemians in 1920s Paris, are, for me, of greater interest, and the way in which they are written has more appeal. Their simple sentence structures, the directness, and the moods they evoke are to my taste. But that's a personal opinion, and the fact is that sufficient people bought *Wide Sargasso Sea* to bring Rhys's name to greater prominence and to provide her with financial security. She didn't write another novel, but she could still turn out fine short-stories. A couple of late ones are worth noting. "Kismet" takes us back to the pre-1914 world of shabby theatre dressing-rooms and the tawdry lives of chorus girls. And there is the wonderfully brief and chilling ghost-story, "I Used to Live Here Once", which ought to be held up as an example to budding writers of how to make an impact with a minimum of words.

There's no doubt that Rhys could be hard work to be close to. Seymour makes it clear that even her most-devoted friends, who had tolerated her drinking and requests for loans that would most likely never be repaid, were glad that she continued to live in Devon: "Absence made it possible for them to retain real tenderness for a stubborn old woman whose child-like need for sympathy and attention could - and increasingly often did – become relentless. What almost certainly would have killed off such unstinting affection was the greater trial of daily proximity". The easy-going George Melly and his wife, with whom Rhys lived for a time, eventually grew tired of her demands and asked her to leave. She spent her final years in Cheriton Fitzpatrick and died after a fall in 1979.

Good writing doesn't excuse bad behaviour, but when all the anecdotes and gossip are done with what remains is, as Rhys herself said, the work. There's no doubt in my mind that her four early novels, and her short stories, constitute a body of writing that deserves to last. I'm not forgetting *Wide Sargasso Sea,* simply stating my preference for the other books. But I have to admit that it may be the one she will be remembered for.

Miranda Seymour's biography has all the information about Rhys's often-chaotic life that a reader might need. And she looks closely at the novels and stories, and shows how they drew on her life for their inspiration. But the point I would make is that it isn't necessary to have that information, nor to know about the real-life characters behind the fictional ones, to enjoy what Rhys produced. She didn't deal in facts and, as Seymour herself says, "It's seldom useful or enlightening to attempt to overanalyse Rhys's fiction". I respect what biographers and academics do, but I like to think that Jean Rhys can be assured that her reputation will rest on her books and not on any kind of notoriety she attracted because of her waywardness and indiscretions.

I USED TO LIVE HERE ONCE: THE HAUNTED LIFE OF JEAN RHYS
By Miranda Seymour
William Collins. 425 pages. £25. ISBN 978-O-OO-835325-4

DEFINING THE AGE : DANIEL BELL, HIS TIME AND OURS

Daniel Bell was one of the New York Intellectuals, a specific group, albeit not one with a fixed membership or agenda. It's possible to place them in a period, roughly 1935 to around 1985, though again I wouldn't want to be dogmatic about the details. The 1940s and 1950s were the key years in many ways and what might be called their house magazine, *Partisan Review*, was read by anyone of consequence in the intellectual world. There were other publications – *Dissent, Commentary, Encounter, Politics*, to name several – but I suspect *Partisan Review* was the one that largely set the pace. Its anti-communist stance was of importance in the battle of ideas during the Cold War.

Bell was born in 1919 in the Lower East Side of New York and grew up in poverty. His father had died when Bell was young, and his mother worked in the garment industry. They (Bell, his mother and brother) lived with relatives in cramped conditions. When he was thirteen he joined the Young People's Socialist League (YPSL), and in 1935 enrolled at the City College of New York (CCNY). It was open to Jews who were often barred from other educational establishments. And it was a hotbed of political radicalism, with different groups gathering in the dining-room alcoves according to their various left-wing leanings. Bell was a socialist of the social democrat persuasion and suspicious of communist intentions. He had been encouraged to read the anarchist Alexander Berkman's memoirs which included an account of the suppression of the Kronstadt sailors' rising in 1921 when Red Army troops under Trotsky's command brutally put down the rebellion. It horrified him.

Moving to Columbia University after graduating from CCNY in 1938 Bell gained an MA, and then decided to go into journalism rather than any further education. He edited the socialist magazine *New Leader* between 1941 and 1945, and in 1948 became Labour Editor at *Fortune*, "the nation's leading business magazine". It was a post he held until 1958. In 1959 he began working on what was to become his first book, *Marxian Socialism in the United States* (1952), an informative history of the numerous groups claiming to represent socialism and the way in which it would be established in America. How and why the dream failed to come to fruition was also dealt with by Bell. Looking at how America was developing, he said : " Whatever the character of that new social structure may be – whether state capitalism, managerial society, or corporative capitalism – by 1950 American socialism as a political and social fact had become simply a notation in the archives of history."

Bell did take up posts in the educational system, teaching sociology at Chicago and Columbia universities, and finally moving to Harvard until his retirement in 1990. He also worked for the Congress for Cultural Freedom (CCF), an organisation which, it turned out, was financed by the CIA as part of its anti-communist cultural programme. The scandal that ensued in intellectual circles when details of CIA involvement came to light also affected magazines like *Partisan Review* and *Encounter*, the latter published in Britain. I think it was in its pages in the late-1950s that I first came across Bell writing about "The Capitalism of the Proletariat? : American Trade Unionism Today". I still have the magazine. He was criticised and condemned for his links to the CCF, and for publishing in *Encounter*, but it always seemed to me that it printed a lot of interesting material which was well worth reading. Critics made it seem as if the entire contents were geared to attacking communism, or at least persuading us that America was always on the side of the angels, but that certainly wasn't ever the case.

The list of Bell's books is quite extensive, with two or three of them standing out for the interest they attracted when published and for the way in which they have retained their value today. Saying that doesn't imply a criticism of his other books. But it is a fact that some of them have material which focused on aspects of the time when they were written – the student activism of the 1960s, for example – but which now may only appeal to cultural historians. However, it needs to be made clear that Bell was primarily an essayist, and his books are often collections of inter-related pieces.

In *The End of Ideology* (1960) Bell put forward a theory of "political deradicalisation". Jan Werner Muller, in an essay, "The End of Ideology, the Long Nineties, and the History of the Present," says that "comprehensive doctrines – ideology in the narrower sense of dogma – appeared to be depleted, if not in the process of disappearing, at the end of the twentieth century". This, in a way, seems to bear out what Bell had predicted years earlier. And the current situation throughout much of the Western world would appear to support the idea that very few people now give allegiance to a particular ideological position. The reasons are complex and don't simply come down to the facts that communism collapsed, and many people in the West are financially more secure than in the past. Even when that security is at risk they're not likely to turn to a party with a specific ideological programme in the hope of making it safe. And few people believe in the notion of utopia and the dream of a better and more-balanced society. I doubt that Edward Bellamy's *Looking Backwards* is likely to be on anyone's reading list these days. And it could be that, contrary to what Marx said, "alienation is a fact of human existence", as PauL Starr puts it in his essay, "Daniel Bell's Three-Dimensional Puzzle". Bell himself wrote: "Alienation is not nihilism but a positive role, a detachment, which guards one against being submerged in any cause".

Bell's views on contemporary society, and it has to be accepted that he's largely looking at the West, can be found in *The Cultural Contradictions of Capitalism* where he expresses doubts about the hedonistic impulse that has taken over throughout Europe and America. In an earlier book about Bell and his ideas, Howard Brick's *Daniel Bell and the Decline of Intellectual Radicalism* (1986), there is a useful summary of what he thinks has happened: "Bell points to the rupture of traditional identity of culture and social structure, whereby a character structure suited to the capitalist norms of productive activity is built upon a Protestant ethic of work motivations, frugality, impulse renunciation, and delayed gratification. Now, as culture in the wake of modernism repudiates impulse renunciation and seeks 'immediacy, impact, sensation, simultaneity' in the boundless cultivation of the self, capitalism has proved 'ideologically impotent', has lost the 'transcendent ethic' that gave it legitimacy". And there is no seemingly viable radical ideology to take its place.

It might be asked what Bell's own position was in terms of politics and other matters. He liked to describe himself as "a socialist in economics, a liberal in politics, and a conservative in culture". It's suggested in the introduction to *Defining the Age* that Bell's ideal may have been "a modified form of capitalism with a strong role for government in managing the economy and protecting workers and consumers". In an engaging memoir of his father Bell's son David says that he was frequently angered by allegations that he had swung to the right and become a neoconservative: "My father insisted that he remained a man of the left, a 'socialist in economics', a 'Menshevik' ".

I'm conscious of the fact that I've raced around *Defining the Age,* Bell's ideas, and those of the various contributors to the book. There is much worth reading in its pages, as for example

Fred Turner's "The Cultural Contradictions of Capitalism, Then and Now", where he takes a close look at "What Daniel Bell Got Wrong", "The Coming of Bohemian Technocracy", and "A New Kind of Capitalism and a New Contradiction". It's a provocative piece and one wonders how Bell might have responded to it. Margaret O'Mara's "Assessing Daniel Bell in the Age of Big Tech" has useful things to say about how Silicon Valley doesn't have all the right answers to his questions.

DEFINING THE AGE : DANIEL BELL, HIS TIME AND OURS
Edited by Paul Starr & Julian E. Zelizer
Columbia University Press. 332 pages. £28. ISBN 978-0-231-20367-8

BETWEEN TWO HELLS : THE IRISH CIVIL WAR

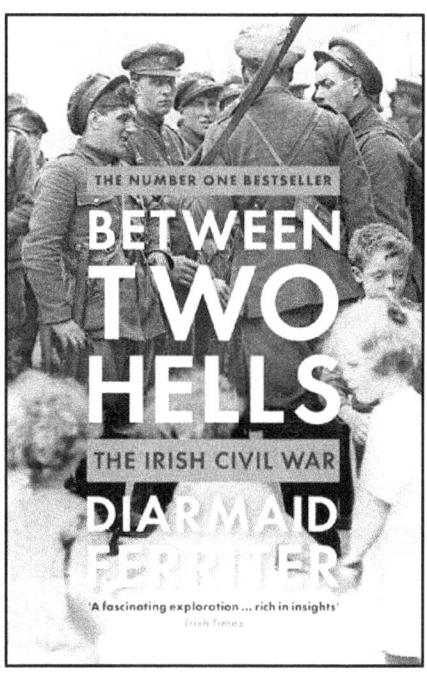

I wonder how many people in England are aware of the fact that there was a civil war in Ireland in the 1920s ? Very few, I suspect. The English, or many of them at least. do sometimes display a woeful ignorance of the island and its problems, and simply wish they didn't exist. As for Irish politics, both in Northern Ireland and the Republic, they can frankly be confusing, depending as they often have done on old loyalties and divisions being carried forward through the generations. Diarmaid Ferriter's book does help to provide clarification of the complex issues initially involved when the Civil War started, and how they influenced what came later.

When the Anglo-Irish Peace Treaty between the British government and the representatives of the provisional Irish Republican government was signed in 1921 it brought an end to the Irish War of Independence. Fought between the forces of the Crown (including the notoriously brutal Black and Tans) and the

Irish Republican Army (IRA) it lasted from 1919 to 1921. The problem was that the Treaty didn't grant the twenty-six counties in the south of Ireland full republican status. They were given self-governing powers as a "free state dominion" and officials were still expected to pledge an oath of allegiance to the King. It was, in the circumstances, probably the best deal that could be expected at the time. And Ferriter says that the Treaty "had fairly broad public support".

However, a sizeable proportion of those who had served with the IRA were opposed to the Treaty. They wanted to continue the struggle for complete independence as a Republic, and for the unification of the whole island. A bitter and violent border war erupted, with paramilitary police units (the "B" Specials among them) being formed to oppose the IRA on the border and in the six counties that made up what became known as Northern Ireland.

In the South the civil war got underway when anti-Treaty volunteers occupied the Four Courts in Dublin in April 1922. Little or no action was taken against them until June when the British government threatened to send in its own troops to defeat the "irregulars", as they were known. Michael Collins, a major figure during the War of Independence, and one of those who signed the Anglo-Irish Treaty, then ordered units of the newly-formed National Army to attack the Four Courts. To do so, lacking their own equipment, they had to use artillery supplied by the British Army. The result was that the buildings, which housed the Public Records Office, were badly damaged and set on fire. Thousands of historic and important documents were destroyed.

The IRA mostly pulled out of Dublin and moved its main activities towards the west, with Munster being a particular base for their operations. Many of the members of the IRA had opposed the Treaty, but not all of them were prepared to fight a war against the new government. Some pro-Treaty IRA members joined the National Army, others, whether pro or anti, just stayed at home and took no part in the fighting. The whole situation was chaotic. The view of one man who was anti-Treaty was that if the English returned he would take up arms again, but in the meantime he had to make a living. Ferriter says he "became a rates collector for Cork County Council".

It needs to be said that both the IRA and the National Army lacked arms and equipment, but the government troops could rely on a supply of suitable material from the British. It was obviously in Britain's interest to support the Dublin government. As for finances the IRA engaged in a spate of raids on post offices and banks. It's tempting to wonder whether or not some of these may have been opportunistic endeavours by people concerned more about personal gain than republican ideals. There were indications of a lack of discipline in the IRA, perhaps because the organisation did not have an effective command structure nor clearly-defined political aims beyond opposing the Treaty. There were sectarian killings. And there is an interesting passage where Ferriter quotes the son of an anti-Treaty IRA fighter as saying that "the civil war had little to do with ideology. The choice of sides in the civil war had, in most cases, little to do with politics. Often it had more to do with personality clashes, the manoeuvrings of cliques and the readiness of troops to follow individual leaders". It was easy to settle old scores in such circumstances.

It quickly became obvious that the IRA could not hope to engage the National Army in any kind of full-scale battle. It was not that the National Army was always better-organised, the rush to recruit sufficient numbers tending to limit the amount of time that could be given to training. A lack of discipline was almost as much of a problem as it was in the IRA. There were complaints of drunkenness and assaults on civilians. Some people even compared them to the Black and Tans.

The IRA reverted to the tactics of guerrilla warfare which they had practised against the British. It was what they did best, and an example of it was the killing of National Army leader Michael Collins in an ambush on a country road. It was a significant blow for pro-Treaty supporters, though it probably helped stiffen their resolve to defeat the IRA. Internment and other measures reduced its effectiveness. It became an offence punishable by death to be found carrying a gun without official permission. The best-known case was that of Erskine Childers, well-known author of *The*

Riddle of the Sands, and an anti-Treaty activist, who was found in the possession of a small pistol presented to him by Michael Collins. He died in front of a firing squad, as did numerous other IRA volunteers.

By April 1923 those in charge of the IRA had realised there was little point in carrying on and the order was given to cease operations. The civil war was over, though some activity, such as armed robberies, lingered on for a few months, and may have been straightforward criminal acts. But, on the whole, "That exhausted legion, though still defiant, just 'hid their arms and went home' ".

A notable aspect of what has been called a "brother against brother" conflict was the extreme savagery that occurred on both sides. The execution of prisoners without trial was not unusual, nor were acts of reprisal. One striking example occurred when National Army soldiers investigating a tip-off about an alleged IRA arms dump triggered a booby-trap. Five were killed and one badly injured. The following day nine Republican prisoners were tied together and a bomb detonated in their midst. One man survived. I've chosen this example to illustrate what I referred to as "savagery" and there are others of a similar nature noted by Ferriter.

The military side of the civil war may have been over, but it carried on politically with Fianna Fáil, and its notable leader, the anti-Treaty Éamon de Valera, and Fine Gael representing the two major parties, though it doesn't do to neglect the Irish Labour Party and Sinn Féin when surveying developments over the years. Nor the activities of the Catholic Church which largely supported the government in Dublin, and often condemned the IRA as " subversive Reds" and "Bolsheviks", because of the advocacy by some of its members of socialist values. What happened in Southern Ireland after the end of hostilities, and later, especially in the 1930s and when a full Republic was declared in 1949, is covered in great detail by Ferriter. He writes clearly about a complex subject.

The Irish Civil War was a relatively small-scale affair if one compares it to similar events in Finland in 1918, Hungary in

1918-20 and the Spanish Civil War, 1936-39. It's difficult to know exactly how many National Army soldiers, IRA volunteers, and civilians died. A figure of 1500 might be about right. For a small country struggling to establish itself it was bad enough.

BETWEEN TWO HELLS : THE IRISH CIVIL WAR

By Diarmaid Ferriter

Profile Books. 328 pages. £9.99. ISBN 978-1-78816-175-6

PAUL POTTS

I was first attracted to the writings of Paul Potts when I came across some of his poems in *New Lyrical Ballads,* an anthology edited by Maurice Carpenter, Jack Lindsay and Honor Arundel, published by Editions Poetry London in 1945. I can't recall where I found the book with its tattered cover and dusty pages. Probably in a second-hand bookshop and most likely in the 1960s. Second-hand bookshops were plentiful in those days. Potts' poems were what I liked – straightforward and open in their sentiments. His work, he said in one of them, was "To sing on-/Until the world is Blackpool/in August/in the afternoon." Reading this I thought how the smart and successful would have sniggered at that reference to Blackpool and its popular image as a gaudy playground for the working-classes. But I grew up not far from Blackpool and went there often, and I knew what Potts meant when he referred to "August/in the afternoon" and its evocation of noisy, good-humoured crowds and cheap entertainments.

I wanted to know more about Potts, so over the years I tracked down nearly all of the few books he'd published and some of his contributions to magazines. And slowly began to establish a picture of the man.

Although often referred to as Canadian, he was born in Berkshire in 1911 to an English father and Irish mother, but moved to Canada when young and was educated there and, after returning to England, at Stonyhurst College. He also attended a Jesuit college in Florence. By the 1930s he was in London and at some point got to know George Orwell and the poet, George Barker. His poems were published in *Poetry London* in 1939, alongside work by Louis MacNeice, David Gascoyne, Dylan Thomas, and Stephen Spender. His first collection, *A Poet's Testament,* was published by the Whitman Press in 1940. It is now a collectors' item. Potts also wrote "Don Quixote on a Bicycle", an insightful appreciation of his friend, George Orwell, which appeared in *London Magazine* and was incorporated into Potts' best-known book, *Dante Called You Beatrice* (Eyre & Spottiswood, 1960), some years later. His poems were also published in *New Masses, Poetry Quarterly*, and other magazines.

Potts was in the army during the Second World War, though there is little available information about his length of service (it would seem that he spent time in the Royal Ulster Rifles and 12th Commando) and exactly what he did. Robert Hewison's *Under Siege: Literary Life in London 1949-45* (Weidenfeld & Nicolson, 1977) suggests that he had been discharged "after passing through the Army's psychiatric hospital at Northfield, outside Birmingham". Hewison seems to have got this information from Rayner Heppenstall's autobiographical novel, *The Lesser Infortune* (Cape, 1953), where Potts appears as a "Canadian poet", and Potts himself in *Dante Called You Beatrice* says that he was "invalided out". It might be worth adding at this point that Potts went to Israel in 1948 to support the Jewish struggle to establish the new state. I don't know if he took part in any actual fighting, but being there was an expression of his deep feelings about little countries such as Israel and the Irish Republic.

A second small collection, *Instead of a Sonnet* appeared from Editions Poetry London in 1944. Although copies of this edition are scarce it has survived in a later version, supplemented by an additional ten poems, published by Tuba Press in 1978. I'm not going to over-rate the poems. Potts himself said of them: "These few poems, if indeed they are poems at all, are not terribly good. The poetry of the English language would be no poorer without them and it is unfortunately no richer because of them". Many people would, no doubt, agree with Potts' opinion of his own work. But for all their faults, real or supposed, there is still something about them that helps to overcome their problems. Perhaps Derek Stanford, who knew Potts in the 1940s and after, summed it up reasonably accurately: "Woodenness of statement and lack of rhythm marred most of the small amount of poetry he published, but there was a small percentage of it which by its economy and simplicity overcame the poet's technical awkwardness". And as evidence he quoted the complete, "Prayer to Our Lady":

> Mary Cohen get for me
> Those things you had yourself
> You wrote a poem
> Had a son
> Lived a proper life

It's a poem that perhaps sums up Potts' yearning for a settled life, despite his bohemian proclivities. If Potts' poetry output was slim and unsteady it was because he was really destined, as he himself said, "to write prose as charged with intensity as true poetry". And with *Dante Called You Beatrice*, published in 1960, he may well have succeeded. I'm not sure how the book is regarded now, but it did attract some attention when it appeared. To quote Derek Stanford again: " there are pages in *Dante Called You Beatrice* and its follow-up, *To Keep a Promise* (for all the book's disfiguring sentimentality), which are among the finest passages written in prose since the war".

The opening lines of *Dante Called You Beatrice* essentially set the tone of the rest of the book:

"This book is an attempt to tell a woman, while I was standing on her carpet, asking her to marry me, just what kind of a man it was who loved her, and what other love he had beyond his love of her. Had she wanted my love she would have had to share it, with all of the poor and each of the lonely."

It's said that the woman referred to was Jean Hore, who rejected Potts and married Philip O'Connor but was later diagnosed as schizophrenic and confined to an institution for fifty years. There is a section in *Dante Called You Beatrice* called "A House with no Address" in which Potts writes about his love for her and his relationship with O'Connor who, like Potts, was well-known in Soho and Fitzrovia. The friendship between Potts and O'Connor is explored in Andrew Barrow's *Quentin & Philip: A Double Portrait* (Macmillan 2002), which is about Quentin Crisp and Philip O'Connor but has quite a few references to Potts. It was a friendship that eventually foundered, with Potts seemingly accusing O'Connor of exploiting Jean Hore for her money, and O'Connor describing Potts as "a complete scoundrel......He did everything he could to ruin Jean and me". Where does the truth lie with two extravagant characters like Potts and O'Connor?

Potts published two more books which, in tone and intention, were similar to *Dante Called You Beatrice,* and can be seen as continuations of it. *To Keep a Promise* (MacGibbon & Kee) was published in 1970 and *Invitation to a Sacrament* (Martin Brian & O'Keefe) in 1973. There is a note in the latter which says that another book, *A Piece of English Prose,* was due to be published in May 1974, but there is no record of it ever appearing. It was a fact that by that date Potts was probably too deep into the alcoholism that would affect his capacity to settle to sustained creative work. I'm not sure of the exact year, but at some point in the late-1970s or early-1980s I happened to be in The French and talking to Jay Landesman when Potts lurched past us. Landesman said something to him about a promised manuscript and got in response what sounded like a dismissive curse. Potts was clearly drunk and in no mood to discuss anything coherently.

It may be that, *Dante Called You Beatrice* apart, what Potts will mainly be remembered for are his appearances as a bohemian character who crops up in numerous accounts of Soho in the 1940s and 1950s. Derek Stanford devotes several pages to him in his *Inside the Forties: Literary Memoirs 1937-1957* (Sidgwick & Jackson, 1977) and indicates how volatile Potts could be at times, with imagined slights bringing about smashed beer glasses and shouted insults. Wrey Gardiner, in *The Flowering Moment* (Grey Walls Press, 1949), says: "I shall never sell out to the little successful journalists. I shall always walk in the gutter with the funny men with the humorous saddened eyes. Fred Marnau and Ruthven Todd and Paul Potts have qualities that no other human beings I know have. The qualities of the grandes pitres".

Mentioning Wrey Gardiner inclines me to point out that he's another neglected figure whose effusive prose style would not find favour today. He edited *Poetry Quarterly* and published Potts' essays about George Barker and the American, William Saroyan: "William Saroyan is in love, in love with nearly everybody and almost everything. Furthermore he uses his sleeve as a blackboard on which to write his love letters. (P.S. - I like Saroyan very much indeed)". And Saroyan is one more writer who probably goes largely unread these days.

Potts crops up more than once in Daniel Farson's *Soho in the Fifties* (Michael Joseph, 1987) where he's noted as frequenting the notorious Colony Club. Farson also mentioned Potts in *The Gilded Gutter Life of Francis Bacon* (Vintage Books, 1994) in relation to the Colony: "His appearance, increasingly like that of a Soho wino, was tolerated with saintly forbearance by Muriel as he smouldered and stank in the corner, for he rarely washed. With her curious instinct she knew that he was all right, a man of some worth in spite of his failure".

There are anecdotes concerning Potts in books about the Colony Room, though they inevitably frequently focus on his misbehaviour. In Darren Coffield' *Tales from the Colony Room: Soho's Lost Bohemia* (Unbound, 2020), a recollection by Jay Landesman perhaps explains the background to the encounter I witnessed in The French. Landesman said that Potts had proposed editing an anthology, *Poems for Poor People*, and they discussed the idea: "His enthusiasm for the project increased in direct ratio to the drinks I was buying. Before the afternoon was over, we had a golden handshake. His advance was possibly the lowest in publishing history.....£5 and free Guinness.....We both knew the book would never happen, but I enjoyed the liquid negotiations".

Another book, Sophie Parkin's splendid *The Colony Room Club 1948-2008: A History of Bohemian Soho* (Palmtree Publishers, 2013), also includes Potts, bringing in the dishevelment of his later years and noting that "Philip O'Connor and Paul Potts were always cadging drinks or getting angry and there was a lot of emotional behaviour around". But it's worth mentioning that "Poet George Barker described his friend Potts as," 'that criminal whose felony is to love everything a bit too much', as well as dreadfully poor, selling his poems for a penny on street corners and often destitute, he was always welcomed by Muriel, despite his smell and rags".

Incidentally, many of the references to Potts describe his appearance as untidy, even dirty and smelly, but a photograph by John Deakin, chronicler of Soho bohemia, taken in the early-1950s, shows a cleaner and smarter Potts.

As well as the various books and magazines I've referred to, it is relevant to draw attention to *The Faber Book of 20th Century Verse* (Faber, 1953, with several later reprints), edited by David Wright and John Heath-Stubbs, where Potts was represented with two poems. And Michael Horovitz included an excerpt from *Dante Called You Beatrice* in *Children of Albion: Poetry of the 'Underground' in Britain* (Penguin Books, 1969), as if to demonstrate that he had some similarities of mood or manner to certain of the new poets and bohemians. Potts' old sparring partner, Philip O'Connor, was also in the anthology, no doubt for the same reason.

Paul Potts died in 1990. His last few years had seen him more or less housebound due to ill-health and living in what would be described as squalor. He died when he fell asleep while smoking and set his bed on fire. Some of the obituaries commented on his role as a Soho character, but others drew attention to the books he had written during his better days. George Barker thought that Potts' real achievement was with his prose because "he found it hard to conform to the rigours of verse". He was right, though lines from a simple poem by Potts stay in my mind longer than most of the poems I come across in books and magazines:

> I want to write something holy
> Holy about life
> Where a kiss is a prayer
> And God is worshipped
> By the way a woman combs her hair.

When Potts died I was often publishing reviews and poems in *Tribune*, the left-wing weekly paper in which he had appeared in the 1940s. It seemed appropriate to commemorate his passing with a short tribute. I make no claims for it as a poem – as Potts said, "The history of the English language would be no poorer without it" - but it served its purpose and I liked to think that in its directness and simplicity it was not unlike some of what Potts himself wrote.

PAUL POTTS (1911-1990)

> I once saw Paul Potts plain,
> in a Soho pub and drunk again.
> A sad decline, perhaps,
> for someone who had the skill
> to write *Dante Called You Beatrice*.
> But while he lived he raged,
> and never gave in like those
> who favoured easy conformity.
> And in our smooth-toned world
> I'll remember his broken voice,
> and say it again and again.
> I once saw Paul Potts plain.

BOHEMIA

Bohemia, they say, is always yesterday. People like to look back nostalgically to a time when life was full of promise, there were more interesting characters around, money didn't seem to matter as much, and it was possible to survive on very little. Or so it seemed. And there may be some truth in it. It costs a lot to be poor these days and rising property and other prices have effectively driven young would-be writers and artists from city centres. Greenwich Village, Montparnasse, Soho have all been gentrified. But there are various reasons for the decline of the bohemian spirit. The American poet Edward Field pointed out that "It was Andy Warhol who declared the end of bohemianism with his camp emphasis on celebrity. Suddenly, becoming successful and famous became the goal of creative artists and the bohemian ideal was finished".

There is probably significance in the fact that John Taylor Williams has chosen to focus his exploration of bohemianism around Cape Cod on the years between 1910 and 1960. A handy fifty year framework, but it also emphasises that, after 1960, things started to change in terms of the sort of people who began to move into the area. And how developments took place that reflected the tastes and interests of the newcomers, rather than those of the bohemians.

Cape Cod is on the Atlantic Coast of the United States and place names such as Falmouth and Barnstaple reflect how it was one of the earliest English settlements in America. I'm not intending to provide a detailed guide to the area and, from the point of view of *The Shores of Bohemia* the three locations that John Taylor Williams deals with are Truro, Wellfleet and Provincetown. The latter is probably the best-known because of its associations with artistic activities. Jig Cook and the Provincetown Players, famous in the history of American theatre, especially for their involvements with Eugene O'Neill, were active there. And, on a personal note, I was aware of Provincetown as a place where writers and artists congregated. I recall picking up one or two copies of *The Provincetown Review* around 1960 or so.

The magazine, edited by William V. Ward, got into trouble when it published a story by Hubert Selby in its third issue. Ward was taken to court and charged with circulating obscene material. It should be noted that Cape Cod had a local population largely made up of Portuguese fisherfolk, who were Catholics, and descendants of the original settlers who were Protestants. They may have sometimes fallen out with each other, but they could come together in their distrust of the "outsiders". The writers and artists rallied around Ward and money was raised for his defence. Expert witnesses like Norman Podhoretz, Allen Tate, and Stanley Kunitz came forward to testify to the literary qualities of the story. They didn't impress the judge, however, and Ward was found guilty and fined. An entertaining account of the episode by Dan Wakefield was published in the February, 1962, issue of the slick New York magazine *Nugget*.

All that occurred at the end of the period Williams is dealing with, and he doesn't refer to it, but I thought it worthwhile bringing it in as an example of how there could sometimes be friction between locals and "outsiders", some of whom had actually lived in the area for several years, though others tended to be summer visitors only. Not everyone could withstand the rigours of the harsh winters along the Atlantic coastline, nor the isolation.

So, let's go back to where Williams starts his story. He chronicles the influx of artists as beginning from around the time that Charles Hawthorne set up his Cape Cod School of Art in Provincetown in 1899. He had previously worked with William Merritt Chase at a Long Island painting school, and when he moved to Cape Cod some of his students followed him. They included Marsden Hartley, Charles Demuth, and Edward Hopper. Norman Rockwell, who was already living in Provincetown, joined them. Williams quotes an aphorism by Hawthorne that sums up his teaching practice: "Painting is just getting one spot of colour in relation to another spot......Let colour make form, do not make form and colour it". Williams says that Hans Hofmann, who had an influential later art school in Provincetown, agreed with Hawthorne "that colour was the key to great painting".

It's suggested that, along with Hawthorne, one of the people responsible for "luring" many Greenwich Village writers and artists to Provincetown was Mary Heaton Vorse. There were, she pointed out, old warehouses and empty cottages which could be rented or even bought cheaply. Vorse had travelled widely in Europe, spoke French, Italian and German, and had lived on Cape Cod since 1907. She was a radical in her politics and a great supporter of the rights of trade unionists, covering numerous strikes and related activities as a labour reporter. She was also familiar with the bohemians of Greenwich Village. Dee Garrison, Vorse's biographer, said of her: "As the respected older-warrior of the pre-1912 Village, Mary Vorse served as a model for the younger men and women enlisting in the ongoing revolt". That revolt was not only political but artistic and exemplified by the 1913 Armory Show which displayed well over 1,000 works by European and American artists. It brought movements such as Fauvism, Cubism and Futurism to the attention of American painters and sculptors.

Williams provides an interesting and useful survey of the social, political and artistic ferment of the years leading up to America's entry into the First World War. It was a time of experimentation in living, so the possibilities of creating a new society, even if only on a small scale, on Cape Cod appealed to many of the Greenwich Village bohemians. They were appalled by the way in which increasing industrialisation had ravaged the country and created slums in major cities and corruption in politics. People like John Reed, Max Eastman and Floyd Dell campaigned against injustices in *The Masses,* at least until the government closed it down in 1917 because of its opposition to American involvement in the European conflict. In Provincetown they could be largely free from police harassment and indulge in affairs and unconventional behaviour. I lost count of the liaisons as people swapped partners, ran off with someone else's husband or wife, or just had one-night stands. And the post-war years didn't see a let-up in the bed-hopping and extra-marital activities. The so-called Jazz Age encouraged people to loosen up, drink a lot, and often behave outrageously.

Frankly, I got a little tired with tales of infidelity, and was more interested in reading about characters like Harry Kemp and Terry Carlin. Kemp, the "Tramp Poet", as he was known, lived In a shack on the dunes, and his work was popular in the 1920s. He'd designed a scheme for a League of Bohemian Republics which would unite and overthrow both capitalism and communism. It was a fanciful idea and never likely to come to fruition. Kemp later declined into alcoholism and died in 1960. But he had written novels, poetry and autobiographical material before the alcohol got the better of him. His *Tramping on Life* is about his experiences hoboing around America. I've hunted for years for a copy of his novel, *Love Among the Cape Enders*, but have never been able to afford to buy it when one becomes available. As for Terry Carlin, perhaps his main claim to fame is that he provided the basis for Larry Slade, a disillusioned one-time anarchist, who sits drinking and philosophising in Eugene O'Neill's great play, *The Iceman Cometh*. He doesn't appear to have been productive as a writer himself though he did contribute to Benjamin Tucker's magazine, *Liberty*, and to Hippolyte Havel's *Revolt*. Havel was the inspiration for the character of Hugo Kalmar in O'Neill's play.

In the 1930s there was what might be called a "radicalisation of bohemia" as the effects of the Depression, coupled with the rising tide of fascism in Europe, began to affect the lives of the bohemians. Friendships fell apart as people identified themselves as socialists, Stalinists, and Trotskyists. Williams has a shaky summary of the Spanish Civil War in which he says that George Orwell served in the communist-controlled International Brigades. He didn't, and fought with the independent POUM (Workers' Party of Marxist Unification) militia which had no connection with the Brigades. The POUM were looked on as Trotskyists by the communists and were eventually suppressed by the Stalinists. And the book Orwell wrote about the Communist Party's "sinister behaviour" in Spain was *Homage to Catalonia* and not *Animal Farm*.

Among the bohemians who had arrived in the 1930s was Jack Phillips, a Harvard graduate from an affluent family, though he politically aligned himself with the Stalinist wing of the Communist Party. Williams describes him as "preternaturally handsome and charming, and women found him irresistible, although all but the last of his five wives abandoned the marriage". The first of the wives was Elizabeth "Libby" Blair, who Phillips met in Paris, where she was studying with Fernand Legér, and married. It might be worth noting that Libby eventually also married five times.

While they were together Jack and Libby had two daughters, Blair and Hayden. Hayden Herrera's *Upper Bohemia* is a graphic and often touching memoir of what it was like growing up with parents who were often never there, and if they were had little time for their children: "To follow their own desire was a moral imperative. Repression, sacrifice, and compromise were cowardly", Hayden says, and "For my mother and her friends, defying all norms of proper behaviour was fashionable. Conformism was beneath contempt". It says something for Herrera's strength of character that she grew up to be a noted art historian, critic, and biographer.

Philips, who became a self-taught established architect, was still active around Cape Cod when things began to return to normal after 1945. New faces were seen in Provincetown, Truro and Wellfleet. Weldon Kees, a significant poet and critic who later disappeared in mysterious circumstances, opened a gallery in Provincetown and ran a series of discussions under the title, "Forum 49", in which subjects such as "What is an Artist" and "French Art v. American Art" were debated. New York was taking over from Paris as the centre of the art world, and there were new movements in poetry, jazz, and other areas that pointed to a general resurgence of artistic activity.

The politics of the Thirties, which had bitterly divided the community, were in decline, but there was a reckoning to be paid. Some Cape Cod residents were caught up in the HUAC investigations and questioned by the FBI. Williams mentions cinematographer Boris Kaufman who, because of having been born in Russia and with two brothers still living there, "had trouble finding work until Elia Kazan hired him in 1954 to film *On the Waterfront*, for which he won an award for cinematography".

Williams also refers to Steve Nelson, a dedicated communist and one-time member of the International Brigades during the Spanish Civil War. He had moved to Truro because other veterans of that conflict, and members of the Communist Party, lived in the area. Williams refers to Nelson's role as a "party enforcer in the International Brigades culling out anarchists and socialists". His "oral biography", *Steve Nelson: American Radical* (University of Pittsburgh Press, 1981) is worth reading for its vivid account of union organising, war in Spain, and life as a Communist Party activist.

Some members of the group described as the New York Intellectuals could also be seen around Cape Cod, including Mary McCarthy and Edmund Wilson. McCarthy's novel, *A Charmed Life*, is set in what can be identified as Wellfleet, and includes fictionalised portraits of Wilson and others. McCarthy's characters were often shown in an unflattering light, and her descriptions of the person supposedly based on Wilson (she had once been married to him) were less than kind. She also satirised the artist and writer Mary Meigs who appears in the book as Dolly

Lamb, "an untalented painter and do-gooder". It seemed to many people cruel and unnecessary. Williams puts it this way: "Always lurking in this highly charged bohemian circle was an underlying tension based on either dangerous liaisons or unsettled intellectual battles". McCarthy had additionally "targeted" the composer Gardner Jencks and his wife Ruth, supposedly friends of hers, which caused their son to say: "I guess she thought her duty was to her art and not to her friends".

There's no doubt that Cape Cod started to show signs of change as the Fifties progressed. There had always been well-to-do people among the bohemians, and they sometimes nursed ambitions to become writers and artists. But many of the latest arrivals weren't of that frame-of-mind. Williams quotes Edmund Wilson reflecting on what was happening: "The technocrats make a striking contrast with the old Jig Cook Provincetown……. They were all writers and painters who were working and freely exchanging ideas; but these people are mostly attached to the government or some university…..They are accountable to some institution".

And Alfred Kazin noted of Joan's Beach, once the playground of the bohemians; "The great beach was replaced every afternoon by the great society. Every year Joan's weathered old beach sank more abjectly into the sand while around it rose the mercilessly stylised avant-garde house of a wealthy Leninist from Philadelphia".Kazin was getting a dig in at Jack Phillips who had designed the house for Luke Wilson, a wealthy communist sympathiser who fled to Rome when questions were asked about his activities and affiliations.

Wilson closes his account in 1960. He could have extended it beyond that date, I'm sure, but there's no doubt that there were noticeable changes after 1960 or so which altered the structure of bohemia. I came across a wonderful comment some years ago by someone who had worked for the old BBC Third programme in the 1950s and before it was disastrously changed to Radio 3 with music predominating. He said the organisation was in those days "full of bohemians disguised as bourgeoisie. Now it's full of bourgeoisie disguised as bohemians". It says a lot about what was happening in society generally, and not just in America. The expansion of higher education, and the development of arts associations and the like, increasingly led to the sort of "institutionalisation" Edmund Wilson was referring to.

There are so many interesting people named in *The Shores of Bohemia* that I would have liked to write about. Daniel Aaron, who was one of the "organisation men" referred to by Wilson, but who wrote the informative *Writers on the Left: Episodes in American Literary Communism*. Robert Nathan, author of the novel, *Portrait of Jennie*, which was adapted into a haunting film starring Joseph Cotton and Jennifer Jones. Edwin O'Connor and his novel, *The Last Hurrah,* about the politics of Catholic Boston. The splendid poet Frank O'Hara. They all deserve greater attention than I can give them.

Others like the radical novelist and critic Waldo Frank who had broken with the Communist Party in 1937 over their treatment of Trotsky, and the well-known Norman Mailer, were in and out of Provincetown.. Many writers, but there were plenty of painters, not all of them necessarily internationally known. Edward Hopper was famous, but is said to have been a sometimes violent heavy drinker who lived on Cape Cod. The lesser-known Ross Moffett is mentioned by Williams and there is, in fact, a photo of him in the book. It wasn't all that long ago that I obtained a copy of Moffett's little book, *Art in Narrow Streets: The First Thirty-Three Years of the Provincetown Art Association 1914-1947* in which the text is sprinkled with pictures of old Provincetown. Moffett was old enough to have studied at Charles Hawthorne's Cape Cod School.

There were the usual oddballs among the bohemians, including the heavy-drinking Frank Shay. He had served in the American Army during the First World War and, Williams says, they (meaning Shay and Harry Kemp) "returned to Provincetown as men who now required a great deal of alcohol to forget". In fact, it's unlikely that Kemp ever saw military service. His biography, *Harry Kemp: The Last Bohemian* by William Brevda makes no mention of it. He didn't need an excuse to get drunk.

Shay had owned the Parnassus, a bookstore in Greenwich Village, and when he closed it down loaded the stock into a "rented wooden-sided station wagon" and set off to sell the books in towns around Cape Cod. The vehicle had a logo, "Parnassus on Wheels", which was the title of a Christopher Morley novel about a travelling bookshop first published in 1917. It, and a follow-up title, *The Haunted Bookshop,* were popular in their day, though it's doubtful if they're widely read now. Morley also had a hit with his novel, *Kitty Foyle*, which was turned into a film starring Ginger Rogers and Dennis Morgan. The screenplay was by Dalton Trumbo, with additional dialogue by Donald Ogden Stewart. Both were later blacklisted when Hollywood purged its communists.

There's a passage in Morley's *Parnassus on Wheels* that has always amused me: "The world is full of great writers about literature, he said, but they're all selfish and aristocratic. Addison, Lamb, Hazlitt, Emerson, Lowell – take any one you choose – they all conceive the love of books as a rare and perfect mystery for the few – a thing of the secluded study where they can sit alone at night with a candle, and a cigar, and a glass of port on the table and a spaniel on the hearthrug". I've met more than a few people who seemed to think that literature is their private preserve and the rest of us shouldn't lay our grubby hands on it.

Williams's final chapter, "Eden's End", says that "The old bohemian Cape began to vanish like Camelot, as did the original world of fishing and farming that had provided the beloved context for bohemian creativity". And he adds: "Through all their political partisanship, artistic creation, lovemaking and drinking, a generation that cared so deeply about the bohemian ethos was evaporating". People placed "a much greater emphasis on monetary success, even if they identified themselves as painters, writers, or architects".

The Shores of Bohemia has much to recommend it, even if sometimes the names tumble over each other. I occasionally lost track of who was related to who, slept with who, fought with who, was an alcoholic (quite a few, according to Williams), and so on. And the photos are disappointing, printed as they are in black and white on the page and not always very clearly. It's a problem with Hayden Herrera's book, too. Still, Williams does have useful notes and a bibliography. Together both books evoke a time when bohemianism had a point beyond merely making copy for publicity purposes.

THE SHORES OF BOHEMIA : A CAPE COD STORY, 1910-1960

By John Taylor Williams

Farrar, Straus and Giroux. 343 pages. $35. ISBN 978-0-374-26275-4

UPPER BOHEMIA : A MEMOIR

By Hayden Herrera

Simon & Schuster. 248 pages. $17.99. ISBN 978-1-9821-0529-7

JAMES CAMPBELL

James Campbell for twenty or so years wrote the N B column on the back pages of the weekly *Times Literary Supplement*. It was lively and always worth reading, both for his own witty comments, but also for the information it provided about often obscure writers, books and magazines. In a way it reflected the interests and experiences of someone who hadn't been through what might be termed a conventional literary education.

Campbell was born in 1951 in Croftfoot, a suburb of Glasgow. His parents were what is often referred to as aspirant working-class, and the young Campbell didn't always match up to what they saw as behaviour befitting an ideal white-collar, middle-class future for their son. He tended to skip school, do poorly when he was there, except in English composition, and mixed with the wrong crowd. He was even arrested for stealing books. much to the annoyance of his father. To make matters worse he left school at fifteen and took a job as an apprentice in a run-down back-alley printing works. The descriptions of the work, the conditions in which it was performed, and Campbell's fellow-workers, are sharp and will ring a bell for anyone who has been employed doing mundane jobs in less than salubrious surroundings.

What proved to be Campbell's salvation were his encounters with Glasgow's folk-music scene and its characters. Along with listening to records of old American blues singers, and making trips to Edinburgh to look for beatniks, the people he encountered in the folk-clubs and pubs were introducing him into a world that wasn't just about work, having a steady girl-friend, and wondering when to get married. It became obvious that Campbell increasingly wanted to be on the "outside" of ordinary life. His father was even more infuriated when he quit his job after three years and decided to travel to India, which is where the hippies and others were heading in the late-Sixties.

I think it needs to be noted that, despite Campbell's involvements, he wasn't blind to his surroundings. He was conscious of the fact that the "old Glasgow was disappearing". He doesn't falsely eulogise the decaying streets and tenements, but "When these neighbourhoods went, their binding spirits, which made people quarrel and occasionally injure to the same degree to which they act on the instinct to shelter and protect, went with them".Reading that I couldn't help thinking about a poem called "King Billy" by the fine Scottish poet, Edwin Morgan. It's about Glasgow in the 1930s, sectarian struggles, poverty, idleness, and razor gangs. Thirty years later an old man dies "So a thousand people stopped the traffic/for the hearse of a folk hero". And if anyone wonders what that was all about, "Deplore what is to be deplored,/and then find out the rest".

Campbell never did make it to India, a combination of factors, including being conned out of his money, intervening to turn him in the direction of Turkey, Greece, Morocco, and a kibbutz in Israel. He worked at various jobs and eventually found his way home to Glasgow, where he decided that his wandering days were over and he needed to settle down to some hard work. He studied for "A" levels so he could enrol at Edinburgh University for a degree in American Literature. When he got it he became editor of *New Edinburgh Review* for four years while also doubling up as a driver for the local Social Services Department. And he was contributing poems and reviews to magazines. The literary life often requires a variety of occupations to provide a reasonable income.

When moving around various countries Campbell had carried with him a copy of Alexander Trocchi's *Cain's Book*, a novel of drug addiction in New York by a fellow-Scot who was much in the news in the Sixties. When he got the opportunity to interview Trocchi, who was then living in London after fleeing America when he was arrested for supplying drugs to a minor (a capital offence at the time), Campbell jumped at the chance. He paints a vivid picture of a man proclaiming the virtues of heroin, along with the promises of his sigma ("the invisible Insurrection of a million minds") project. Campbell's girlfriend had accompanied him to the interview with Trocchi and he says that she was less impressed and said she "could smell evil about his person". I only met Trocchi once and likewise had an uneasy feeling about him. As for sigma it seemed to me about as practical as the old bohemian Harry Kemp's scheme for an alliance of the Republics of Bohemia which would overthrow both capitalism and communism.

Campbell had a better experience when he first got to know James Baldwin, and his account of how their relationship developed over the years is well worth reading. In time Campbell, of course, wrote one of the best books about him, *Talking at the Gates: A Life of James Baldwin,* which has recently been reissued. He obviously admired Baldwin as a writer in many ways, though he wasn't unaware to his occasional shortcomings as a person. But when he writes of an encounter with Baldwin that it "is one of my most precious memories" you know that he means it.

Campbell's memoir comes to a halt just about when he started working part-time at the *Times Literary Supplement*, and in due course became the J.C. of the NB column of that publication. I know quite a few people who, when the *TLS* arrived each week, immediately turned to the back page to see what J.C. was writing about. As I mentioned earlier, he seemed to have the knack of locating writers and books and magazines that were too often forgotten or overlooked or otherwise neglected by many other critics and commentators.

Just Go Down to the Road is an engaging memoir. I've out of necessity had to leave out his experiences at Lewes Prison (a visitor and not an inmate, I hasten to add) which resulted in his book, *Gate Fever: Voices From a Prison.*and his interview with the novelist, John Fowles. And later there were excellent books on the post-war Parisian scene (*Paris Interzone)* and the Beats (*This is the Beat Generation*), and a fine collection of essays and reviews in *Syncopation,* all of which displayed a close awareness of the lives of writers and their work. The memoir helps to round out our awareness of James Campbell's life and work.

JUST GO DOWN TO THE ROAD : A MEMOIR OF TRAVEL AND TROUBLE

By James Campbell

Polygon. 279 pages. £14.99. ISBN 978-1-84697-529-5

MINA LOY : APOLOGY OF GENIUS

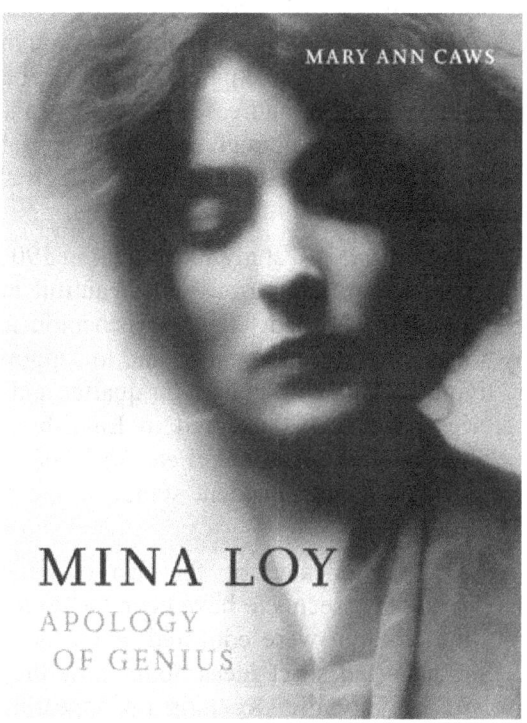

Mina Loy was one of those legendary figures at the heart of modernism in its heyday, but who, I suspect, very few people have read in any depth. They may have read about her, and it could be that, for many who have come across Loy, the life is possibly more interesting than the work. She knew the right people, was in the right places at the right time, and attracted the right sort of attention. Saying that may make her seem like an opportunist, but I don't think it's true to suggest she simply hopped on the latest bandwagons. She was far too much of an individual for that.

Loy was born Mina Gertrude Lowy in London in 1882 and was the first of three daughters. Her parents were Sigmund Felix Lowy, "a tailor of Hungarian Jewish heritage", and Julia Bryan, "a British Methodist". Mary Ann Caws' book is not a biography, so I'm doing no more than sketching in some basic details. But it may be worth noting that the description of Loy's father as a Jewish tailor could suggest Whitechapel, sweat shops, and poverty. It wasn't the case and Loy's parents appear to have been affluent enough to have lived in addresses in Hampstead. And to allow Mina to attend art school, though they drew the line at the Slade and she went to one in St John's Wood which she later described as "the worst art school in London".

She was also given permission to study in Munich in 1900. It was there she would have seen the notorious and beautiful Franziska zu Revenlow, a countess who had left her aristocratic family to have a child by a man she refused to name, and to support herself and her son by living in Munich's bohemian quarter and writing. Some of her stories have been published in English under the title, *The Guesthouse at the Sign of the Teetering Globe* (Rixdorf Editions, Berlin, 2017). Her independent stance would no doubt have appealed to Loy.

Loy's childhood was complicated by the fact of her parents' mixed religions. Her mother seems to have been the dominant one in terms of how the children were educated and which religion they followed. She also had strict ideas about how they had to conduct themselves in daily life. Keeping up appearances was seen as of key importance. A full account of Loy's early years can be found in Carolyn Burke's *Becoming Modern: The Life of Mina Loy* (Farrar, Straus and Giroux, New York, 1996) should anyone want further details.

From the point of view of Caws' book she refers to lines in Loy's poetry which touch on the relationship between her father and mother. And, in fact, this is largely her approach throughout *Apology of Genius*. She draws heavily on *The Last Lunar Baedeker,* the collection with its free verse techniques and structures on which Loy's reputation rests, to show how her writing followed the events of her life. There is a poem, "Anglo-Mongrels and the Rose", originally published in *The Little Review* in Spring 1923, which is about Loy's parents and the England they and she inhabited. I'm looking at a copy of the magazine as I write this, and the lines in the poem about "Sundays when/England closed the eyes of every/commercial enterprise/but the church" amuse me. It wasn't much different when I was growing up in England in the 1940s.

It was inevitable that Loy would go to Paris, where she studied with Whistler and it was there that she met the free-spirited bohemian painter and photographer Stephen Haweis, who seduced her. She was four months pregnant when they married in 1903. He proved to be unreliable, and Caws quotes from a poem, "Parturition", which has references to "The irresponsibility of the male" and "He is running upstairs", which, according to Caws, was to be with his mistress while his wife gave birth to a girl who died a few months later. The marriage does seem to have been one of convenience more than anything, and Loy had an affair and a daughter with the wonderfully named Dr Joël Le Savourex, who "treated her neurasthenics" after her first child died.

Loy and Haweis moved to Florence, where she came across Italian Futurists like Marinetti ("a bombastic superman", though she was impressed by his energy) and Giovanni Papini, with whom she had an affair. And she mixed with the people who gathered around Violet Paget (described by one of her admirers as "deeply learned and eloquent") who wrote erudite supernatural fiction under the name Vernon Lee. Loy's spiritual inclinations were often to a higher, if not supernatural, form of existence, though a strain of realism runs through her writing. It may be relevant that she maintained a strong allegiance to Christian Science throughout her life, something that enabled her to form a close friendship in America with the artist, Joseph Cornell.

In order to make money Loy designed magazine covers and created theatre sets, as well as producing lampshades and dress designs. Some of these activities were to provide a source of income for much of her life. She eventually had enough money to take her to New York where she fell in with Walter Arensberg's coterie. It was said of Arensberg and his wife that they "not only collected art, but the artists as well". Marcel Duchamp was one of their friends, and so was Arthur Cravan. There is a painting by André Raffray spread over two pages of Caws' book and it shows an assembly at the Arensberg's apartment which includes, among others, Picabia, Joseph Stella, Cravan, Loy, and the eccentric Baroness Elsa von Freytag Loringhoven, whose appearance and antics are described in memoirs and histories of the period. But it was Arthur Cravan that Loy was interested in.

Cravan, a nephew of Oscar Wilde and sometimes given to imitating him, had used a variety of names and had a variety of adventures, though it's not always possible to know for sure just who he was and what he had done. One thing that is a fact, however, is that he had a well-publicised boxing match in Spain with the black fighter, Jack Johnson, one-time heavy-weight world champion. Was it a publicity stunt with a fake sixth-round knock-out by Johnson, by then past his prime, and just designed to make money for him and Cravan?

Loy and Cravan married in Mexico in 1918 and planned to live in Buenos Aires. She travelled by ship, and he set out to make his way there in a small boat. He never arrived, and it has always been assumed that he must have drowned. Loy searched for him but neither he nor any evidence of what had happened ever turned up. Given his past record some people might have wanted to assume that he'd deliberately organised a disappearance. But if so it's more than likely that he would have resurfaced somewhere, if only under another name. He never did.

Loy's next move was to Paris and encounters with the expatriates, including Robert McAlmon, who she had previously met in New York. Carolyn Burke says that his short sketch, "A Poetess" (included in *A Hasty Bunch*, first published in 1922 and reprinted by Southern Illinois University Press in 1977), is most likely a prose portrait of Loy.

She also met up with the Surrealists, though I doubt that she ever really connected closely with them. She knew the leading figures in the movement, and the rest of the art world of Paris, and was photographed with Djuna Barnes by Man Ray. She had an affair with a German Surrealist artist, Richard Oelze, though she didn't speak kindly of a character based on him in her novel, *Insel*, which only saw print many years after her death. It has been said that her intention in *Insel* was to "banalise the Surrealist milieu of

1930s Paris". She had done something similar with her comments on Futurism some years earlier. Caws does not have a high opinion of the novel, describing it as "not worth the time of reading", and that "It becomes well nigh impossible to understand some paragraphs".

By 1936 Loy was back in New York, and it's from this point that she started to drift into obscurity. The social and political atmosphere of the Thirties was vastly different to that of the 1920s. It's difficult to imagine Loy in a world of proletarian novels, radical magazines, and paintings which emphasised protest and left-wing opinions. A good-looking, well-dressed woman might have been out-of-place in a strike meeting or on a picket-line, though to be fair some did turn up in such circumstances to demonstrate their affinity with the working-class. But not Loy who began her withdrawal into the almost-solitary life that often marked her late-years. Only a few people – Djuna Barnes, Berenice Abbott – knew where she was and tried to keep in touch, and only one or two others – Kenneth Rexroth, Jonathan Williams – continued to draw attention to her work. But it was years before it was reprinted. She appears to have survived with support from her daughters and friends.

I said that it's difficult to envisage Loy identifying with striking workers or political dissidents, but likewise she continued to stand aside from bourgeois manners and morality. She lived in close proximity to the Bowery area of New York and mixed with its drunks and down-and-outs. Her poem, "Hot Cross Bums", celebrates them in its idiosyncratic way: "So wonder why /defeat/by dignity of the majority/oft reveals/in close-up of inferno faces/a nobler origin/than practicality's elite".

Loy's two daughters were living in Aspen, Colorado, and when it became obvious that she could not continue to live comfortably and safely in New York she was persuaded to move closer to them in 1953. The rise of interest in the 1950s in the Beats, Black Mountain Poets, and others, with their precursors in earlier avant-gardes and bohemias, brought about a revival of some older poets like Walter Lowenfels and Mina Loy. Jonathan Williams reprinted work by both of them, including *The Last Lunar*

Baedeker, and in 1961 and 1962 Gilbert Neiman used some of Loy's poems in issues of *Between Worlds*, a magazine he edited from the Inter American University in Puerto Rico. They were the first opportunity I had to read her work, though I knew her name from accounts of Paris in the Twenties. Loy died in Aspen in 1966.

I'm not going to claim that I've always found Loy's poems easy to read and understand. But there has usually been something there that has continued to draw me to them. She had a love of words and their sounds and sometimes the meaning is almost lost as the sounds take over. But then there is a return to reality which anchors the poem. I hadn't looked at Loy's work for some time, and Caws' enthusiastic comments on her poetry caused me to find my old copies of *Between Worlds* and refresh my memory of first coming across it.

Caws' enthusiasm carries her book along, and it is hard to resist it. She doesn't restrict herself to looking at the poems. There is Loy's art work, which admittedly I've overlooked because, apart from some reproductions in the book, I haven't had an opportunity to see it. She views Loy as "unusual, to put it mildly, but admirable", and her "very peculiarity was priceless". "She was never 'striking a pose', but rather inhabiting her own personality". There's also a passage, a little too long to quote in full, where Caws refers to Loy's "usual ease and elegance" when seen in photographs. The selection in the book by photographers like Man Ray and Lee Miller, points to the truth in what Caws says.

Some people might object to this focus on Loy's physical appearance and ask what it has to do with her poems? Is it a case where the life and looks take over from the literary accomplishments? Our own age, with its shallow emphasis on celebrity, doesn't ask much from people it admires other than to look good. But Loy did a lot more than simply dress well and catch the eye. Caws is as affirmative about the work as she is about Loy's appearance. She is, in fact, occasionally carried away to the point where words and phrases like "poetic genius", "epic", and "Mina Loy had one of the most outstandingly open panoramas of a brain ever evolved" are scattered around the text. And she claims that Loy and Tristan Tzara were "two great poets". I have doubts whenever I see the words "great" and "genius" used too often, no matter who they're applied to. It seems to me enough that someone's work is of interest and I find pleasure in reading it.

But I don't want to detract from the very real and readable qualities that Mary Ann Caws *Mina Loy: Apology of Genius* has to offer. It's refreshing to read something by someone who doesn't lay claims to total detachment, and is prepared to perhaps stand open to criticism by being outspoken in her admiration for Loy and her work. I can forgive the occasional lapses into hyperbole. They're sincere and well-meant. The book has notes, a short but useful bibliography, and is well-illustrated with photos and reproductions of art works. Also, and it's a virtue in my opinion, it doesn't need to extend beyond its 223 pages when making a convincing case for Mina Loy as a poet worth reviving and reading.

MINA LOY : APOLOGY OF GENIUS
By Mary Ann Caws
Reaktion Books. 223 pages. £20. ISBN 978-1-78914-554-0

THE LITTLE ART COLONY AND US MODERNISM : CARMEL, PROVINCETOWN, TAOS

Art colonies came in various shapes and sizes. They were a notable feature of artistic life in Europe and America prior to the First World War, and some continued after 1914. But many had been in coastal locations and the war had particularly affected them. Added to which few people could travel to them, even if they continued to have some sort of relevance in terms of artistic activity. The point of a colony was to give people the opportunity to meet others with similar interests and develop their work in a sympathetic atmosphere. It may not have always worked out like that, creative people often having a tendency to compete and argue when they feel that they have been snubbed or slighted in any way.

There was, also, the problem of colonies becoming too popular in terms of the hordes of people visiting them. It's significant that the number of art colonies expanded as the nineteenth century saw the rise of a middle-class with the time and money to spend on their developing interest in art, not only from the point of view of creating it but also of appreciating it. And, for many people, there was the entertainment value of increasingly looking on artists as some sort of rare breed who lived free-and-easy lives devoid of the everyday responsibilities that beset other people. The bohemian idea, both for the beholder and the practitioner, was largely a product of industrial capitalism.

It's possible to add other reasons for the growth of art colonies. The introduction of easier ways of carrying paint in tubes, and the availability of portable easels, made painting outdoors much easier. Of particular importance was the extension of the railway network to locations that were previously thought of as difficult to access. It was easier for artists to get to coastal villages that had once seemed isolated. They could, if necessary, reside there just for a few summer months and then escape back to the comforts of the city when winter came in. It was convenient to keep in touch with galleries and dealers if there were regular rail services to major cities. And people perhaps likely to purchase paintings could travel by train to view what artists were producing.

Geneva M. Gano's book focuses on three American art colonies. They were originally among the many that sprang up across the United States at a time when unfettered capitalism seemed unstoppable in its determination to impose its values on everyone and everything. This led to vast disparities of wealth and the violent social conflict that caused. There may be some irony in the fact that many, if not most, of the artists and their patrons who lived in or visited the art colonies, and were often critical of rampant capitalism, were the beneficiaries of funds created from that source.

It was necessary to have some money to be able to move to Carmel or Provincetown or Taos in the first place. A patron might provide it, or it could be from a private income, and sometimes from selling a painting or two. Gano makes the point that, in Jack London's novel *The Valley of the Moon*, two working-class characters who visit Carmel, while searching for an alternative to life in the factories and warehouses of the cities, see it as "a playground for bohemian leisure" and decide not to settle there. The "modernism" in the title of Gano's book refers not only to that suggested by developments in the arts, but also to the widespread influence of the growth of a capitalist economy.

Gano's approach is to present a general outline of the development of each of her chosen colonies and the effect that the arrival of the artists had on the original inhabitants, and in turn, the impact that the advent of tourism had on the artists. She then adds lengthy analyses of relevant works by major figures related to the colonies. With Carmel she looks at Robinson Jeffers, for Provincetown its Eugene O'Neill, and for Taos, D.H. Lawrence. My only complaint about this method would be that not enough attention is paid to other writers and artists in the communities involved. The result then tends to be that it's difficult to decide if sufficient work of quality was created in a wider sense. The reader may find it difficult to understand whether or not it went beyond the ordinary and added anything of value to the world-wide continuity of artistic modernism.

From Gano's account of Carmel it would seem that, almost from the start, its role as a haven for artists was under threat from real estate developers and other local businessmen. And from tourism. She quotes from a journalist who, as early as 1892, was noting the fact that "the whole area had been transformed into a veritable picnicking ground for the whole state" and the genuine bohemians were being pushed out. And there's the later lament by Robinson Jeffers in his poem, "Carmel Point", when he refers to "This beautiful place defaced with a crop of suburban houses".

Similar problems of business interests intervening and too many tourists arriving were experienced in Provincetown. Charles Hawthorne had established an art school there in 1899, and the writer Mary Heaton Vorse bought a house in the town in 1905 and encouraged friends and contacts from Greenwich Village to visit and sometimes settle along Cape Cod. The local economy, primarily centred around fishing, was in decline, and it was obviously to the advantage of real estate developers and businesses to look for alternative sources of income. Renting and selling properties to artists and writers boomed and astute promoters began to advertise the idea of Provincetown as a bohemian outpost where painters and poets could be seen at play.

I think that, in many ways, Provincetown might be a livelier subject for commentary than Carmel. The range of creative artists and others who either lived in the area, or spent some time there, was wider and reflected the fact that New York was within manageable distance as far as travel was concerned. Numerous relatively well-known painters and writers could congregate not only in Provincetown itself but also in neighbouring towns like Truro and Wellfleet. But Provincetown was essentially the centre of activities and as such was where tourists aimed for. Inevitably, the tourists, and the well-to-do who had little interest in the arts but liked the idea of living around Cape Cod, began to take over, with the result that many of the genuinely creative people drifted away. There can never be a bohemia if property prices and the general cost of living prevent struggling painters and poets, and the idiosyncratic and eccentric types who cluster around them, from living cheaply and getting together.

Gano looks in some detail at the role played in the Provincetown art colony by the Provincetown Players. Founded by George Cram Cook and Susan Glaspell, with Mary Heaton Vorse, Neith Boyce, and one or two others in close support, the Players' original intention was to present mostly short plays largely written by members of the local bohemian community. It initially had "no aim except the amusement of its members", and the people who wrote the plays often acted in them. Scenery, where it existed, was functional. Should anyone want to sample the kind of work written and performed by some of those involved there is an excellent selection of short plays in *The Provincetown Players,* edited by Barbara Ozieblo, published by Sheffield Academic Press, 1994.

Most of the plays are probably forgotten now, but Eugene O'Neill's *Bound East For Cardiff*, is remembered as an early work by someone who became famous and not only in America. He doesn't appear to have written anything that referred specifically to Provincetown and its inhabitants, and Gano devotes most of her comments on O'Neill to *the Emperor Jones,* the play which effectively brought him to the attention of critics and wider audiences. Daring to feature a black actor in the leading role it was launched in Greenwich Village, moved to Broadway, and extensively toured the country at a time when the Ku Klux Klan was active. Not all Provincetown's supposed liberals were colour blind, and limits on what blacks could do were in operation in many towns and cities. Gano points out that it was written while O'Neill was living on Cape Cod. Her analysis of the play is perceptive. O'Neill, of course, was ambitious and Provincetown was simply one rung on the ladder to success. Not everyone was as idealistic as George Cram Cook.

Both Carmel and Provincetown were coastal locations with developing transport facilities, but when Mabel Dodge Sterne (as she was then) "discovered" Taos she couldn't have chosen a more isolated place from the point of view of access. Set in the New Mexico desert, its nearest train depot was over twenty miles away and road travel meant "a long rough trip". The isolation seemed to attract "a creative class of painters, writers, lovers of Nature and students of American history". But Gano suggests that Taos wasn't perhaps as isolated as we might think. It was, she says, "a long-established, cosmopolitan site of transnational commerce and intercultural exchange". It wasn't a complete cultural backwater, and as soon as artists and writers began to arrive in force commercial interests were quick to use their presence for advertising purposes.

Mabel Dodge Luhan, as she became when she married a local resident, Tony Luhan, had the money to live in comfort and invite artists, writers, and others to spend long, and hopefully productive periods in Taos. Marsden Hartley and Andrew Dasburg were among the first visitors, followed by Leo Stein, Willa Cather, Jean Toomer, Carl Jung, and Georgia O'Keefe. Gano indicates that they were attempting to "escape" from "a repellent modernity epitomised by the European war fuelled by a capitalism run amok and stoked by technological advances". What they were seeking in Taos was not only a refuge from industrial society and war, but also a kind of spiritual awakening that they might find among the original inhabitants of the area.

The Pueblo Indians, whose traditional ceremonial dances and practices were frowned on by the authorities, seemed to offer something far beyond the mere physical satisfactions of the everyday. But their activities were under threat from the "two most reprehensible elements of mass modernity: aggressive and ongoing governmental suppression and a voracious uncontrolled capitalism". The artists and writers, or "anarcho-bohemians", as Gano describes them, empathised with the dancers, having suffered their own "political persecution and cultural suppression" when the government banned certain publications, limited freedom of expression, and introduced conscription after America decided to go to war in 1917.

When D.H. Lawrence arrived in Taos he was in search of his own refuge from modern society. His short novel, *St Mawr*, looked at in some detail by Gano, tells the story of Lou, a sophisticated but disillusioned young woman who flees from polite society in London and elsewhere and seeks salvation in the American South West. But, "as Lawrence finally shows us, Lou's attempted escape from the modern world system can only be unsuccessful. As the reader is gradually made aware, there is nowhere beyond or outside of this system to escape to. Even at the world's most apparently pristine and unmolested margins and edges, buying and selling is the rule of the day".

Gano closes her book with some brief comments on Taos today where it's possible to book into the Frieda Lawrence or Georgia O'Keefe room for the night at the Mabel Dodge Luhan house. And attend a creative retreat or workshop. She also mentions a new "art colony" in Marfa, Texas, with "nineteen permanent art galleries, multiple non-profit foundations devoted to the arts, internationally celebrated music and arts festivals", plus restaurants and the like. This truly is the age of the arts administrator and not the artist.

The Little Art Colony and US Modernism is a useful and provocative book, well-researched and coherently argued. My own feeling, for what it's worth, is that art colonies, like bohemia (other than in its individual "state of mind" sense), are essentially a thing of the past. They depended on spontaneity for their creation and can't be constructed by institutions. They had their day and reading about them is always fascinating and likely to fill one with nostalgia for a perhaps shabbier but more open time. But the bureaucrats have taken over and creative people are now subject to their whims and wishes for bigger audiences and greater profits.

THE LITTLE ART COLONY AND US MODERNISM :
CARMEL, PROVINCETOWN, TAOS

By Geneva M. Gano

Edinburgh University Press. 296 pages. £24.99. ISBN 978-1-4744-3976-3

QUEER ST IVES AND OTHER STORIES

St Ives has a fascinating history as an art colony, and more than one book has focused on what happened there in the years following the Second World War. Painters and sculptors like Barbara Hepworth, Denis Mitchell, Patrick Heron, Peter Lanyon, and others, made the small coastal town a centre of international attention in terms of developments in the arts. It's obvious that there must have been a number of lesbians and homosexuals among the populace, whether locals or outsiders, but it needs to be remembered that it was a time (the 1940s through to well into the 1960s) when it was safer to hide one's sexual proclivities which, in the case of gay men, could lead to prosecution and imprisonment. And even just on an everyday level a hint of deviance could result in provocation and physical assaults. Beating up a queer was seen as normal and not to be condemned in the northern industrial town where I grew up in the 1940s and 1950s.

At the centre of Ian Massey's book is John Milne, a sculptor born in 1931 into a working-class family in Eccles, a town now incorporated into the Greater Manchester conurbation. His father was a tailor who worked from home and his mother took in boarders at what Massey says was a "substantial semi-detached house". Milne had shown some talent for drawing but, due to pressure from his father, initially went to Salford Technical College to study on the Junior Building Course, He was unhappy at the thought of a career in the building trades and his mother, aware that he wanted to be an artist, and with assistance from the Head of the School of Art, managed to have him transferred to the Art course.

Massey says that "Upon his completion of his general training in art and design, Milne decided to specialise in sculpture, a choice resulting from his fascination with the work of the Romanian Constantin Brancusi, which he had come across in photographic reproduction". Described as "a driven and productive student", he exhibited locally. Insofar as his personality was concerned, Massey refers to him being "highly sensitive in nature" with "nothing in common with the rest of his family" who "shared none of his interests in classical music and poetry and found themselves bemused by him".

It was inevitable that Milne would make friends and contacts among similarly-minded people, and "Manchester had a rich cultural scene in the post-war world of the late 1940s". He got to know students whose hang-out was "The Kardomah on Deansgate, a subterranean coffee house with arched and vaulted recesses". Massey's evocation of the bohemian scene in the city is helped along by his use of novels by Tony Warren, perhaps best-known for his links to *Coronation Street*. His *The Lights of Manchester* mentions "Magda Schiffer…a Manchester bohemian legend" and Massey says she was based on the real-life Käthe Schuftan who, Milne later recalled, "had been a strong and encouraging influence on him during his student years". A German Jew she had left when Hitler came to power and she was under suspicion because of her political commitments and the fact of her art work being unacceptable to the Nazis.

I haven't the space to mention all the artists, writers and others included in Massey's survey of the post-1945 Manchester scene, though I was intrigued to see the painter Rowley Smart referred to in passing. He had died in the 1930s but people who had known him were still in the city. It's worth reading this section of the book for its own sake, and not just because of its relevance to Milne's life. But it was because of his involvement in the bohemian world, and the homosexual aspect of it, that in 1951 Milne met Cosmo Rodewald, a wealthy American who was "a lecturer in classical history at Manchester University". Sixteen years older than Milne he was "highly cultured" and a "discreet philanthropist". He was to be of importance in his life, in one way or another, for many years.

It would appear that Milne was more than well treated by Rodewald, with trips to Paris, Greece, and Turkey. In the words of Victor Sayer, who became Rodewald's lifelong partner, "John was spoilt rotten by Cosmo", and he recalled arguments between them when Milne "became yet more demanding". Milne also studied in Paris for a time, enrolling at the prestigious La Grande Chaumière which was under the directorship of Ossip Zadkine. But he was disappointed in the teaching methods, finding them too traditional and restrictive. It was abstraction he was looking towards. On the other hand, being in Paris meant that he could get closer to the work of Giacometti and especially Brancusi, whose carvings in marble and wood particularly impressed him.

Late in 1952 Milne journeyed south to St Ives where he was to become an assistant (unpaid at first) to the well-known Barbara Hepworth. Massey says it's not clear how he established contact with Hepworth in the first place. Clearly it was, for Milne, an opportunity to work alongside an already-established sculptor and study her methods as well as developing his own. What wouldn't have been in his mind was that St Ives would be his home for the rest of his life. Milne stayed with Hepworth for eighteen months and then left, determined to set up on his own as a sculptor. In 1956 the ever-generous Rodewald bought Trewyn (described by

Massey as a "large double-fronted house on three floors") for Milne, the idea being that he could boost whatever income he had from his sculptures by taking in paying guests.

One of those guests was Julian Nixon, who might be worthy of a book himself. He was a flamboyant gay, variously described as "just a camp little queen" and "living in a delusional world". He had been arrested in 1954 with a number of other men and charged with gross indecency. This was when the police were conducting a campaign of surveillance and harassment against gay men and the press was particularly virulent in its comments on homosexuality. Most of Nixon's co-defendants went to prison, one committed suicide before he could be sentenced, and Nixon himself was bound over for two years provided he spent twelve months in a mental hospital.

I don't want to spend too much time on Nixon's subsequent career. He seems to have survived by living off others, including elderly well-to-do ladies, trying to sue the writer Norman Levine for damages by claiming he'd been libelled in one of his stories, and even attempting to sue Milne for damages for "alienation of affection" of a young man who Nixon had brought to stay with him at Trewyn and who, he said, Milne had enticed away. In both cases he was persuaded by legal experts against going to court and possibly having his own shady past and activities brought to light.

It's of relevance to note that Massey is of the opinion that Milne's hedonistic life-style probably worked against him completing a substantial body of work: "For the greater part of his career, Milne's production of sculpture was sporadic", Because of the support provided by Cosmo Rodewald there was little pressure on Milne to sell his work. And, Massey adds, he had periods of "mental instability" and made several suicide attempts, including one following the tragic death of Barbara Hepworth in a fire at her studio.

I mentioned earlier Milne's hedonism, which not only included trips to North Africa in search of sex, something that many gays who could afford it did in the late-40s and 1950s, but also any number of "scandalous" parties at Trewyn and other locations in and around St Ives. Some have gained almost-legendary status. The Canadian writer Norman Levine who lived for many years in St Ives, and whose novel, *From a Seaside Town*, is a key document in the literary history of the area, wrote a long story or novella called *Playground* with various easily-identifiable people portrayed in fictional form. This is the story in which Julian Nixon claimed to have been libelled. One of the other characters, a man called Starkie, commits suicide after arguing with his partner and other people at a party. Starkie was closely based on Edde Craze, a St Ives garage owner who mixed with the bohemian crowd and died in just the same way as Levine's supposed fictional person. There was a lot of ill-feeling in the town towards the bohemians, local people blaming them for persuading Craze to participate in their antics.

It's only fair to say that, despite Milne's tendency to let other distractions get in the way of his creative work, he did produce some excellent sculptures. He exhibited in Britain, across the Continent, and in the United States. He was influenced by Brancusi and by Hepworth and her long-term assistant and fine sculptor, Denis Mitchell. Was Milne's work distinctive enough to act as an influence"? I'll let Massey provide the answer: "Did his work influence that of other artists? Not in any profound sense, although his formal repertoire finds certain echoes in sculpture made during the decades since his death, and he remains admired and collected. And while not of the first rank, in his twenty-five years or so as a mature artist he created a body of work that, at its considerable best, has a definite place in the crowded field of postwar British sculpture".

Milne's final years were not happy ones, He had an exhibition at the Gilbert Parr Gallery in April, 1978, but from a personal point of view he was not in good shape. Massey says "In his later years Milne was reliant not only on alcohol but on drugs". He was often in debt, and alienated various friends by making constant demands for support. This was certainly the case with Cosmo Rodewald who Milne would phone in the middle of the night when he was drunk and beg for help. According to someone who knew them both: "He was in a desperate state, very pissed, very emotional....In the end he became a very neurotic drunk – he really needed medical treatment I think".

Mine died on 24th June, 1978. There were suggestions that, because of his known previous attempts, he had committed suicide, but the inquest verdict was that it was an accidental death caused by an overdose of alcohol and barbiturates.

Queer St Ives and Other Stories is a fascinating book. As well as providing an account of John Milne's life it throws light on an aspect of the culture of St Ives that has not been looked at in any depth in the past. Ian Massey manages to pack in a great deal of information about interesting individuals like the artist Marlow Moss, somewhat overlooked and, according to Massey, "frozen out" of membership of the Penwith Society of Arts due to opposition from Ben Nicholson and Barbara Hepworth who "saw Moss as an interloper, a threat to their primacy, both in St Ives and beyond". Moss had known Mondrian and produced purely abstract works before Nicholson and Hepworth.

There is also Ida Kar who visited St Ives in 1961 on an assignment for the *Tatler* magazine, and included John Milne among the artists she photographed. There is a particularly good picture of him in his studio in the book *Ida Kar: Bohemian Photographer*, published by the National Portrait Gallery, London in 2011, to accompany an exhibition of her work.

And then, of course, the very informative chapter on the post-war cultural and homosexual scenes, often intertwined, in Manchester. Not to mention St Ives fringe figures like Julian Nixon. And walk on parts by Keith Vaughan and Francis Bacon who described St Ives as "a stronghold of really dreary abstract stuff". It all adds up to a stimulating mixture that is enhanced by a first-rate selection of photographs of some of the people involved, and reproductions of art works, together with notes and a useful bibliography.

QUEER ST IVES AND OTHER STORIES
By Ian Massey
Ridinghouse. 253 pages. £30. ISBN 978-1-909932-69-2

COLD WAR COUNTERFEIT SPIES : TALES OF ESPIONAGE; GENUINE OR BOGUS?

I was once on a train travelling North and couldn't help overhearing the man seated across the aisle telling a young woman sitting opposite him about his adventures as an officer in the Territorial Army. They included some sort of training with the SAS and visits to France where he had a relationship with the daughter of a high-ranking French Army officer he'd met at a reception at the British Embassy in Paris. He was plausible and dropped enough factual hints to give his account a touch of authenticity. I didn't believe him, though, and wrote him off as just another sad fantasist.

But I did sometimes later wonder if there had been any kind of truth in his story? Perhaps he had experienced at least some of what he referred to, hence the occasional references to locations and the like, and had then suffered a breakdown or some other misfortune that had caused him to confuse fact and fantasy? After all, I hadn't been in a position to challenge what he said.

The man may have been merely a harmless crank, and never likely to take his tales beyond trying to impress young ladies on trains. But there are people who extend their fantasies into print and persuade publishers to advertise their myth-making as being accurate accounts of fighting against great odds, achieving miraculous rescues deep inside enemy territory, and somehow surviving extremes of weather that would quickly kill off most ordinary people. They no doubt appeal to armchair warriors who can imagine themselves in such situations but coming out of them unscathed, while sometimes having had the opportunity along the way to hop into bed with an attractive agent.

One of the more bizarre stories that Nigel West examines is that of Lawrence Gardella whose book, the curiously-titled *Sing a Song to Jenny Next,* purports to be the true story of how, at the time of the Korean War in the early-1950s, he was one of a seven-man unit parachuted into Manchuria to attack a Chinese nuclear facility. They teamed up with Nationalist guerrillas and a Scot who had lived in China since the 1930s. The mission successfully accomplished, despite having to fight off hordes of enemy troops, Gardella made his escape by somehow travelling a thousand miles across China in twenty-two days, reaching the coast to be picked up by submarine, and eventually arriving home in America where he was decorated by President Truman. But he was sworn to secrecy. Officially, the operation had never taken place. It was only in 1981, just before Gardella died, that he decided to speak out and his book was published. I forgot to add that among the Chinese guerrillas who helped Gardella was the attractive Dragon Lady, whose favours he managed to enjoy at one point.

West takes Gardella's tale to pieces, and links it to another similar account by Lieutenant-Colonel Arthur T. Boyd, published in 2008, in which he "revealed in *Operation Broken Reed* that in 1952 he had been selected for a clandestine assignment". This involved venturing deep into enemy territory and resulted in some curious encounters. But Boyd doesn't seem to have found it necessary to have killed dozens of Chinese or North Korean communists while following orders in yet another highly-secret operation that may never have existed. Like the one Gardella undertook, it appears to be completely absent from all the CIA, Marine Corps, and other military records. West closely questions the facts referred to by both men, and sums up the mysteries surrounding Gardella's and Boyd's books when he says, "In retrospect, *Operation Broken Reed* appears to have much in common with *Sing a Song to Jenny Next,* and each seems as bogus as the other, although Colonel Boyd at least has the excuse that he has suffered from a psychiatric disorder".

It's obvious that some people with little or no involvement in military or espionage situations may want to create a false impression to make themselves look good. But why would someone who already has a genuine record in these matters need to fabricate supposed incidents that could easily be disproved? Sir Ranulph Twisleton-Wyckham Fiennes Bt. Is a colourful personality with a reputation for adventuring in various parts of the world. West says that he "fought in Oman and in 1975 wrote a well-received account of the conflict, *Where Soldiers Fear to Tread*". But Fiennes then authored *The Feathermen,* about four British soldiers who had participated in an ambush in Qum in October 1969. This was "during the 'secret war' fought in the mountains of Dhofar, to protect the Gulf states from communist insurgents". This truly was a real "secret war".

If Fiennes was to be believed the four soldiers concerned became the targets of hitmen hired by a rich Dubai merchant whose son had been killed in the ambush. One of the four died when a helicopter he was piloting crashed into the sea. An accident? No, said Fiennes, it was the result of a time-bomb planted in the helicopter, A second soldier died in a road accident. It wasn't, it was a planned murder, as was the death of a third soldier who, according to the inquest, died of hypothermia while taking part in an exercise on the Brecon Beacons. Fiennes himself claims to have been targeted by the hired assassins and was only saved by the intervention of some volunteers recruited by SAS's wartime founder, David Stirling. As West says, the story has a "veneer of authenticity" due to Fiennes' "stature, but also because almost all the names in the book are authentic". He's perhaps being kind when he adds that Fiennes' friends "regard *The Feathermen* as an aberration……but are tolerant of his eccentricity because of his many accomplishments".

Northern Ireland inevitably comes into consideration, which isn't surprising when one considers the amount of delusion, confusion, collusion, and other factors at play there during the Troubles. West inspects a book called *The Nemesis File* by a Sergeant Paul Bruce, "supposedly an authentic account of how the SAS had murdered numerous terrorist suspects in Northern Ireland, and then buried the evidence". Bruce was actually a vehicle mechanic in the Royal Electrical and Mechanical Engineers who claimed he was transferred to the SAS and took part in undercover operations. But West reckons that the SAS troopers were not really active to any great extent in Northern Ireland in 1971 and 1972, when Bruce said he was there. And it turned out that Bruce was actually "a psychiatric patient named Paul Inman, a former soldier from Weston-Super-Mare who had a long history of mental illness". It further transpired that *The Nemesis File* had actually been written "not by Inman but by Nicholas Davies, a former *Daily Mirror* journalist" with a somewhat questionable background in arms dealing. The book was later acknowledged as a work of fiction and not fact.

There is much more in *Cold War Counterfeit Spies* to intrigue those who sometimes wonder if the security services, branches of the police and armed forces, and even some government departments do get up to some decidedly dodgy things. I can remember the furore that erupted over the death of the peace campaigner Hilda Murrell who, in 1984, was found dead in a field a few miles away from her home. Gary Murray described himself as "a former MI5 undercover agent", and in his book, *Enemies of the State* it was suggested that she might have been killed by a private investigator who broke into her house while collecting information about anti-nuclear activists for the Atomic Energy Authority. The police took the view that it was more than likely a case of an ordinary burglary that went wrong. Some years later, in 2003, a local man who had been sixteen when Murrell was killed, was charged with the crime and convicted on the basis of DNA and fingerprint evidence.

I don't suppose West's investigations (his book was first published in 2016) will deter anyone, fantasist or not, from wanting to embroider on the truth and even totally construct what might be called alternative facts. Nor will it stop anyone reading bogus tales and believing in conspiracy theories and distrusting what the authorities say. And some fantasists do tell a good story.

COLD WAR COUNTERFEIT SPIES : TALES OF ESPIONAGE; GENUINE OR BOGUS?

By Nigel West

Frontline Books (Pen & Sword). 252 pages. £14.99. ISBN 9-781-39907-509-1

TROTSKY : THE PASSIONATE REVOLUTIONARY

Years ago I met Reg Groves, author of a book called *The Balham Group,* a history of a small gathering of early British Trotskyists he had been involved with in the 1930s. It would have been in the 1970s when I first had the opportunity to talk to Groves, and there had been something of an upsurge of interest in Trotskyism and other left-wing alternatives to capitalism. The so-called "underground" bookshops that flourished at the time had racks of publications offering a variety of views on current problems.

And past problems, too. It often seemed to me that the Trotskyist magazines and papers were particularly inclined towards resurrecting old arguments. They involved the different factions that existed in what had never been much more than a limited, if dedicated, number of devotees of Trotsky's ideas. The Left, it seems, has always been prone to dissension within its ranks, but the Trotskyists appeared to have taken the art of factionalism to greater levels than most. Splits and miniscule groups with only a handful of members were par for the course, and most managed to produce a publication of one sort or another. In them they put forward their arguments for having the only correct interpretations of what Trotsky had said and intended. There is a story, "The Party", by Isaac Rosenfeld, a one-time American Trotskyist, which satirises such groups: "the fact is that the party has existed separately for only seven years; it split off from the parent body, which in turn was born by separation from an earlier party and so on".

Leon Trotsky, as he was known, was born Lev Davidovich Bronstein in 1879 in a rural area of Southern Ukraine. His father was a wealthy landowner, despite the restrictions placed on Jews owning or even renting very large areas of land. His mother was better educated than his father, subscribed to a lending library, and gave her children (Trotsky had a brother and two sisters) opportunities to take an interest in the arts. Trotsky spent seven years at St Paul's School in Odessa, though at one point he was briefly expelled for taking part in a demonstration against an unpopular teacher. But he was an extremely successful student with maximum marks in every subject. While in Odessa he lived with the Spentzer family who introduced him to the work of a variety of writers. He later said, "It was a good intellectual family. I owe it a lot".

Allan Todd notes that, at this stage of his life, Trotsky looked and behaved like "a typical bourgeois cosmopolitan youth". But he was noticing the very real inequalities in Russian society, and was aware that his comfortable way of life was derived from wealth created by the peasants his father employed and exploited. He argued with his father about this, sometimes in front of the peasants, and Todd says he "already displayed tendencies towards a lack of discretion and an inclination to contradict".

In 1895 Trotsky moved to a school in Nikolaev, a town used by the police as a useful place to settle and observe political revolutionaries. For Trotsky it was an opportunity to develop his political thinking. He met people linked to the Narodniks, the promoters of a form of agrarian socialism and, in many ways, the forerunners of the Socialist Revolutionaries (SRs) who initially played a prominent part in the 1917 events in Russia. They were not Marxists, and neither was Trotsky at that time.

It was when he became a student at the university in Odessa that he began to take greater note of Marxist theories. He helped form the South Russian Workers' Union (SRWU) which, despite its title, consisted mainly of "student activist intellectuals". Trotsky had already come to the attention of the police and he was arrested in 1898 and exiled to Irkutsk. He associated with the Mensheviks, who tended to be less in favour of tight central control than the Bolsheviks. It was in 1903 that he began to use the name he became known by, Leon Trotsky. I'm deliberately moving quickly through his activities, such as escaping from exile, travelling to various European cities – Zurich, Vienna, Paris, London – meeting Lenin, and being nicknamed "The Pen" because of the frequency and quality of his numerous essays and articles for the radical press. It all necessitated his leaving behind a wife and two daughters when he chose to become an active revolutionary. It's worth noting that Todd remarks how Trotsky's intellectual "brilliance" sometimes annoyed those who were less gifted than he was. He could come across to them as arrogant.

Although still allying mostly with the Mensheviks, Trotsky was also displaying a growing commitment to Marxism by attacking other groups in the wider revolutionary movement such as the Narodniks and the anarchists. He was active during the 1905 Revolution in St Petersburg, arrested, and sent to Siberia. He escaped and made his way to Finland. He had, by this time, formed a relationship with Natalya Sedova, "a seasoned revolutionary" who was to become his lifelong companion. Again, it's necessary to move at a fast pace through the years leading up to 1917. Trotsky wrote steadily, sometimes as a literary and art critic, and was a war correspondent during the Balkan conflicts of 1912/13. Like many hopeful revolutionaries he was taken aback when, in 1914, the workers of the world didn't unite, but instead turned on each other and supported the war programmes of their respective countries. The slogan, "Workers of the World Unite" now had a hollow ring to it.

He kept moving through the usual locations – Vienna, Zurich, Paris – though the war situation made it increasingly difficult to settle in any one place. At one point he was in New York. When, in 1917, it became obvious that something was afoot in Russia he left the United States and headed to Petrograd, as St Petersburg had been renamed once war with Germany broke out. Arriving there he was acclaimed by the crowds of workers and soldiers who were demonstrating in the streets. He was particularly popular among the sailors of the Kronstadt naval base.

Trotsky was still not formally a Bolshevik, but identified with them as the insurrection developed. It was largely his plan that ensured the success of the overthrow of the Kerensky government in November 1917. And there's no doubt that Trotsky was responsible for the formation of the "new" army that eventually defeated the various White armies that attempted, with the help of interventionist British, American, French and Japanese forces, to defeat the Bolsheviks. Todd mentions Trotsky's harsh methods when imposing discipline on the troops, with deserters shot. It was a harshness that also came out when he later suppressed a rising by sailors at Kronstadt who were protesting against increasingly rigid controls imposed by the Bolsheviks.

It was when the fighting finished that Trotsky's troubles began. Lenin was ill and would soon die, and Stalin, who had fallen out with Trotsky during the war years, was General Secretary of the party and building a power base within it. It's a fascinating period to study, assuming one can follow all the twists and turns at the meetings, and the scheming that went on in private. What it came down to in the end is that Trotsky, for all his high intellect, was outflanked by Stalin. The increasing bureaucratisation within the party gave Stalin the opportunities to appoint his own people to key positions. And it's more than likely that Trotsky made the mistake of assuming that because Stalin wasn't an intellectual he wasn't intelligent. It's a mistake frequently made by intellectuals whose arrogance turns people against them. Trotsky had dismissed Stalin as a "nonentity" and described him as "the gravedigger of the revolution". And it would seem that Trotsky simply hadn't the kind of mind set that can cultivate personal contacts and use them to good advantage when wanting to take control. There was also the basic clash between Stalin's idea of Socialism in One Country and Trotsky's theory of Permanent Revolution which suggested that, unless there were revolutions in other countries, the revolution in Russia would stagnate.

In the end Trotsky was outmanoeuvred and forced into external exile. Many countries refused to give him sanctuary, and after brief sojourns in Turkey and Norway he was offered refuge in Mexico, which then had a left-wing government. It also had a powerful communist party which would prove troublesome to Trotsky. It's from this point that the legend of Trotsky as the true revolutionary holding out against the tyranny of Stalinism, and leader of small bands of dedicated Trotskyists, began to take hold. Volunteer guards came from the United States and elsewhere to protect him against possible attacks. It was assumed, if not directly known, that he was on Stalin's hit-list. Members of Trotsky's family still living in Russia were arrested and executed, and his son, Lyova, active in Paris as Trotsky's advocate, died in mysterious circumstances. A Stalinist agent, Mark Zborowski using the name Etienne, had infiltrated Lyova's organisation and seemed reliable but regularly passed information to Moscow.

There had been attempts on Trotsky's life, especially that led by David Sequeiros, the Mexican artist and fervent communist. The final one came in 1940 when Frank Jacson cultivated a relationship with Sylvia Agelof, an American Trotskyist in Mexico, and through her gained access to Trotsky. Jacson was actually Ramon Mercader, a Spaniard and an NKVD operative. The story of how he drove an ice-pick into Trotsky's head is well-known. Mercader himself was overpowered by Trotsky's guards and was later tried and sentenced to twenty years in a Mexican prison.

I'm not sure what the state-of-play is now with regard to supporters of Trotsky. No doubt there are some out there, but we hear little of them these days. And it's also worth wondering how his reputation stands in general? I don't think many people would now be inclined to take his teachings to heart. And I have doubts about what he would have done had he ever been in a position of authority. I suspect he may have been pushed by circumstances into adopting some brutal methods and measures. He was hardly liberal-minded during the difficult early days of the Bolshevik take-over and wanted to militarise the unions and apply conscription to the workers. And there is his undeniable ruthless record with regard to military discipline and the suppression of the Kronstadt rebellion. Power corrupts and absolute power corrupts absolutely.

I can understand why he has had some appeal over the years. An intellectual who is also a man of action, and actually participates in world-shaking events, might well appear attractive to those whose own activities go little beyond talking and writing about the possibilities of revolution. Am I being cynical in saying this? Perhaps, but it is possible that, for some, following a dream that may never become reality is a good way of seeming to be spotless. Others engaged in the dirty business of struggling to achieve even minor changes will inevitably come out stained and be accused of compromising.

Trotsky is a fascinating figure to follow on paper. He would have loved to have been in a position to concentrate on writing. His range of interests – he could easily and knowingly converse about art and literature with the Mexican muralist Diego Rivera or the French surrealist André Breton – could take him beyond the world of revolutionary politics. But events determined which course he had to follow and how and why he came to his tragic end.

Allan Todd provides a brisk account of Trotsky's life and achievements, and also indicates that he had some failings as a person and as a possible leader of a country beset by numerous problems, both internal and external. His book has notes, many of which point to the importance of Isaac Deutscher's work in documenting Trotsky's story. There's a very short bibliography (to be fair numerous books are referred to in the notes), and some illustrations.

TROTSKY : THE PASSIONATE REVOLUTIONARY
By Allan Todd
Pen & Sword Book. 227 pages. £25. ISBN 978-139901-076-4

KIKI MAN RAY : ART, LOVE AND RIVALRY IN 1920s PARIS

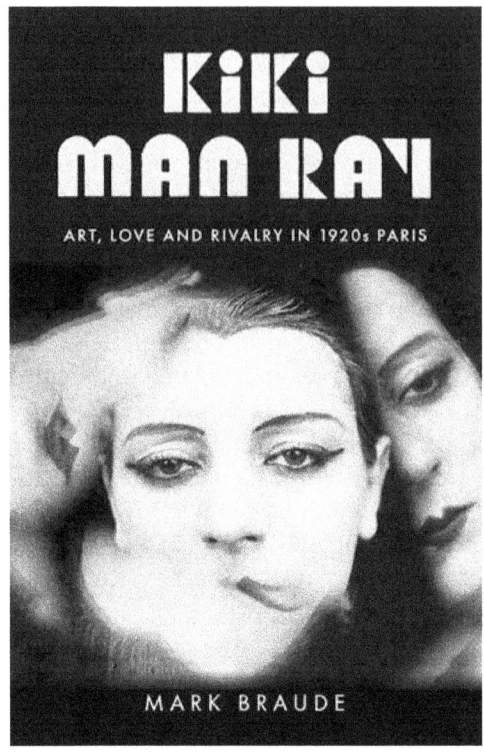

Paris in the 1920s. A legendary time, with novels, memoirs, literary histories, walking guides, and additional material comprising a library that on its own might fully occupy someone for a lifetime. The names tumble from the pages, some of them well-known, others perhaps of only passing interest. One name that does often occur is that of Kiki, a celebrity in her day when she was usually referred to as Kiki of Montparnasse. But who was she?

She was born Alice Ernestine Prin on 2nd October, 1901 in Châtillon-sur-Seine, "a village in Burgundy 150 miles southeast of Paris". She grew up in poverty, not knowing for sure who her father was, and with a mother who left her in the care of her grandmother and moved to Paris. Alice had a somewhat disjointed education at the village school, where she at least learned to read and write, and then reunited with her mother when she was twelve. She was only briefly at school in Paris, leaving when she was thirteen, the then legal age for going to work. Mark Braude makes the point that she loved to read and was especially fond of the *Fantômas* books and their tales of the "misadventures of the brilliant occasionally murderous arch-villain Fantômas". These books were also popular with the Surrealists who Alice, when she became Kiki, would later encounter in Paris.

Following a series of mundane jobs, one of which involved disinfecting boots from dead soldiers so that they could be issued to troops at the front, she somehow fell in with a sculptor who asked her to model for him. His studio was at the Impasse Ronsin, "a hive of artists' studios and workshops", where the Romanian Constantin Brancusi also lived. There were other encounters with sculptors, painters, and a Brazilian diplomat who introduced her to cocaine. She also learned that the Café de la Rotonde was a good place to get to know artists and pick up modelling jobs. She became familiar with La Ruche, the rackety collection of studios where many artists lived, and by 1918 was residing there with the painter Maurice (Moishe) Mendjizky. There are several of his paintings of Kiki (she had by then adopted that name), a couple of them nude studies, in the book. She seems to have lived with Mendjizky for three or four years. She also modelled for Moise Kisling, and met Modigliani, Utrillo, and Soutine. It's more than probable that she posed for all of them.

It's obvious that, by 1921 or so, Kiki would have been a streetwise young woman and able to stand up for herself in any argument. Her initial encounter with Man Ray came after a scene in a café where Kiki had been refused service because she wasn't wearing a hat, a standard requirement in those days for ladies who wanted to appear respectable. A friend, the artist Marie Vassilieff, intervened and invited Kiki to sit at her table, where she was with an American. It was Man Ray, and it would seem that he and Kiki immediately took to each other.

Man Ray's real name was Emmanuel Radnitzky and he was born in Philadelphia in 1890. When he was seven his family moved to Brooklyn. He was a bright student and, according to Braude, won a scholarship to study architecture at New York University. But he decided not to go there and instead got a job as an engraver. He switched to "doing layouts and lettering at a publishing house". His real ambition was to become an artist. He visited art galleries in New York and was particularly fond of 291, the gallery run by photographer Alfred Steiglitz. It was there that he first encountered names then new to him – Rodin, Brancusi, and Picasso, "the one who touched him deepest of all with his Cubist acrobatics, trying to make the fourth dimension of time visible on a two-dimensional surface". Manny, as he was known, also picked up copies of Steiglitz's magazine, *Camera Work*.

He saw the 1913 Armoury exhibition, which introduced many European artists to an American audience, became friends with Marcel Duchamp, married a poet named Donna Lacour (also known as Adon Lacroix), and met William Carlos Williams, and Alfred Kreymborg. A move to Greenwich Village brought him into contact with Djuna Barnes, Mina Loy, and others. Dada had hit New York and Braude says that "Man Ray appreciated how the Dadaists wanted to alienate themselves from the times and places they happened to be living in".

With all that he had experienced in New York, much of it with a European base, it was probably inevitable that he would go to Paris, and perhaps be fated to meet Kiki. By late-1921 they were living together. She continued to work as a model, while he took on commercial photography jobs to boost their combined income. There is a suggestion that he occasionally also turned his camera hand to pornography as a means of making money. Kiki had started painting, no doubt influenced by what she had seen in various artists' studios, and a couple of her watercolours were bought by Henri-Pierre Roché, a well-known art dealer. Braude tells us Roché wrote that "with their summery tones and quick lines they reminded him of Matisse".

Kiki was, no doubt, one of the queens of the Rotonde and enjoyed living it up, but she appears to have been quite practical-minded when it came to the domestic arrangements with Man Ray. She shopped and cooked, and organised his workdays and his appointments book. He may have been making a living by doing portraits and fashion work, but he was constantly experimenting and anxious to produce more creative material. He developed what he referred to as "Rayographs", a process defined as "photographic prints made by laying objects onto photographic paper and exposing it to light". It's this kind of work that he's mostly remembered for, though he always wanted, but never really received, recognition for his paintings.

Both Man Ray and Kiki were caught up in the early days of Surrealism and attended sessions where André Breton, Louis Aragon, Robert Desnos, and others indulged in automatic writing and derangement of the senses. Kiki was not impressed and, in her down-to-earth way, dismissed what they were doing: "She thought of them as silly kids from good families playing at being dangerous by poking around in the hidden depths of the mind". And she felt that as a group "they dealt too heavily in theories and abstractions". As Braude puts it, "They were Surrealists. Kiki was a realist".

The relationship between Kiki and Man Ray was always turbulent. At one point she walked out and went to New York with a journalist she'd met and who is known to posterity only as "Mike". Their association didn't last long and Mike eventually left her. She had to contact Man Ray to ask him to send her money so she could get back to Paris. The reason she'd given for leaving him in the first place was that, though she loved him, he didn't love her. Braude quotes a comment that May Ray supposedly made when she raised the question of love: "Love? What's that? Huh, idiot? We don't love, we screw".

It was in 1924 that Man Ray posed Kiki in what has become one of his most famous images. Called "La Violon d'Ingres" we see a near-naked Kiki with her back to the camera, head turned to profile, and with two "f-holes" tattooed on her back. It's the stuff of a thousand postcards and, like the "Mona Lisa", has been parodied more than once. But the original is an enticing photo and raises questions about what it means. Braude's comments are apt:

"There's no effort to fool. The f-holes have been rendered too clearly superficial for that. Instead we're being challenged to hold both their visual artifice (we know those markings don't belong to that woman's body) and their analogical effectiveness (but her body does look like a cello) in our heads at the same time". The photo was used in the final issue of the Surrealist magazine, *Littérature*.

By the mid-1920s Kiki was singing in a bar called The Jockey owned by Hilaire Hiler, an American artist and writer. It was obvious that, young as she still was, her "voice was weary, burning and broken" from years of smoke and drink. She was also increasingly reliant on cocaine to help her cope with the pressures of constantly performing. There is a group photograph taken outside The Jockey in which Kiki appears, along with, among others, Ezra Pound, Tristan Tzara, Man Ray, and the beautiful Mina Loy. The latter seems to steal the limelight, kneeling as she does and looking over at the crouching Man Ray with a smile on her face as if he's just said or done something amusing.

In February 1925 Kiki paid a visit to Villefranche-sur-Mer, a small town on the Riviera, staying at the Welcome Hotel. Braude refers to the town as "seedy Villefranche with its small but lively port", and says that Kiki "settled in at the Welcome's lobby bar, a natural among the pimps, petty thieves, counterfeiters, hustlers, and *filles de joie* ('pleasure girls', as French sex workers were called). She could swear as colourfully as any of the seamen and knew dirtier songs". But she got into trouble and was arrested for assaulting a policeman. She was lucky not to be sent to prison.

In early 1927 Kiki and Man Ray made a trip to New York where she met members of his family. When they returned to Paris she had her first solo show of her paintings at the Au Sacre du Printemps gallery. It wasn't a large exhibition but all of the twenty-seven canvases on display were sold. It was around this time that Sisley Huddleston, an English journalist well-known as a commentator on the Parisian artistic scene, described the show as "the sensation not only of Montparnasse but *tout Paris*".

She may have been riding high in some ways, but her relationship with Man Ray was coming to an end. Braude suggests that there may have been a degree of professional jealousy on his part due to her increased popularity, but also perhaps a resentment because she was no longer available to do the shopping, cooking, washing and other routine tasks while he spent time photographing and painting. Whatever the reason they'd split up by 1929.

It didn't take Kiki long to link up with someone else and she moved in with Henri Broca, a cartoonist. They started a magazine, *Paris – Montparnasse*, and she began to work on her memoirs. They were published in French in a limited de-luxe edition, and later by Edward Titus in an English edition, with the translation by Samuel Putnam. Titus, the husband of the immensely wealthy Helena Rubinstein, had a bookshop, At the Sign of The Black Manikin, in Paris, and had also taken over as editor of *This Quarter*, a magazine previously edited by Ethel Moorhead and the ill-fated Ernest Walsh.

As an added attraction for the English edition Titus persuaded Ernest Hemingway to write an introduction in which the noted American writer said that Kiki's book marked the end of an era. Unfortunately, many of the copies that Titus sent to America were seized by Customs officials on the grounds of obscenity. Braude notes that, years later, in the 1950s, a pirated edition using the Titus original was published in New York by the notorious pornographer Samuel Roth.

It was true, it was the end of an era. 1929 brought the Wall Street Crash and the onset of the Great Depression. Kiki and Broca's magazine closed down in 1930, and Broca, increasingly subject to mental health problems, was diagnosed as suffering from schizophrenia and committed to a sanatorium. Kiki's own health issues were a matter for concern. She was advised to stop drinking, but this pushed her into using cocaine more often. She carried on painting and had what was to be her final show in January, 1931 at "an informal gallery space" in the garden of a large house owned by a wealthy young collector. Braude says that her paintings "retained the same casual feel as her earlier work, though she now showed greater skill in rendering perspective and scale". And he refers to "L'Acrobate" as "a feast of colour and movement" and describes it as "the finest of all her paintings".

It's reproduced in the book, and seems naïve but with a certain amount of charm.

In 1932 Kiki teamed up with André Laroque, "a minor tax official" and part-time piano and accordion player, who accompanied her when she sang in clubs and bars. Her modelling career had declined and although she had appeared in minor roles in a few films there was no further screen work for her after 1933. There were a handful of recordings by Kiki and Laroque in the late-1930s, but her addiction to cocaine (Braude thinks she was also using heroin) continued to cause her to be unreliable as a performer. Braude sums up the situation in these words: "Kiki's name pops up rarely in the 1940s, most often in the back pages of newspapers advertising an appearance in some local dives". He adds that: "There is evidence pointing to Kiki living in the Loire valley with a plumber between 1941 and 1944". The war years are otherwise an undocumented period in her life.

She returned to Paris after the War and met Laroque who tried to help by paying her bills, knowing that if he gave her money she would spend it on drink and drugs. She was arrested in 1946 for "creating false prescriptions for psychotropic substances".Laroque was living with someone else but insisted, despite opposition from his partner, that Kiki move in with them so that he could look after her. She still made appearances in clubs and the American writer Kay Boyle, who had known Kiki in the 1920s, recalled seeing her "singing in various little night-clubs, and remembering nothing from one night to the next", which Boyle put down to the drug-taking. She would ask Boyle the same questions about old friends each time they met.

There were other equally sad accounts of Kiki's post-1945 activities. The English artist Ronald Searle pictured her in his *Paris Sketchbook*: "In Searle's line drawing of Kiki, who would then have been forty-eight or forty-nine, her hair is withered and her face ravaged and emaciated". She met Man Ray again when he was in Paris in 1952 and told him she was ill. He gave her some money and "She came by his studio a few times, then disappeared". In March 1953 she collapsed in the street and was rushed to a nearby hospital but died. She was buried in the "massive Thiais cemetery, where in the alabaster vaults of the Jardin de la Fraternitié the penniless and unidentifiable may be buried without charge. Her friends were unable to raise enough money to see her buried in the Montparnasse cemetery, a hope she'd expressed while alive".

Braude quotes a passage by the Canadian poet John Glassco, another of those who'd encountered Kiki in the Paris of the Twenties: "Kiki was always a *savagesse* who didn't care what happened to her. It is terrible, to *us*, to compare her as she was in Modigliani's and Kisling's paintings and in Man Ray's photographs, with what she became.....But I don't think it bothered her at all..........She used to say 'Modi and (Kisling) have done me; what more can a tart want than that? I look at their pretty pictures and I think: *That's me, you know*' ".

One of the advantages of Braude's book is that, focusing as it does on Kiki and Man Ray, it doesn't repeat the usual stories about what various American expatriates got up to in Paris. Man Ray was American, but on the whole chose not to mix too closely with his fellow countrymen. It could be that his links to the Surrealists and their ideas set him apart from the others. He obviously knew people like Hemingway, Malcolm Cowley, and Robert McAlmon, and it may have been a case of being with them, but not of them. Braude brings them out of the wings where necessary, but it's Kiki who is centre stage and he does a good job of telling her story. And should anyone want to delve further into the world that Kiki lived in there are ample notes and references to numerous books that will provide all the required information.

KIKI MAN RAY : ART, LOVE AND RIVALRY IN 1920s PARIS
By Mark Braude
Two Roads (John Murray Press). 290 pages. £20. ISBN 978-1-529-30048-2

www.ingramcontent.com/pod-product-compliance
Lightning Source LLC
Chambersburg PA
CBHW071652160426
43195CB00012B/1437